BESTSELLING
BOOK SERIES

Building a Web Site For Dummies, 3rd Edition

W9-ABQ-610

Cheat Sheet

The Seven Rules of Site Design

Rule #1: The Web is for reaching out to people.

Rule #2: Keep your Web pages lean and clean.

Rule #3: Don't make your visitors jump through hoops.

Rule #4: Never make an unnecessary link.

Rule #5: Always group necessary items together.

Rule #6: If you can give visitors an option, do so.

Rule #7: It's your Web site. It's your vision. Do it your way.

Web Site Design Tips

- Make your content as useful as possible.
- Use appealing graphics, but make sure that they support the content.
- Give your pages a consistent appearance.
- Install a search feature.
- Update your pages often so that people have a reason to return frequently.
- Stick to your topic.
- Know your audience and strive to please them.

CGI/Perl Resources

Site Name	Web Site
CGI Extremes	www.cgiextremes.com
CGI Made Really Easy	www.jmarshall.com/easy/cgi
CGI Resource Index	www.cgi-resources.com
CGI: Why Things Don't Work	www.raingod.com/raingod/resources/Programming/Perl/Notes/CGIDebugging.html
FREEPerlCode.com	www.freeperlcode.com
Matt Kruse's Intro to CGI	www.mattkruse.com/info/cgi
Matt's Script Archive	http://worldwidemart.com/scripts
Perl Primer	www.webdesigns1.com/perl
ScriptSearch	www.scriptsearch.com
WDVL: The Perl You Need to Know	http://wdvl.com/Authoring/Languages/Perl/PerlfortheWeb
www.perl.com	www.perl.com

Miscellaneous Resources

Site Name	Web Site
DevX.com	www.devx.com
Google Groups	http://groups.google.com
International Webmasters Association	www.iwanet.org
Internet FAQ Archives	www.faqs.org
Internet Related Technologies	www.irt.org
Internet Traffic Report	www.internettrafficreport.com
Internet World	www.iw.com
Webmaster Tools Central	www.webmastertoolscentral.com
Webmaster World News	www.webmasterworld.com
Webmonkey	http://hotwired.lycos.com/webmonkey/index.html

For Dummies: Bestselling Book Series for Beginners

Building a Web Site For Dummies, 3rd Edition

Cheat Sheet

HTML Resources

Site Name	Web Site
Builder.com	www.builder.com
HTML Goodies	www.htmlgoodies.com
HTML Specification	www.w3.org/TR/html401
HTML Station	www.december.com/html
HTML Writers Guild	www.hwg.org
HTMLcenter	www.htmlcenter.com/tutorials/index.cfm
Index DOT Html	www.eskimo.com/~bloo/indexdot/html/index.html
Introduction to HTML	www.wdvl.com/Authoring/HTML/Intro
Validome Validation Services	www.validome.org
W3C Markup Validation Service	http://validator.w3.org
Web Developer's Virtual Library	www.wdvl.com
WebReference.com	www.webreference.com
XHTML Specification	www.w3.org/TR/xhtml1
XHTML vs. HTML	www.w3schools.com/xhtml/xhtml_html.asp
XHTML.org	www.xhtml.org
XML Specification	www.w3.org/TR/2006/REC-xml11-20060816
XML.com	www.xml.com

Java and JavaScript Resources

Site Name	Web Site
April's A1 JavaScript(TM) Resources	http://a1javascripts.com
Freewarejava.com	http://freewarejava.com
Java Boutique	http://javaboutique.internet.com
JavaScript.com	www.javascript.com
JavaScript City	www.javascriptcity.com
JavaScript Kit	www.javascriptkit.com
JavaScript Search	www.javascriptsearch.com
JavaScript Source	http://javascript.internet.com
JavaScript Tutorial	www.w3schools.com/js
WebReference JavaScript Articles	www.webreference.com/programming/javascript/index.html
Web Teacher JavaScript Tutorial	www.webteacher.com/javascript

For Dummies: Bestselling Book Series for Beginners

Building a
Web Site

FOR

DUMMIES®

3RD EDITION

by **David A. Crowder**

Wiley Publishing, Inc.

Building a Web Site For Dummies® 3rd Edition

Published by
Wiley Publishing, Inc.
111 River Street
Hoboken, NJ 07030-5774

www.wiley.com

Copyright © 2007 by Wiley Publishing, Inc., Indianapolis, Indiana

Published by Wiley Publishing, Inc., Indianapolis, Indiana
Published simultaneously in Canada

For general information on our other products and services, please contact our Customer Care Department within the U.S. at 800-762-2974, outside the U.S. at 317-572-3993, or fax 317-572-4002.

For technical support, please visit www.wiley.com/techsupport.

Wiley also publishes its books in a variety of electronic formats. Some content that appears in print may not be available in electronic books.

Library of Congress Control Number: 2007935023

ISBN: 978-0-470-14928-7

Manufactured in the United States of America

10 9 8 7 6 5 4 3

WILEY

About the Author

David A. Crowder has authored or coauthored more than 20 books on subjects ranging from computers to historical mysteries, including popular bestsellers such as *Building a Web Site For Dummies* and *CliffsNotes Getting on the Internet.* He was selling hypertext systems back in the days when you had to explain to people what the word meant. He's been involved in the online community since its inception and is the recipient of several awards for his work, including *NetGuide Magazine*'s Gold Site Award.

He is the son of a teacher and a college president, and his dedication to spreading knowledge, especially about the computer revolution, goes beyond his writing. He also founded three Internet mailing lists (discussion groups), JavaScript Talk, Java Talk, and Delphi Talk, all of which were sold to Ziff-Davis. One of his most treasured memories is the message he received from an old-timer on one of those lists who said that he had never seen such a free and open exchange of information since the days when computers were built by hobbyists in home workshops.

When he isn't writing, he spends his time with his wife Angela, wandering through villages in the Andes or frolicking in the Caribbean surf.

Dedication

For Angela. *Eres mi sol, nena, eres mi luna.*

Author's Acknowledgments

Thanks are due to Steven Hayes, Jean Rogers, Heidi Unger, and Jim Kelly, my fine editors, who were there for me every step of the way. Sometimes the relationship between writers and editors is smooth as silk, and sometimes it's tempestuous, but it always results in a better book through the give-and-take of the writing/editing process — and I'm grateful for the critiques and contributions of all the members of the Wiley team. I also leaned heavily on the expertise of Laura Moss-Hollister, my permissions editor, who helped me put together all the marvelous material on the CD-ROM that accompanies this book. All helped to make this the best book we could put together for you. And they're just the tip of the iceberg: About a zillion people work their tails off anonymously and behind the scenes at Wiley to bring you the finest books they can possibly produce. My hat is off to all of them, from the top editors to the humblest laborer on the loading dock. Last, but by no means least, I'd like to say how much I appreciate all the hard work done by my literary agent, Robert G. Diforio, without whose help I would be lost in the intricacies of the publishing world.

Publisher's Acknowledgments

We're proud of this book; please send us your comments through our online registration form located at www.dummies.com/register/.

Some of the people who helped bring this book to market include the following:

Acquisitions, Editorial, and Media Development

Project Editor: Jean Rogers

Executive Editor: Steven Hayes

Copy Editor: Heidi Unger

Technical Editor: James Kelly

Editorial Manager: Kevin Kirschner

Media Project Supervisor: Laura Moss-Hollister OR Laura Atkinson

Media Development Specialist: Angela Denny, Josh Frank, Kate Jenkins, OR Kit Malone

Media Development Associate Producer: Richard Graves

Editorial Assistant: Amanda Foxworth

Sr. Editorial Assistant: Cherie Case

Cartoons: Rich Tennant (www.the5thwave.com)

Composition Services

Project Coordinator: Heather Kolter, Kristie Rees

Layout and Graphics: Stacie Brooks, Carl Byers, Joyce Haughey, Stephanie D. Jumper, Alicia B. South, Christine Williams

Proofreaders: John Greenough, Jessica Kramer, Penny Stuart

Indexer: Potomac Indexing, LLC

Anniversary Logo Design: Richard Pacifico

Special Help: Jessica Parker

Publishing and Editorial for Technology Dummies

Richard Swadley, Vice President and Executive Group Publisher

Andy Cummings, Vice President and Publisher

Mary Bednarek, Executive Acquisitions Director

Mary C. Corder, Editorial Director

Publishing for Consumer Dummies

Diane Graves Steele, Vice President and Publisher

Joyce Pepple, Acquisitions Director

Composition Services

Gerry Fahey, Vice President of Production Services

Debbie Stailey, Director of Composition Services

Contents at a Glance

Table of Contents

Introduction

Maybe you already have your own Web site and you're not quite satisfied with it. Or perhaps you're still in the planning stages and want to know what you can do to make your site as good as it can be. You've been to Web sites that have all the bells and whistles, and you wouldn't be human if you weren't just a wee bit envious. Well, now you can have it all, too. In *Building a Web Site For Dummies,* 3rd Edition, I show you some of the best stuff around, and I tell you just how to go about putting it on your site.

About This Book

This isn't just another Web-design book. It's special. Really. I set out to write the one book I'd want by my side if I were looking to set up a really fancy Web site and not break the bank doing it. I tracked down and tested zillions of Web site enhancements and selected the top of the line to share with you. And I'm honestly proud of the results. I've authored or coauthored more than 20 books on computers and the Internet, and this one is my hands-down favorite.

It's full of things you're sure to love. It's packed with fun stuff, but it's got plenty of serious stuff, too, like how to get past the hype and really make money through your Web site. You'll wonder how in the world you ever got along without having these features on your Web site.

How to Use This Book

Keep this book next to your computer and never lend it to anybody. It's far too precious for that. Make your friends buy their own copies. If you need to make space on your bookshelf, throw away anything else you own to make room for it. When you travel, take it with you. Hold it in your arms at night and tell it how much you love it.

Each chapter is a stand-alone entity. (Don't you just love that word?) You don't have to read the whole thing, and it's a rare person who will read the book from cover to cover right off the bat. Go ahead — hit the table of contents or the index and jump to the parts you're most interested in. But don't forget to explore the rest of the book after you're done with the parts that excite you most. You won't regret spending the time — you'll find wonders in every chapter.

Foolish Assumptions

I assume that you have a favorite Web-page creation program — whether it's Dreamweaver, plain old Notepad, or the UNIX-based text editor, `vi` — and you know how to use it. So when I say to copy and paste text or save your file, you know what you need to do. Just in case you don't have a good Web-authoring program, I include a passel of HTML editors on the CD-ROM that accompanies this book.

Conventions Used in This Book

It's all organized; I promise. Even though it's rather plebeian compared with finding free content for your site, lots of people worked very hard to make sure that this book follows some straightforward rules and typographical conventions.

Code listings, of which there are plenty, look like this:

```
<HTML>
<HEAD>
<SCRIPT>
. . .
</SCRIPT>
<TITLE>
. . .
</TITLE>
</HEAD>
. . .
```

HTML elements in this book are in uppercase, and their attributes are in lowercase, as in this example:

```
<INPUT type="hidden" name="answer" value="yes">
```

If the value of an attribute is in normal type, you enter it exactly as shown. If it's in italics, it's only a placeholder value, and you need to replace it with a real value. In the following example, you replace *myownimage* with the name of the image file you intend to use:

```
<IMG src="myownimage">
```

Whenever you see the URL for one of the top sites I've tracked down, it appears in a special typeface within the paragraph, like this: `www.dummies.com`. Or it may appear on a separate line, like this:

```
www.dummies.com
```

How This Book Is Organized

This book is divided into eight parts. I organized it that way, with a little help from the folks you see in the Acknowledgments. You did read the Acknowledgments, didn't you? Don't tell me that you're the kind of person who reads the Introduction but doesn't read the Acknowledgments. Please tell me that you didn't miss the Dedication, too?

Each part has chapters in it. And each chapter has headings and subheadings. All the sections under these headings and subheadings have text that enlightens the heart and soul. Here, take a look.

Part I: Planning and Designing Your Web Site

Part I spills the secrets of how to plan a successful site from the ground up and shows you how to transform a bunch of Web pages into a coherent Web site.

Part II: Building Your Site

Part II tosses in a quick refresher course in basic HTML and then goes into more depth with WYSIWYG site creation, Cascading Style Sheets, and different ways to add search features to your site.

Part III: Adding Sparkle to Your Site

Part III gives you a ton of ways to make your site work, look, and sound great. It covers the different ways that you add new features to your Web site and shows you where to get great graphics and multimedia.

Part IV: From Blogs to Toons — Good Content Makes Contented Visitors

Part IV is about getting your visitors involved in your site so that they keep coming back for more. It shows how to get feedback from your site visitors with message boards and chat rooms. If that's not enough, you'll find fun and games and a guide to getting fresh content for your site via RSS, as well as a guide to the wonderful world of blogging.

Part V: Raking In the Bucks

Part V takes a look at making money from your site. It explodes the myths about Internet income and shows you how to really make a profit, how to get a credit card merchant account, and how to work both ends of the affiliates game.

Part VI: Publishing and Publicizing Your Site

Part VI shows you all you need to know about getting your site online and helping people find it. It covers Web-hosting options, getting listed in search engines, and establishing reciprocal links with other sites. It also shows how to keep in touch with your visitors without falling into the spam trap and how to keep your site in tip-top shape.

Part VII: The Part of Tens

Part VII is The Part of Tens. Well, it just wouldn't be a *For Dummies* book without The Part of Tens at the end, right? This part comprises three chapters, so you've got 30 extra bits here that tell you all sorts of wonderful things, like where to go for Web site design advice and ways to add value to your site.

Part VIII: Appendixes

Appendix A is a glossary of all the tech terms that might leave you baffled, and Appendix B is a guide to what's on the CD-ROM that's tucked into the back of this book.

About the CD-ROM

I've put together plenty of nice stuff for you on the CD-ROM that accompanies this book. You'll find all sorts of things that make jazzing up your Web site easy — programs for Windows and programs for Macs. And wherever possible, I included the Web site add-ins discussed in the book, including some Java applets that'll knock your socks off.

Icons Used in This Book

The icons in the margins of this book point out items of special interest. Keep an eye out for them — they're important.

Psst! Listen, pal, I wouldn't tell just anybody about this, but here's a way to make things a bit easier or get a little bit more out of it.

Time to tiptoe on eggshells. Make one false step, and things can get pretty messy.

You don't really need to know this stuff, but I just like to show off sometimes. Humor me.

Well, of course, it's all memorable material. But these bits are ones you'll especially want to keep in mind.

You don't need to bother downloading this applet or feature because it's already been done for you and is included on this book's CD-ROM.

Where to Go from Here

Well, keep turning pages, of course. And use the material to make your own Web site the hottest thing there ever was.

One of the hardest parts about getting this book together was categorizing the material in it. Many times, a Web site add-in could've been slotted into a different chapter than the one it ended up in because it had multiple features or attributes. So when you're visiting any of the sites that I mention in this book, be sure to take a good look around. A site that has a great chat room might also have a fine affiliates program. One that offers a good series of Java applets could have some solid tutorials on Web design. A site that has good information on dedicated servers may have the best e-commerce solution for you. I encourage you to browse up a storm.

Part I
Planning and Designing Your Web Site

The 5th Wave   By Rich Tennant

RURAL WEB DESIGN

"What you want to do, is balance the image of the pick-up truck sittin' behind your home page, with a busted washing machine in the foreground."

In this part . . .

1 start off by covering all the things that you need to know to put together a Web site. Chapter 1 shows you the differences between a bunch of Web pages and a coherent Web site, while Chapter 2 spills the secrets of planning a successful site from the ground up.

Chapter 1

The Zen of Sites

. . . .

In This Chapter

▶ Creating unity of content

▶ Building visitor loyalty

▶ Unearthing your personal creativity

. . . .

"You're a really good Web designer," I told a client's Webmaster once. He shrugged it off and went on to the next topic on the meeting's agenda. Whether he was just being modest or thought that I was playing corporate politics with cheap compliments, I don't know. I meant what I said, however, and the reason is simple. It wasn't that his pages were filled with nice graphics. It wasn't that the elements were finely balanced. It wasn't that the JavaScript pop-ups added an involving level of interactivity.

None of these things — neither individually nor in combination — can make a site fly. The reason I was impressed with the Webmaster's work was because he clearly understood that a Web site isn't just a bunch of pages that happen to reside on the same server. Building a quality Web site requires careful planning. This chapter introduces you to the basic elements of designing sites, achieving visitor satisfaction, and being creative.

Achieving Unity: What Makes a Site Truly a Site

No matter what technology you use to build your site, you can make it a great one — or a real loser. You can base it on HTML (HyperText Markup Language), CFML (ColdFusion Markup Language), ASP (Active Server Pages), DHTML (Dynamic HTML), AJAX (Asynchronous JavaScript and XML), or any other alphabetical wonders you care to work with. It may sound blasphemous to a world that's used to worshipping at the altars of the latest high-tech advances, but the real secret to making a Web site work is simple human insight.

Determining the underlying theme

Long before you set out to choose background colors or font types or graphical styles, you must get a solid grasp on the theme of your site. The *theme* is the unifying idea on which everything else on your site rests. Sometimes, the theme is simple and obvious. For a corporate recruiting site, the theme is why this company is the best place to work. For a genealogical site, the theme is the history of a single family and its offshoots.

Other times, the theme is a bit more complex. For an e-commerce site, you may choose a theme of great prices and saving money. If you're aiming for a different market, however, you may charge high prices and base your theme on either higher-quality products or just plain snob appeal. The underlying mechanics of both sites may well be identical — navigational methods, order-processing systems, and so on — but the sites' editorial content and graphical look and feel would be totally different.

Your low-cost bargain site may, for example, have bright and simple graphics that show a happy-go-lucky cartoon character using scissors to whack dollars in half. The high-roller site, on the other hand, would do well with richer, deeper colors. Although both sites, as in any selling situation, need to display photographs of their products, the higher-priced site is most likely to appeal to its intended audience with photographs of well-dressed people using its products in sophisticated settings.

Setting limits on content

If you've ever participated in newsgroups or mailings lists, you know how annoying it is when someone gets way off topic. There you are on `alt.citrus.cosmetics`, trying to find out the latest tips for using orange juice as a hair conditioner, and some guy starts blathering about the high price of gasoline or which cell phone company has the best roaming plan. It's usually not very long before someone else reminds him that's not what he's there for.

When it comes to the material on your site, unless you're part of a Web development team, you alone are responsible for staying on topic. This is the flip side of determining your theme — determining where to stop and what not to cover.

Take an e-commerce site devoted to personal electronics, for example. You'd need to decide whether to sell the entire spectrum of available devices or to target a specific niche, such as MP3 players or digital cameras. For a religious site, you may need to choose among covering the activities of your local church, the wider issue of the tenets of the sect to which it belongs, or the broadest range of world religious beliefs. If you don't know in advance what you're going to do — and not do — you're really hampering yourself. Designing a Web site is much easier if you know what specific parameters your efforts must meet.

Keeping Them Coming Back

Practically every human endeavor depends on repeat customers. Even if you're not selling anything, the number and frequency of return visits are generally good indicators of success or failure.

If you're going to make your site into a place that people want to visit again and again, you need to think from two perspectives. You have to wear your developer's hat, of course, but you also need to look at your site from a visitor's perspective. Put aside your awareness of the site's structure and mechanics; approach the site as though you just stumbled across it and have never seen it before.

Ask others whose judgment you trust to visit and critique your site. You don't have to change things to suit them, but getting outside perspectives on your work never hurts.

Creating a comfortable site

Keeping visitors around for even a little while, let alone making them want to return, depends on the level of comfort that you provide. If visitors aren't comfortable moving around your site to begin with, what makes you think that they'll add it to their favorites list and come back for a return engagement? In creating comfort in your Web site, you need to consider the following questions:

- ✔ **Does the site maintain a consistent layout from page to page?** If not, you'll create stress and annoyance for your visitors.

- ✔ **Is the type and style of content consistent over time?** This point is a critical one. A large part of visitor comfort comes from always finding what they expect when they visit your site.

- ✔ **Is it easy to navigate from one page or section to another?** Visitors usually don't appreciate being forced to jump through hoops or follow a preset path. See Chapter 6 for site navigation tips.

- ✔ **If the site is larger than a few pages, does it include a search feature?** Most people are either legitimately busy or just plain impatient. Unless your site enables visitors to run a search so that they can quickly and easily find the material they're looking for, you run the risk that they simply won't bother to use your site. (See Chapter 6 for how to add a search feature.)

Keeping your site fresh

If your material never changes, the odds are pretty good that most people won't come back to it very often, if ever. Unless your sole topic is a rock-solid reference subject, you can't get away with anything less than constant updating. Sure, the *Oxford English Dictionary* can come out with a new edition only every few generations. (The first edition came out in 1928 and the second one in 1989, with only two supplements in between.) But such cases are very rare. Even if you deal with a modern high-tech equivalent, such as a site on the Java programming language or the current HTML standard, you need to stay on your toes.

If your core material is something that doesn't change often, you need to add some peripheral material that you can replace more frequently. Consider adding a Tip of the Day, fresh links, a Did You Know? column, or something along those lines so that you can avoid offering only stale content to your return visitors.

How often you need to update your site depends partially on your topic and partially on your site policy. With sites that deal with volatile topics such as breaking international news, you need to update on an hourly basis at a minimum. On the other hand, sites that analyze the news can stand a more leisurely pace — daily, weekly, or even monthly — because their scope is considerably wider.

Even if your topic doesn't absolutely demand a certain update schedule, you should still establish a regular policy for how often you add fresh material to your site. Whatever schedule you establish, make sure you stick with it. Remember the comfort factor and bear in mind that your site's visitors will be less comfortable if they don't know what to expect from you. Consistency on your side helps build trust on theirs.

A Web site must change at least once a month to keep visitors interested in coming back to it.

Tapping Creativity

Although much of what goes into making a Web site function is pretty much simple, mechanical, left-brain stuff, there's another level — creativity. You need to reach that level to stretch beyond the basics and create a site that really shines. Fortunately, you can use a lot of simple techniques to get from here (the basics) to there (an extraordinary site).

The Web 2.0

When the World Wide Web first got started, it was pretty much a one-way street — Webmasters like you always made the decisions about what would appear and how it could be used. As the Web has evolved, however, it has taken on some important new characteristics.

Today, some of the Web's most popular sites aren't so much controlled by their Webmasters as they are by their users. Places like YouTube and MySpace are hotbeds for the users' self-expression and, indeed, that is their reason for existence. The new trend that has led to the phrase "Web 2.0" is user-generated content, supplemented by social networking.

Of course, the majority of Web sites are still generated almost totally by either individuals or small teams working together, but the public's hunger for its own chance to shine is seemingly insatiable — and it's something you might want to keep in mind as you design your own Web site. Wikipedia and the other wikis are collaborative efforts, and the old personal home page has largely given way to *blogs* — Web logs, or personalized diaries that can be syndicated and sent to others automatically. (See Chapter 11 for more information on blogs.)

You don't need to sit around in a lotus position, chanting mantras in order to tap into your hidden creative resources. If that's your particular cup of tea, by all means do it, but whatever means you employ, the goal's the same — to stop doing just plain thinking and reach a different level of understanding.

Now, I've got nothing against day-to-day thinking. I do a fair amount of it myself. But *standard* thinking means that you're using only half of your brainpower. People's brains have two halves. The left brain is the one that people "live in" most of the time — the one that handles numbers and words and sees everything as sequential. The right brain, on the other hand, sees everything as symbols and images that are free-floating and nonsequential.

People actually have five brains, not just two, but I promised my editor that I wouldn't use the word *paleomammalian* in this book.

The basic upshot of all this right-brain/left-brain stuff is that the left brain is such a loudmouth that you don't often hear what your right brain says. And it's got so much to tell you. Because the right side of the brain isn't stuck in the same patterns as the left brain, it gives you an entirely different perspective on the world — and on your work — that can often provide valuable insights and show you patterns that you didn't even realize existed. Perhaps your right brain can identify the perfect background color to go with a particular topic or the kind of navigation buttons that would appeal most to your audience — things that would be very difficult to achieve by linear thinking alone.

At any rate, your right brain is there for you to use, free of charge, and you ignore it at your peril. So how do you muzzle the left brain long enough to hear what the right brain has to say? Here's a handful of tips:

✔ **Meditate:** You can use an official, ritualistic method of meditation, if you want, where you study for years under a guru. Or, you can just sit in a comfortable chair and let your mind drift. If your left brain just refuses to stop chattering, try subvocalizing or humming nonsense syllables such as "dum-de-dum" to override it, or listen to music to occupy its attention.

✔ **Brainstorm:** If you're fortunate enough to be a member of a loose, relaxed team, sit around with other team members and shoot the breeze about the problem. Feel free to get off topic. Let the humor roll — nonsense often leads to sensible results.

✔ **Doodle:** If you're on your own, take your mind off the straight-and-narrow path by drawing whatever pattern comes to mind. Try doodling with your left hand (if you're right-handed) to jog your right brain into action. It's an odd fact that your left brain controls the right side of your body, and the right brain controls the left side.

✔ **Do other things:** Engage in an activity that has nothing — nothing at all — to do with your work. Play solitaire. Read a novel. Play a video game. After you take a break from your nonwork activity, the answer to your problem often comes to your mind.

✔ **Take a nap:** Your right brain often speaks to you when you're in an unconscious or semiconscious state. You may well wake up with all the inspiration that you need.

Online Sources for Creative Thinking

Table 1-1 lists some places on the World Wide Web where you can find more information on the topics that are covered in this chapter.

Table 1-1	Online Resources on Creativity
Web Site Name	*Web Address*
BrainWaves Center	www.brainwaves.com
WebsiteTips: Creativity and Inspiration	www.websitetips.com/design/ creativity.shtml
Drawing on the Right Side of the Brain	www.drawright.com
Funderstanding: Right Brain vs. Left Brain	www.funderstanding.com/ right_left_brain.cfm

Chapter 2

Pouring the Foundation

In This Chapter

▶ Determining your site's purpose

▶ Analyzing the audience

▶ Identifying your support needs

▶ Appealing to visitors

▶ Keeping your site lean

*P*eople argue about what the number-one factor in quality Web site design is, and they probably always will. Some say great graphics are the key. Others say worthwhile information is everything. Still others think that ease of use is the most important factor. I'm not so sure that there's such a thing as a linear ranking for these kinds of things. After all, a good-looking site that doesn't work well is useless. A site with a combination of good content and lousy graphics is nothing to crow about either.

In this chapter, I walk you through the fundamental things that you should consider as you create your Web site. And at the end of the chapter, I give you seven basic rules for creating Web sites that work. Take 'em with a grain of salt, and remember, you're the ultimate judge.

Drafting a Plan

Are you publicizing a political candidate? Trumpeting your favorite cause? Looking for a job? Selling shoe polish? Notice the verbs in each example. They're the key factors in determining your site's *purpose,* as opposed to its *topic.*

What do you want to accomplish?

Just having a topic isn't enough — you need a purpose, too. The *topic* is merely what the site is about; the *purpose* is what the site does. Say, for example, that you want to create a site about penguins. Okay, that's a nice starting point. You like penguins — they're cute, unusual, and pretty interesting; many people share your interest in them. But why do you want to create a Web site about them? Do you have something to say? Do you have information to give, an opinion to share, or a particular point of view that you want to put across?

You don't need to have a PhD in aquatic ornithology to create such a site. Maybe you just like funny-looking birds that swim. But you still need a purpose, or the site just won't work out in the long run. Perhaps you spent ages plowing through the search engines, and you've gathered together the world's greatest collection of penguin links. But why did you go to all that trouble? What's your purpose?

If the purpose for creating a penguin site is for your own personal enjoyment, you really don't need to do much with the site. In fact, you can just create a Web page on your own hard drive or even settle for leaving the links in your Web browser's bookmarks. If you do want your page on the World Wide Web, however, you need to take into account the needs of your potential visitors, as well as your own needs for creating such a site.

Suppose that you're putting your penguin page on the Web for the purpose of sharing everything you know about these birds with the world. How does that purpose change your approach to site design? You need to include more on the Web site than a bare list of links, for one thing. Everything that you do with the site must help people understand its purpose. If you're setting up your own domain name, for example, you want to pick one that clearly describes your site's content — like www.penguinfacts.com. (Grab it quick — it still wasn't taken at press time.)

The purpose of your site trickles down through each step that you take in creating it. You want the title of each page in the site to specify how it supports the site's purpose. The textual content of each page needs to lead naturally into some specific aspect of the topic that furthers your goal. Each graphical image must be just the right one to drive home or emphasize a critical point.

Who do you want to reach?

Who are the people you expect to visit your site? What geographical or cultural groups do you want the site to appeal to? Without at least a general idea of your potential audience, you can't have much of an idea about what type of site to create.

If data is available about the audience for similar sites, you want to track it down. But where do you find it? Surprisingly, most of it's available from the people you're competing with. (Even if you're not running a commercial site, similar sites are your competitors.) Anyone who's been involved in any type of corporate intelligence work would be shocked at the way people on the World Wide Web casually throw around valuable information, instead of keeping it under lock and key.

Many sites offer links to their visitor data. Even a quick perusal of the server logs (which automatically record information about visitors) can provide you with priceless insights into the sort of people who visit sites similar to the one you're creating. If the sites you want information on don't list links to their log data, send an e-mail message to the Webmaster asking how to access it. Most Webmasters aren't the slightest bit security-conscious about their customer data, and you may be surprised at how many of them are more than willing to spill the beans about their visitors.

What outside help do you need?

How much of your own time and effort are you going to put into your Web site? Presumably, you're going to at least control the general design and make the key decisions about content, or you wouldn't be reading this book. Most likely, you'll do the actual page creation as well. If not, you need to make sure that the people who *are* doing the coding know what they're doing and exactly what you expect of them.

When searching for qualified people to create your Web site, don't rely on college degrees, paper certifications, and the like. Here are a few tips for finding out how good they really are:

- ✔ Make candidates show you their previous work. If they don't have a CD-ROM or DVD with samples of their work, or if they can't show you sites on the Web that they've worked on, forget it.

- ✔ Explore their other Web sites. Make notes on anything that raises a question in your mind and ask for an explanation later.

- ✔ Test everything that you can to determine whether a candidate has the necessary skills and experience to implement the features you want to include on your site. In particular, make sure that all the links work (see Chapter 18 for helpful tools) — a site that has many broken links is a poorly maintained one.

If your site means anything to you at all, do *not* place it in the hands of your Aunt Sophie's extremely clever cousin who, although he's only 11 years old, knows just *all sorts of things* about computers.

Beyond the question of creating the Web pages and other files that make up your site, you need to consider where the site itself will reside. Chapter 15 contains more details on this point, but you basically have to decide if you're going to commit to the task of running your own Web server or house your site on someone else's server. The advantage of doing it yourself is that you maintain total control. The advantage of leasing either an entire Web server or space on a virtual Web server is that you have about 20 million fewer things to worry about, leaving you free to concentrate on your main task — managing your site.

Examining Page-Building Programs

These days, everyone wants to jump on the Web bandwagon, and it seems like every program under the sun can be used to make Web pages. You can use word processors such as Microsoft Word and dedicated page-creation software such as Adobe Dreamweaver, Amaya, or HotDog. Every program has its quirks, and not all of them produce high-quality, clean HTML code.

Leaving out the Johnny-come-latelies (such as word processors that tack HTML onto their older functions), two basic kinds of page-building programs are available:

- **Text editor:** Kind of like a word processor without the frills.

- **WYSIWYG (What you see is what you get) program:** Lets you develop the Web page visually instead of by working directly with the code. The main advantage of this approach is that what you see on the screen as you're working is the same as you would see if viewing the Web page in a browser.

Proponents of pure text editors and WYSIWYG enthusiasts can get about as raucous defending their favorite approaches as a bunch of baseball fans can get about the World Series. The plain fact, though, is that sometimes you'll want to use one type of editor, and sometimes you'll prefer the other kind of program. The following sections describe the differences between these two types of programs.

Text editors

HTML files are simple text files. They contain nothing but the plain old letters, symbols, and numbers that you find on your keyboard. HTML is so simple, in fact, that you don't need any kind of specialized Web-page-building program. You can create Web pages perfectly well by using nothing but Windows Notepad — assuming that you have enough knowledge of the HTML language that you can type it without making any mistakes. (See Figure 2-1.)

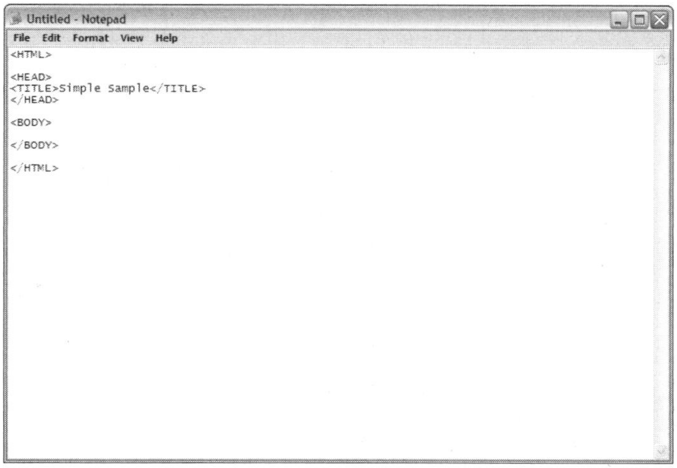

Figure 2-1:
Windows Notepad is really all you need to make a great Web page.

You don't have to settle for total simplicity, however, to get the raw power of working directly with the HTML source code. A number of high-powered text editors (such as CoffeeCup HTML Editor) are designed specifically for creating HTML code.

Table 2-1 shows where to find several additional text editors that also make creating Web pages easy.

Table 2-1	HTML Editors
Program	*Web Address*
Arachnophilia	`www.arachnoid.com/arachnophilia`
CoffeeCup HTML Editor	`www.coffeecup.com`
HotDog Professional	`www.sausage.com/hotdog-professional.html`
HTML Assistant Pro	`http://exit0.com`

WYSIWYG programs

WYSIWYG programs are easy for novices to use in the early stages of Web site creation, but they can quickly prove less than satisfactory. The reason for both factors is the same: The program makes a bunch of choices for you. Although this feature may seem like a comfort at first, it quickly becomes a limitation. If you go for a WYSIWYG program, make sure that it's sophisticated enough that you can still use it as your skills advance.

Most WYSIWYG programs have at least some degree of depth beneath their surface simplicity. They let you set the attributes for every element, in case you don't like the default choices. Dreamweaver (shown in Figure 2-2) gives you the best of both worlds because it comes with its own built-in text editor. That means that you can enjoy both the quickness of WYSIWYG creation and the total control of text editing in the same page-creation session. Table 2-2 lists several WYSIWYG programs that you can use to build Web pages, along with the Web addresses where you can find them (or information about them), and I suggest checking out *Dreamweaver CS3 For Dummies,* by Janine Warner (Wiley Publishing).

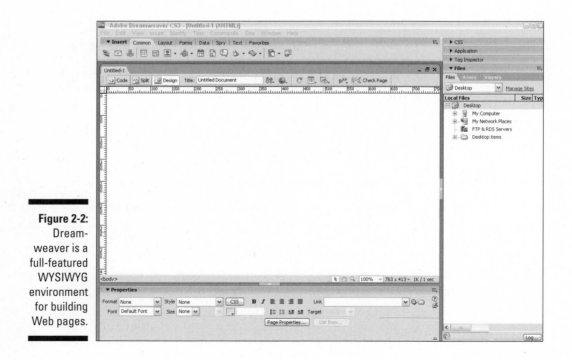

Figure 2-2:
Dreamweaver is a full-featured WYSIWYG environment for building Web pages.

Table 2-2	WYSIWYG Programs
Program	*Web Address*
HotDog PageWiz	`www.sausage.com/hotdog-pagewiz.html`
InnovaStudio	`www.innovastudio.com/editor.asp`
Web Studio	`www.webstudio.com`
Whizzywig	`www.unverse.net/whizzywig-cross-browser-html-editor.html`

Designing the Look of Your Site

All great art depends on having every necessary component in place and nothing — not one thing — that you don't need there. Great literature doesn't add extraneous characters or pad its plot lines. Great paintings don't have extra brush strokes or colors thrown in for no particular reason. When you're practicing the art of Web design, strive for that kind of purity.

Appealing to your audience

The audience — which is made up of the visitors you hope to attract to your site — determines the content. To set some basic limits, think of these visitors as being at a beginning, an intermediate, or an advanced level, and gauge your content accordingly. If you're aiming advanced content at a beginning audience or vice versa, you're looking at failure from the word go.

Not only does your audience determine your content, but its preferences influence your visual-design requirements as well. If your audience consists of high-school students whose interests revolve mainly around the latest musical sensations, you need a far different look than if it consists of retired naval officers who want to know about international events.

For the young music lovers, for example, you need to strike a tone that's lighthearted and exciting, both in your words and graphics. Brighter colors and a more relaxed and informal tone for the text are the call here. For the old salts, though, you need to take a heavier approach, with darker, duller colors and a middling-formal approach to language.

Whatever the group you're aiming for, ask yourself the following questions:

- ✓ **How do they communicate with one another?** Roller hockey players don't communicate quite the same way as cartographers do. What are the level and style of language usage in the group? Do its members have a particular jargon, slang, or regional dialect? If so, can you use it comfortably and correctly?

- ✓ **What kind and color of clothes do they wear?** This kind of information tells you volumes about their preferences. People who are willing to wear suits and ties in midsummer don't think the same way as those who prefer casual clothing. The colors they wear also indicate the color ranges they're likely to feel comfortable with on your site.

- ✓ **What's their worldview?** For many people, the world consists of their apartment or house; the road between it and their workplace; their cubicle, office, or factory floor; and a couple of restaurants somewhere along that pathway. For others, the world consists only of Wall Street and the Asian financial markets. For some, the world is a series of airports, cell phones, and e-mail messages. Anything that exists outside your audience's worldview is invisible to them and probably doesn't belong on your Web site.

Find out all that you can — from what kind of cars your visitors drive to the hours they wake and sleep. Any kind of information that you can nail down about your visitors and their lives helps you to understand them, and that understanding can't help but improve your site's appeal.

Avoiding clutter

If you're one of those people who keeps a perfectly clean desk where your speakers line up exactly perpendicular to the edge of your monitor, whose laundry basket is more than occasionally empty, and who always knows where to find everything that you own, I probably can't tell you much about organization. If you're like the rest of us, however, read on.

Far too many Webmasters seem to think that the best kind of Web page is one that has everything in the world crammed into it. It's like a novel that introduces 27 characters in the first two pages — the overkill ruins it, and your mind is left swimming.

Perhaps you absolutely must put together a Web page containing a dozen frames, several JavaScript pop-ups, numerous Java applets running in the background, and a bunch of animated GIFs that move around the screen by using Cascading Style Sheets (CSS) positioning. If so, please, please, _don't_ put in an image map, too.

The line between losing and winning is very fine if you're considering using Web gadgetry. Without it, most sites seem a bit on the dull side, and Web designers exhibit a really strong keep-up-with-the-Joneses streak that usually results in a frenzy of site changes whenever some new technique becomes popular. Too much of a good thing — or too many good things in one place — can, however, become a real problem.

The key is to remember your site's purpose as you're designing any page. If anything you're considering adding to the page doesn't serve that purpose, don't add it. If you discover some fun or glitzy gizmo that you simply *must* put on a page — and I show you plenty in this book to tempt you — first determine if you can make it fit in with what you already have on that page. If you absolutely can't fit it in, but you still want to add it, maybe you can take something else out to make room for it.

This doesn't mean that you can't have more than one unusual feature on a page — just make sure that you follow a path of moderation.

The Big Rules for Planning Your Site

Here are some short lines to condense the information in this chapter down to a few rules that I think are pretty good guidelines, going by my own experience as both designer and visitor. Make these rules a part of your very being. Do them in calligraphy and hang them on your wall. Use a wood-burning kit to engrave them on your desk. Tattoo them backward on your forehead so that you see them in the mirror every morning.

- **Rule #1:** The Web is for reaching out to people.
- **Rule #2:** Keep your Web pages lean and clean.
- **Rule #3:** Know who your visitors are and what they want.

    Remember that design and content are more a matter of art than science, which means that your own gut feelings count more than anything else. If someone tells you that your design decisions are wrong, and that person is someone whose input you respect, you certainly want to give that opinion some consideration. But if you're firmly convinced that you're right, never let anyone else's concepts override your own. This brings me to The Big Rule:

- **Rule #4:** It's your Web site. It's your vision. Do it your way.

Online Sources for Web Design

Table 2-3 lists some places on the World Wide Web where you can find more information on the topics that were covered in this chapter.

Table 2-3	Online Resources for Web Design
Web Site Name	*Web Address*
Beginners Web Design Tutorial	`www.how-to-build-websites.com`
useit.com	`www.useit.com`
Web Pages That Suck	`www.webpagesthatsuck.com`
Web Style Guide	`www.webstyleguide.com/ index.html?/contents.html`

Part II
Building Your Site

The 5th Wave   By Rich Tennant

"It's a site devoted to the 'Limp Korn Chilies' rock group. It has videos of all their performances in concert halls, hotel rooms and airport terminals."

In this part . . .

1 go beyond the planning stage and get into the nitty-gritty of making your Web site work. Chapter 3 is a quick refresher course in basic HTML. Chapter 4 shows you how to use a WYSIWYG editor to visually design your pages. Chapter 5 introduces the powerful tool of Cascading Style Sheets (CSS). And Chapter 6 shows you how to design for site navigation and set up your own search engine.

Chapter 3

Web Page Construction 101

*T*his chapter's here just in case you need a refresher on basic Web-page building before plunging ahead into all the wonderful add-ons that are covered in the rest of the book. Here, I touch on how you use HTML to create Web pages and populate those pages with text and images. I show you how to format text, set the colors on your Web page, set up links between pages with both text and images, and guide you to some great programs for creating image maps.

Even if you already know all about these things, you may want to browse through the chapter and check out some of the Web sites listed in the tables.

Tagging Along with HTML

Web pages are built primarily by writing instructions in *HyperText Markup Language* (HTML). HTML is a simple programming language; its main aim is to tell a Web browser, such as Microsoft Internet Explorer, how a Web page should look on-screen. What I cover in this chapter is the bare minimum that you need to know to create Web pages and link them to make a Web site. If you're interested in going deeper into HTML, check out *HTML 4 For Dummies*, 5th edition, by Ed Tittel and Mary Burmeister (Wiley Publishing).

You can find the HTML 4.01 specification at `www.w3.org/TR/html401`.

HTML is composed of *elements*. A paragraph or an image, for example, is an element. Elements, in turn, are composed of tags, attributes, and — sometimes — content. Here's a little more information about each of those:

- ✔ **Tags:** A tag is a simple descriptive term that tells a Web browser what element it's dealing with.

  • *Start tag:* The beginning of each element is shown by the name of that element within angle braces; this is called a *start tag.* The start tag for a paragraph, for example, is `<P>`; for an image, it's `<IMG>`.

  • *End tag:* The end of an element is shown by the *end tag,* which is just like the start tag except that the end tag has a slash before the element's name. The end tag for a paragraph, therefore, is `</P>`. Some elements, such as `IMG`, don't have end tags.

- ✔ **Attributes:** An attribute is a modification of the basic element. You specify the width and height of an image, for example, by adding attributes to the tag, as in the following example:

  ```
  <IMG width="100" height="30">
  ```

- ✔ **Content:** Content is anything that goes between the start tag and the end tag, as in the following example:

  ```
  <P>This is the content of this paragraph.</P>
  ```

The tags and attributes that you need most often are covered in more depth in the rest of this chapter, but the basics I just covered help you to understand the choices that you face among different Web-page-building programs.

Determining Your Web Page Structure

The two basic kinds of Web page structures are *regular* and *framed.* Regular gets better mileage on highways, and framed looks nice on a wall. No? Okay. A regular Web page is a stand-alone structure, as shown in Figure 3-1.

Frames, on the other hand, enable you to place more than one Web page on-screen at a time. To the visitor, a framed site appears as one coherent whole, no different from a regular page, something like the horizontally framed example shown in Figure 3-2. (Frames can run vertically, too.) Frames give you more capabilities, such as simultaneously showing many Web pages in a typical browser — and a few extra headaches like making them work with search engines as well.

Figure 3-1:
A regular
Web page is
composed
of a single
HTML file.

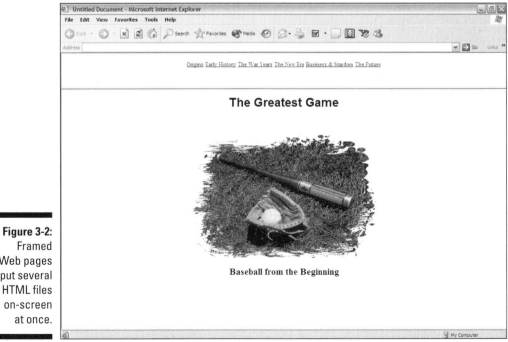

Figure 3-2:
Framed
Web pages
put several
HTML files
on-screen
at once.

Normal elements

As mentioned in the section "Tagging Along with HTML," earlier in this chapter, Web pages are built with *elements*. A typical Web page features a basic structure of three elements: HTML, HEAD, and BODY. The HTML element contains both the HEAD and BODY elements, as the following example demonstrates:

```
<HTML>

<HEAD>
</HEAD>

<BODY>
</BODY>

</HTML>
```

You can make a Web page without using the HTML, HEAD, and BODY tags, but I don't recommend it. It's technically possible and even legitimate under the HTML standard. However, leaving them out can't help anything, and putting them in helps you to keep the other elements in their proper places.

All the code for everything that's visible on the Web page goes into the BODY element. The HEAD element contains information such as the page's title, which goes between the <TITLE> and </TITLE> tags like this:

```
<HEAD>
<TITLE>This is the page title.</TITLE>
</HEAD>
```

The title doesn't appear on the actual Web page — it's displayed in the title bar at the top of the visitor's Web browser.

Frames and framesets

Framed sites work a bit differently than regular sites do. You build them out of *framesets*, which set off different areas of the screen. Each one of these areas is known as a *frame*, and each frame contains its own Web page. The following HTML code sets up the pair of frames that you see in Figure 3-3:

```
<HTML>

<FRAMESET cols="80,*">
  <FRAME name="leftFrame" src="navigation.html">
  <FRAME name="mainFrame" src="main.html">
</FRAMESET>

</HTML>
```

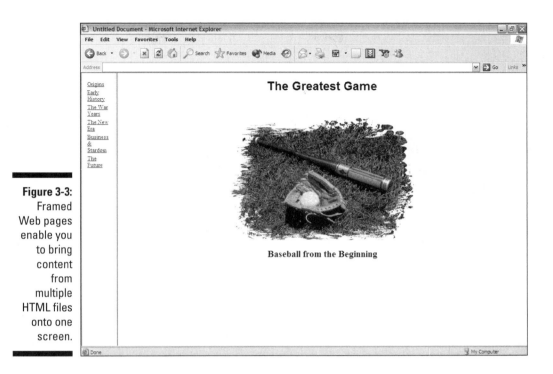

Figure 3-3:
Framed
Web pages
enable you
to bring
content
from
multiple
HTML files
onto one
screen.

The "80, *" in the preceding code listing means that you're setting aside 80 pixels for the first frame, and the rest of the screen is available for the second frame. You can also specify a specific pixel amount for the second frame if you want. Another option is to specify a percentage of the screen for each frame rather than exact pixel sizes, as in the following example:

```
<FRAMESET cols="20%,*">
```

To create horizontal frames instead of vertical frames, you use the `rows` attribute instead of `cols` in the first frameset tag. Everything else works just the same way.

Getting Wordy

Words are the foremost method of communication on the World Wide Web, and it's a rare Web page indeed that hasn't got a passel of 'em scattered all over it.

In the examples that are provided in the following sections, I show the basic code necessary for creating the particular elements that I talk about.

Paragraphs

Paragraph elements are what you normally use to place text on a Web page. You put the text between the `<P>` and `</P>` tags, as in the following example:

```
<P>This is where the textual content goes.</P>
```

Technically, the end tag for a P element is optional in HTML. You don't need to include it, although most Web-page creation programs add it automatically.

Web browsers automatically add a bit of space between paragraphs. If you want some extra space, you can add it by using the line break, or BR, element, as the following example shows:

```
<P>This is the first paragraph.</P>
<BR>
<P>This paragraph has a space above it.</P>
```

Figure 3-4 shows the results of using the BR element.

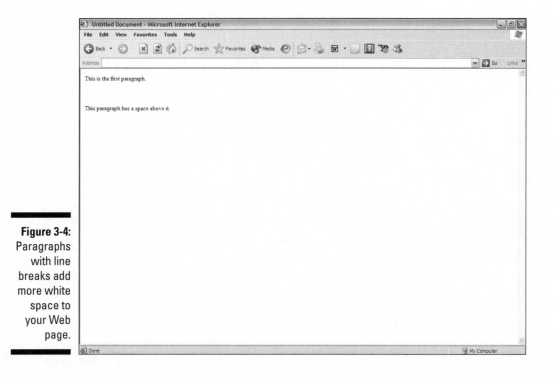

Figure 3-4:
Paragraphs with line breaks add more white space to your Web page.

You can usually get away with using an empty P element — one with no content between the start and end tags — to create a blank line between paragraphs instead of using a BR element. Unfortunately, this technique doesn't work for all Web browsers. Because empty P elements aren't allowed under the HTML standard, browsers that strictly follow the standard ignore them and don't insert a blank line.

If you want the best of both worlds, the standard solution to this problem is to put some invisible content into the P element. Because Web browsers ignore plain white space, you can't just press your spacebar. What you need to do is put in a nonbreaking space with a special code . Here's how you do it:

```
<P>This is the first paragraph.</P>
<P> </P>
<P>This paragraph has a space above it.</P>
```

If you use a nonbreaking space, make sure that you include the semicolon at the end. If you don't, you end up with the characters   on-screen rather than a blank space.

Headings

Headings are also elements that contain text. Different headings create different sizes of text and make that text bold. HTML uses half a dozen heading elements, ranging from the humongous H1 size all the way down to the teeny-weeny H6. You can probably guess that H2, H3, H4, and H5 are between H1 and H6 in size, so I won't bother to explain that.

You use headings to differentiate one section of text from another. Smaller headings designate subsections under larger headings. Say, for example, that you're running a news Web site. You use H1 for the main headline and follow it with the text in P elements. Any subheads in the article use H2 headings, any subheads under those headings use H3, and so on, as the following example demonstrates:

```
<H1>Clown Runs Amok</H1>
    <P>In a surprising development today, Clown of the Year
    Toby O'Dell-Gonzalez went on a rampage through the
    Hideyoshi Circus, spraying at least 17 elephants with
    whipped cream.</P>
<H2>Echoes Earlier Incident</H2>
    <P>Highly placed sources within the circus confirm that
    this is not the first time the famed performer has
    committed such an act. "Toby just kind of has a thing
    about dairy products," said one of the co-owners of the
    circus.</P>
```

Figure 3-5 shows how the preceding code listing looks on your Web page.

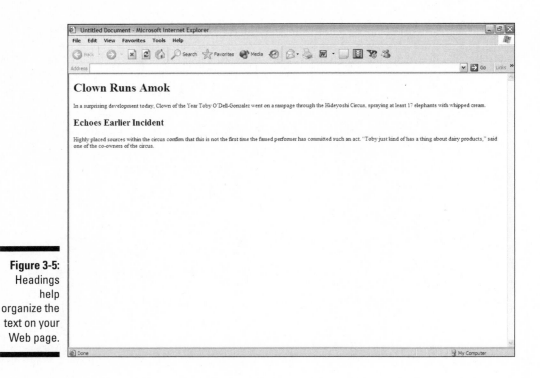

Fonts

Font is a fancy term that describes the way a letter is shaped. **This** word is in a different font than **this** one is. You can just go with the default fonts — those fonts that are automatically set in the Web browser — or you can specify which fonts you want. For casual Web page development, the default fonts work just fine, but you may find that you prefer to make your own choices to get just the right look.

Two elements that you use most often for altering fonts are B and I. These elements set the enclosed lettering to bold or italic print, respectively, as in the following example:

```
<P>This is normal print. <B>This is bold print.</B>
        <I>This is italicized print.</I></P>
```

You can also use the FONT element to set the *face* of the text, which is the basic appearance of the lettering (whether it's Arial, Times New Roman, and so on), as well as the size and color. (See the section "Using Color," later in this chapter, for more information on setting color.) The following example shows how to use the FONT element to set face, size, and color:

```
<P><FONT face="Arial, Helvetica, sans-serif" size="5"
   color="blue">This is blue-colored Helvetica in
   size 5.</FONT>
<FONT face="Times New Roman, Times, serif" size="3"
   color="red">This is red-colored Times Roman in
   size 3.</FONT>
<FONT face="Courier New, Courier, mono" size="7"
   color="black">This is black-colored Courier in
   size 7.</FONT></P>
```

Figure 3-6 shows the results of the two preceding code examples.

Although I used the FONT element on whole sentences in the code example, you can also apply it to smaller stretches of text — even to a single character.

The reason for the face attribute's several choices is that many different computer systems are hooked up to the Internet, and Windows doesn't offer the same options that Macs or UNIX boxes do. If the font you specify isn't available, the visitor's Web browser makes its best guess about what font to substitute. By offering a series of font options for the browser to use, you improve the chances of a visitor seeing just what you intended. The preceding code example includes all you need to cover the three main types of font faces common on the World Wide Web.

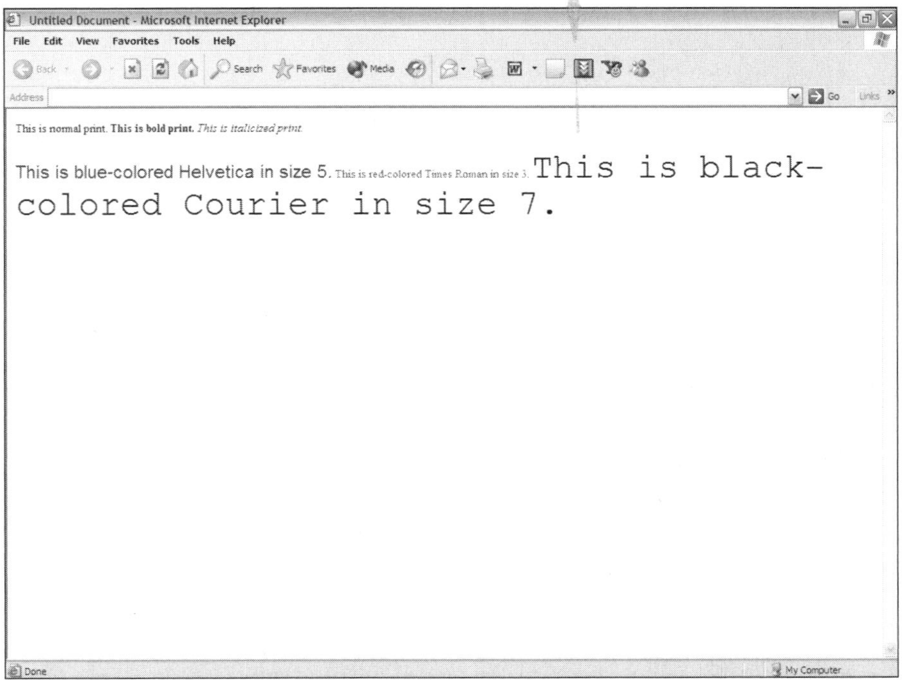

Figure 3-6:
You use the FONT element to make your text appear in different fonts.

Lines

Okay, a horizontal line isn't really a word, but this part of the book is the least unlikely place I can think of to discuss this element. In HTML, these lines are technically known as *horizontal rules,* so the element that represents them is called HR. Horizontal rules visually separate one section of a page from another, underline an image, and do just about anything you normally do with lines.

You can set the width of horizontal rules as either a percentage of the width of the screen or as an exact pixel value. The default width value of a horizontal line is 100 percent of the screen width, so if you don't specify the value of the width attribute, that's what you get. To specify a width of 50 percent, for example, use the following code:

```
<HR width="50%">
```

To specify a width of 400 pixels, you do it like this instead:

```
<HR width="400">
```

You use the size attribute to set the height, or thickness, of the line, as the following example shows:

```
<HR size="6">
```

By default, the line is hollow, or *shaded.* (The hollow line is called *shaded* because back in the days when Web pages weren't so colorful and all you had to work with was black text on a medium gray background, hollow horizontal lines appeared to sink into the page, creating a shaded, or 3-D, effect. Against most other background colors, the effect isn't apparent.) To make a line solid, you need to add the noshade attribute, as in the following example:

```
<HR noshade>
```

The following code creates the Web page shown in Figure 3-7:

```
<HR>
<HR width="100%">
<HR width="50%">
<HR width="200">
<HR width="400">
<HR size="10">
<HR size="6" noshade>
```

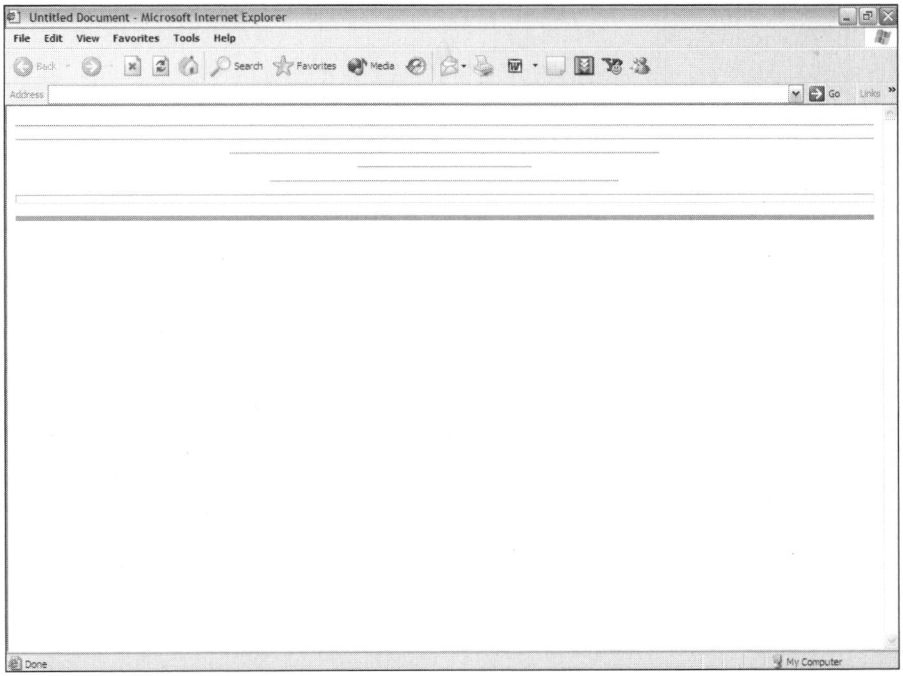

![Untitled Document - Microsoft Internet Explorer window]

Figure 3-7:
Different
width and
size values
change the
appearance
of horizontal
rules.

Many Web designers use graphics, such as GIF files, to create horizontal lines instead of relying on HTML. See the clip art sources in the section "Picturing It: Using Images," later in this chapter, for some examples.

Using Color

Unless you're really into television reruns or artsy photography, you probably don't see much of anything in black and white these days. The world's a colorful place, and you may disappoint your visitors if you don't use color on your Web site.

I touch on color in the earlier section "Fonts," but you can use color in many places. As time goes by, you will doubtlessly be able to color every element in HTML.

If you use *Cascading Style Sheets* (CSS), you have much more control over color than you do with normal HTML. There's an introduction to CSS in Chapter 5 of this book, and you can find out even more in the book *Creating Web Sites Bible,* by yours truly and my colleague Andrew Bailey (Wiley Publishing).

If you read the section "Fonts," earlier in this chapter, you already know that you can set the color of a particular set of letters, but you can also set the base color for all the text as well as for a page's background and its links. The links use three different colors: one for links a visitor hasn't clicked, one for links that he or she is clicking, and one for links already visited.

You can accomplish all these color changes by setting the values for various attributes of the BODY element:

- ✔ text   Text color
- ✔ bgcolor   Background color
- ✔ link   Unvisited link color
- ✔ vlink   Visited link color
- ✔ alink   Color for a link that someone's clicking (the *active link*)

Setting all these attributes at once looks like this:

```
<BODY text="black" bgcolor="white" link="blue" vlink="red"
      alink="purple">
```

Creating Links

When it comes to the World Wide Web, *links* (which connect different files) are everything. Without them, the Web wouldn't exist. You create links with the A (anchor) element. That element's href (hypertext reference) attribute gives the Web address of the file you want to link to. This address is called a *URL,* which is short for uniform resource locator. Here's what a link looks like in HTML:

```
<A href="http://www.dummies.com/">content</A>
```

The part that reads *content* is where you put words or images that people can click to go to the linked file. This content appears by default as blue underlined letters if it's a text link or as a blue outlined image if it's an image link.

Picturing It: Using Images

You can have a Web page with nothing but words on it, but most people think that's a bit dull. It's pretty rare to find a site that's not filled with images of one kind or another. When it comes to placing images on the World Wide Web, you need to use graphics files in one of three common formats: *GIF, JPEG* (also called *JPG*), or *PNG.* (Chapter 7 covers these file formats in more depth.)

Where do you get images? You can create them from scratch, or you can download ready-to-use files from some of the Web sites listed in Table 3-1. If you use other people's images — and most Web designers do — make sure that you first read all the fine print on their Web sites. Unless it states otherwise, the original artist owns the copyright on an image. You can't use it without permission. Fortunately, the vast majority of artists on the Web are eager to give that permission in exchange for nothing more than a link from your Web site back to theirs. This arrangement gives them free publicity and gives you free, high-quality artwork. Everybody's happy.

If the artist isn't willing to let you display copyrighted art in exchange for a link, you may need to pay to use the image. Sometimes, too, the image is free to use on noncommercial sites but costs money to use on commercial ones. To reemphasize the point, *make sure that you read the fine print.* Don't — I repeat, *don't* — just grab an image that's not free, use it, and figure that you can get away with it. You can do that — after all, you can download any image that you can see in a Web browser — but you're cheating the artist and running the risk of serious repercussions, like federal charges. Plenty of freely available art is out there. Stick with it, and you're unlikely to run into problems.

Table 3-1	Clip Art Sources
Web Site Name	*Web Address*
Animation Arthouse	www.animation.arthouse.org
Barry's Clipart Server	www.barrysclipart.com
Clipart Connection	www.clipartconnection.com
CoolArchive Free Clip Art	www.coolarchive.com
Graphic Maps	www.graphicmaps.com/clipart.htm

Images

The most common item other than text on Web pages is the *image,* represented by the IMG element. The only absolutely required attribute for that element is the src attribute, which specifies the name and, if the file is located somewhere other than in the same directory as the HTML file that links to it, the location of the graphics file.

Thus, you code the simplest image on a Web page (see Figure 3-8) like this:

```
<IMG src="seated16.jpg">
```

Figure 3-8:
This image
of some
bored
people is in
a JPEG file
format.

To specify a graphics file in another folder, you need to add the path to the folder, as in the following example:

```
<IMG src="pets/seated16.jpg">
```

If the graphics file is on another Web server entirely, you need to add the full path to that URL, as follows:

```
<IMG src="http://www.anotherserver.com/seated16.jpg">
```

I mention in the section "Creating Links," earlier in this chapter, that you can use an image as a link just as you can use text for one. To do so, just put the IMG element right between the start and end tags for the A element, as the following example shows:

```
<A href="http://www.dummies.com/"><IMG src="seated16.jpg"></A>
```

IMG elements don't have an end tag.

Background images

A background image follows the same rules as a regular image, except that you create it by using the background attribute of the BODY element rather than an IMG element, as shown in the following example:

```
<BODY background="guitar2.jpg">
```

Background images *tile,* which means they repeat themselves across the page until they reach the edge of the screen. Then they begin tiling again in the next available space below the first line of images and so on, until they fill the entire page from side to side and top to bottom. Because of this characteristic, most people prefer to use small background images, like the guitars shown in Figure 3-9.

Choose background images with care. Make sure that they don't interfere with the other elements on the Web page. You want the color muted, the lines indistinct, and the content supportive of the overall theme.

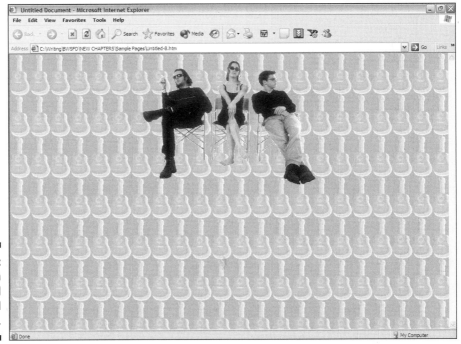

Figure 3-9:
A page with
a tiled
background
image.

Image maps

Image links are discussed in the preceding sections on linking and images. However, you can also use a special kind of image link called *image mapping*. If you use a normal image link, you have one link that goes with one image. By using image mapping, you can add several links to a single image.

By using an image-mapping program, you draw shapes over specific areas within an existing image. You then assign a particular URL to each of these areas. When visitors click the part of the image that links to a URL, they're sent to that URL. You may, for example, use a map of the world as your image map. When your visitors click England or Scotland, they go to a page about the U.K. If they click Africa, they go to a page about that continent. And so on and so on. . . .

You don't need to stay purely geographical, however. You can just as easily take a diagram of the human body and click the abdomen to go to a page about appendectomies or click the mouth to go to a page about dentistry. Any kind of logical connection works with image maps.

Many graphics programs, such as Fireworks, include image-mapping capabilities. If you don't own one of those programs, you may want to check out some of the image-mapping programs that are listed in Table 3-2.

Table 3-2	Image-Mapping Programs
Program	*Web Address*
CoffeeCup Image Mapper	www.coffeecup.com/image-mapper
Image Mapper	www.pcoward.com/imagemapper
Mapedit	www.boutell.com/mapedit

Online Sources for Web Page Building

Table 3-3 lists some places on the World Wide Web where you can find more information about the topics that were covered in this chapter.

Table 3-3	Online Resources for Web Page Building
Web Site Name	*Web Address*
HTML 4.01 Specification	`www.w3.org/TR/html401/`
HTML Goodies	`www.htmlgoodies.com`
HTML Writers Guild	`www.hwg.org`
Index DOT Html	`www.eskimo.com/~bloo/indexdot/html/index.html`
Introduction to HTML	`www.wdvl.com/Authoring/HTML/Intro/`

Chapter 4

Working with WYSIWYG

*W*YSIWYG (What You See Is What You Get) programs are easy for novices to use in the early stages of Web site creation, but they can quickly prove less than satisfactory. The reason for both factors is the same: The program makes a bunch of choices for you. Although this feature may seem like a comfort at first, it can quickly become a limitation. If you go for a WYSIWYG program, make sure that it's sophisticated enough that you can still use it as your skills advance.

Most WYSIWYG programs have at least some degree of depth beneath their surface simplicity. Dreamweaver (the topic of this chapter), for example, lets you set the attributes for every element, in case you don't like the default choices, giving you the best of both worlds, allowing you to create visually while working under the hood with the base code. That means that you can enjoy both the quickness of WYSIWYG creation and the total control of text editing in the same page-creation session.

Dreamweaver, shown in Figure 4-1, is the main choice of most professional Web designers, but it isn't the only possible choice. Table 4-1 lists several WYSIWYG programs that you can use to build Web pages, along with the Web addresses where you can find them (or information about them).

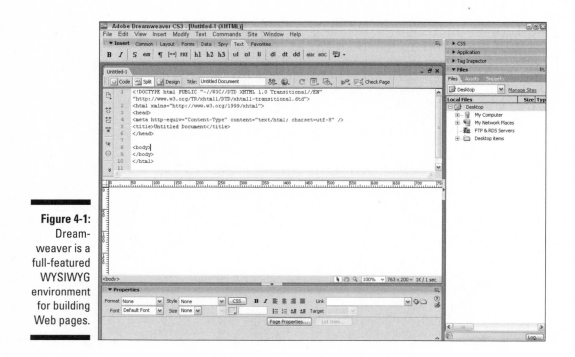

Figure 4-1:
Dream-
weaver is a
full-featured
WYSIWYG
environment
for building
Web pages.

Creating the Basic Page in Dreamweaver

After you understand what's going on under the hood of a Web page, as
discussed in the previous chapters, it's time to sit back and let Adobe
Dreamweaver (formerly Macromedia Dreamweaver, but that's how things
go in the world of computers) do a little magic for you.

Don't worry about doing anything fancy here; I cover site design in other
chapters. For now, just play around with Dreamweaver and experience the
joy of working with a truly excellent program (one of my personal favorites,
seriously). In the next few sections, I walk you through using it to set page
properties and work with text and links. Of course, you should feel free to
experiment with different values, colors, and so on, as you familiarize yourself with the program.

Setting the page properties

In Chapter 3, I explain how to set the page title and page background with the
normal HTML approach. Here's how to set page properties in Dreamweaver:

1. **In the Properties panel at the bottom of the Dreamweaver workspace
(refer to Figure 4-1), click the Page Properties button.**

The Page Properties dialog box appears.

2. **If you want to change the text color, click in the Text Color box to open a drop-down palette, as shown in Figure 4-2. Choose a color from the palette that appears by clicking it.**

   If you want to change the background color, click in the Background Color box and then choose a color from that palette.

   Alternatively, you can simply type the hexadecimal number of the color into the text box.

   If you're not sure what the number is, take a look at the color chart at www.colorcombo.com/400_table.html.

3. **If you want to add a background image, click the Browse button and then navigate to the image file and select it.**

4. **On the Category menu on the left side of the Page Properties dialog box, select Title/Encoding.**

   The Title/Encoding options appear in the Page Properties dialog box, as shown in Figure 4-3.

5. **In the newly displayed options, delete the words Untitled Document from the Title text box and then type the title for your Web page.**

6. **Click the OK button to complete the process.**

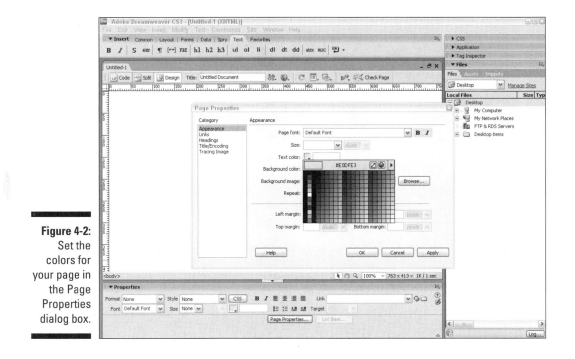

Figure 4-2:
Set the colors for your page in the Page Properties dialog box.

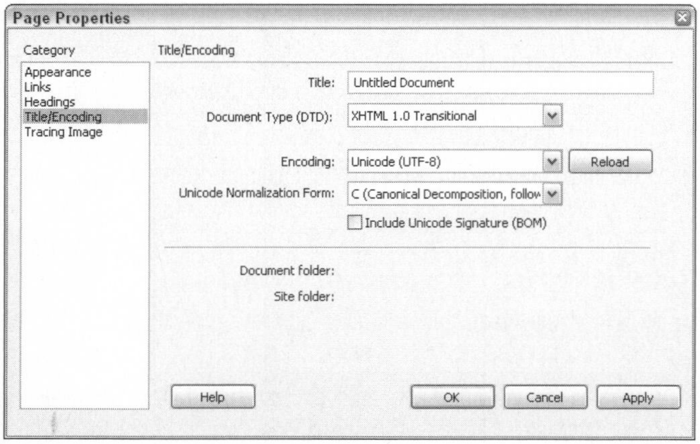

Page Properties

Category	**Title/Encoding**
Appearance	Title: [Untitled Document]
Links	
Headings	Document Type (DTD): [XHTML 1.0 Transitional ▾]
Title/Encoding	
Tracing Image	Encoding: [Unicode (UTF-8) ▾] [Reload]
	Unicode Normalization Form: [C (Canonical Decomposition, follow ▾]
	☐ Include Unicode Signature (BOM)
	Document folder:
	Site folder:

[Help]   [OK] [Cancel] [Apply]

Figure 4-3:
Changing
the title of
your Web
page.

Working with text and links

The Insert bar, which is located just below the menu bar, has several options that you can choose from, each of which changes the set of buttons that appears on the bar. By default, you see the Common Insert bar. To reveal the buttons you use for formatting text, click the Text tab. The Insert bar changes to reveal the text buttons shown in Figure 4-4.

When the Text Insert bar is selected, these are some of the formatting options available in the Properties panel (shown at the bottom of Figure 4-4):

- ✔ **Format:** Select a paragraph style.
- ✔ **Font:** Specify the type of lettering (Arial, Courier, and so on)
- ✔ **Size:** Set the size of the font.
- ✔ **Text color box:** Select the text color. The text color box is located just to the right of Size, but it doesn't have a label.
- ✔ **Link:** If you want to make the selected text into a link, simply type the URL of the linked page into the Link text box (or click the folder icon to browse to the file).

You can add bold or italic formatting only with the main buttons on the toolbar. To add *or* remove this formatting, use the buttons in the Properties panel instead.

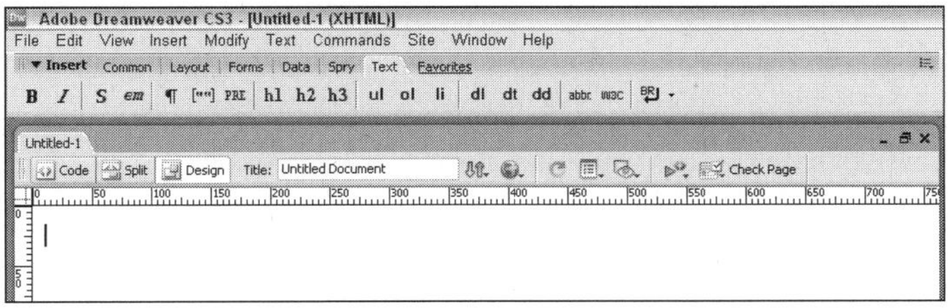

Figure 4-4:
The text
buttons are
now on the
Insert bar.

Adding images

Adding images in Dreamweaver is much easier than typing all the information in by hand in a text editor. Follow these steps to add images in Dreamweaver:

1. **Click the Image button on the Common toolbar. (It's the one with a little tree on it.) In the drop-down menu that appears, select Image.**

   The Select Image Source dialog box, shown in Figure 4-5, appears.

2. **Navigate to the image file or enter the location.**

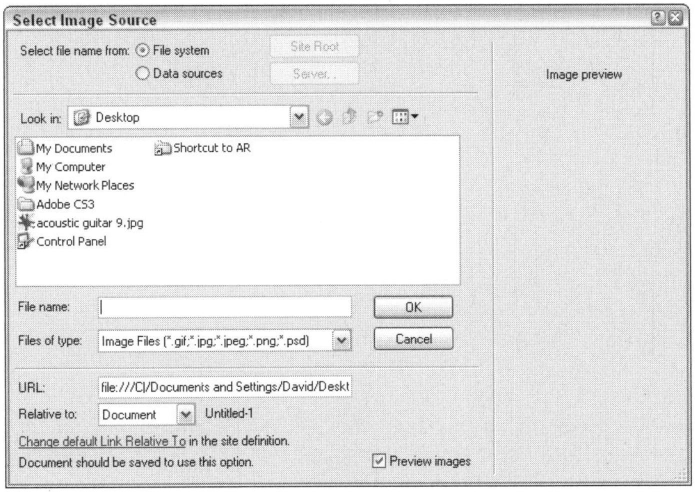

Figure 4-5:
Choosing an
image.

3. **Click the OK button.**

4. **Enter some alternate text (for non-visual browsers) in the dialog box shown in Figure 4-6, and then click the OK button.**

   The image now appears on your Web page in Dreamweaver.

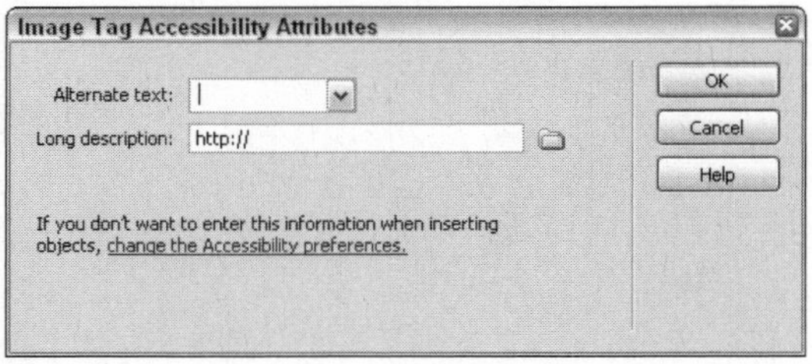

Figure 4-6:
Adding alternate text.

5. **If the image isn't automatically selected when it's inserted, you need to click it.**

   The Properties panel presents you with various image information and options, as shown in Figure 4-7. Dreamweaver automatically enters the height and width information for you.

6. **If you want to resize the image, type the new height and width in the appropriate text boxes in the Property Inspector or move the corners and sides of the image on-screen with your mouse.**

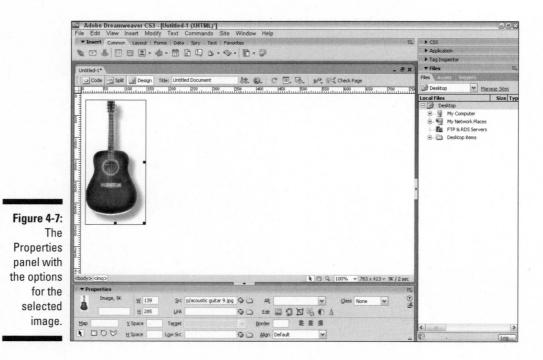

Figure 4-7:
The Properties panel with the options for the selected image.

Jumping into Code View

Dreamweaver isn't just a WYSIWYG editor; it has a built-in code editor as well, thus satisfying the needs of both those who don't want to be bothered with the details and those who like to tinker around "beneath the hood."

There are three ways to see Dreamweaver, or rather the pages that you're creating in it: Design View (the default, WYSIWYG, view), Code View (the actual HTML, XHTML, or whatever language you're using), and a combination of the two.

It's an easy matter to switch among the views: Simply select View⇨Design, View⇨Code, or View⇨Code and Design. Refer to Figure 4-7 to see the Design View in Dreamweaver. Figure 4-8 shows the Code View, and Figure 4-9 shows the Code and Design View.

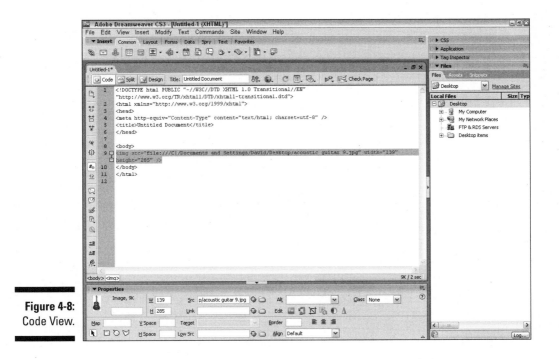

Figure 4-8: Code View.

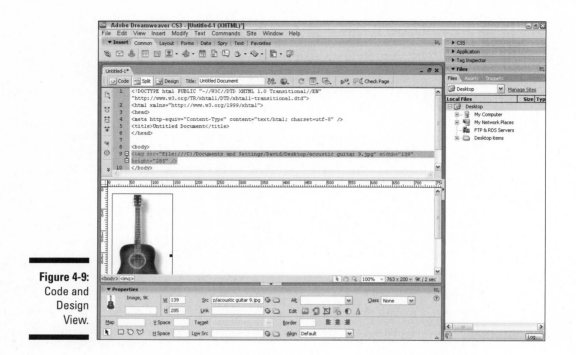

Figure 4-9:
Code and
Design
View.

Online Sources for WYSIWYG

Table 4-1 lists some places on the World Wide Web where you can find more information about the topics that are covered in this chapter.

Table 4-1	WYSIWYG Programs
Program	*Web Address*
Microsoft Expression Web	`http://www.microsoft.com/Expression/products/overview.aspx?key=web`
Adobe Dreamweaver	`www.adobe.com/products/dreamweaver`
HotDog PageWiz	`www.sausage.com/hotdog-pagewiz.html`
Web Studio	`www.webstudio.com`

Chapter 5

Cascading Style Sheets

· ·

· ·

*H*TML was designed to specify the appearance of a Web page, but the initial implementation left a lot to be desired. In the name of standardization (admittedly, a laudable goal at the time), a great deal of creative control was left behind. An `<H1>` element, for example, would always look the same no matter what the designer wanted to show with it. It would always be the same size, the same color, the same font, and so forth.

With the advent of Cascading Style Sheets (CSS), however, all that changed. Suddenly, Webmasters could make anything on a Web page behave any way they wanted it to. This led, naturally, to both a greater degree of creative license and more than a little bit of confusion.

In this chapter, I'll cover the basics of CSS and how you can use it to make your own Web pages dance to the tune of your dreams. There is SO much that you can do with CSS that is beyond the scope of this book, however, that I highly recommend that — after you read this chapter, of course — you rush out to the bookstore and get a copy of *CSS Web Design For Dummies* by Richard Mansfield (Wiley Publishing).

That said, let's take a look at CSS and the kinds of things that you can accomplish with it.

Merging CSS and HTML

There are three ways to add CSS to your Web pages:

✔ **Inline styles:** With this method, the effect is totally localized. That is to say, the style you create with this method applies only to the element that contains it and to nothing else on the Web page. An inline style is the simplest kind of CSS, but lacks much flexibility. It uses the `style` attribute to add CSS. An inline style that sets the color *only* for the H1 element *in which it is declared* looks like this:

```
<H1 style="color: blue">This is a major heading in
    blue.</H1>
```

✔ **Style declaration:** This permits you to use the full range of CSS, applying it throughout a single Web page, but it's of limited utility when dealing with a large number of pages on a significant Web site. Such a declaration must occur within the HEAD element of the HTML document. A style declaration takes the form of:

```
<HEAD>
<STYLE>
H1
{color:blue}
</STYLE>
</HEAD>
```

After such a declaration, the text in all H1 elements on this Web page will be blue in color.

✔ **Separate `.css` file:** This file is linked to the `.html` files on your Web site. With this approach, all the creative elements (color, font size, and the like) are specified in a different file (`.css`) from the ones that define the content of the Web pages on your site (`.html`). This has a tremendous advantage over either of the other two approaches: One `.css` file can control the appearance of multiple Web pages. Let's say, for example, that you have a Web site with 87 pages. You can readily imagine the amount of effort involved if you have to go into each and every one of those Web pages and manually alter all the CSS properties you'd entered into each of them. Now imagine that there's just one `.css` file that you have to change to effect a new style on every single Web page in your site. You get the picture, right?

A `.css` file isn't anything fancy. It's just a plain text file, like a regular `.html` file. You can create one in anything from Windows Notepad to the fanciest Web page editor. Just make sure to give it an extension of `.css` (if your program doesn't already do that for you), and you'll be fine.

All you have to do is put a link to the .css file in each of your Web pages and, after that, any change in the linked file is reflected automatically in all your Web pages.

Here's how it's done:

1. **Create the .css file with the variables relating to font size and color or whatever other features you wish to specify.**

2. **Create the .html files that define the content of your site.**

3. **In the HEAD element of each Web page on your site, add the following lines of code:**

```
<HEAD>
<LINK rel=stylesheet href="file.css" type="text/css">
</HEAD>
```

Of course, you replace the *file* part with the name of your actual .css file.

4. **Upload both the .css and .html files to your Web server.**

There. You're done.

After that, to change the appearance of every page on your site, just alter the .css file and upload the new version. Yep, simple as that. No kidding.

You can add several different .css files to one .html file by simply listing them all. Say you have three different style files that apply to your site. The following code would add them all:

```
<HEAD>
<LINK rel=stylesheet href="file1.css" type="text/css">
<LINK rel=stylesheet href="file2.css" type="text/css">
<LINK rel=stylesheet href="file3.css" type="text/css">
</HEAD>
```

Perhaps the hardest thing to keep in mind when dealing with a separate .css file is also the simplest: that you don't use the <STYLE> tag. In fact, a .css file doesn't use any HTML at all. Ever. Other than that, the syntax is exactly the same. Take a look at how the code changes between the two:

✔ **Declared style:**

```
<HEAD>
<STYLE>
H1
{color:blue}
</STYLE>
</HEAD>
```

✔ **Separate file:**

```
H1 {
color:blue
}
```

There's actually a fourth level of CSS, but Webmasters have no control over it. A visitor to your site can specify in his Web browser that his own personal style sheet be used instead of any that is intended on the site.

Selectors, Classes, and IDs

Cascading Style Sheets — hmm — the *style sheets* part of that seems pretty obvious. Well, with a little struggle, maybe. I honestly cannot tell you why the inventors decided on *sheets* instead of *files* or some other more common term — that's just one of life's little mysteries. But the *style* part, at least, should be obvious: it's a way of establishing the style (appearance) of your Web pages, giving you much more control than standard HTML does. The *cascading* part is, after a moment's reflection on the way CSS works, also obvious: The style formatting flows from the top down, just the same as a waterfall or cascade does. (Perhaps its originators had a *sheet of water* in mind. . . .)

The preceding section describes three methods of adding CSS to your Web pages. The top in this case is a separate .css file, the next level down the cascade is a general style declaration and, at the bottom of the cascade, you find your inline styles. Each of these is interpreted in that order.

Whether you realize it, you've already learned about using *selectors* in CSS. A *selector* is simply the name of the element or elements that you're altering. The H1 element that was used in the preceding examples, for instance, is a selector.

What if you don't want to change all instances of an element, but just want to change some instances of them? That's where classes and IDs come in. You create a class in either a style declaration in the HEAD element or in a separate .css file. The syntax is, by now, familiar:

```
<HEAD>
<STYLE>
.class1 {color:blue}
.class2 {font-family:Arial, Helvetica, sans-serif}
</STYLE>
</HEAD>
```

If this is done in a separate .css file, leave out the HTML parts (HEAD and STYLE).

This declares that any element that is assigned `class1` will be blue while any element that is assigned `class2` will be Arial. (The other terms in that font family are the most likely similar fonts in descending order. Any modern operating system will recognize at least one of them and, therefore, display something close to what the Web site designer intended.)

The `.class` definition is CSS. You recall that CSS and HTML aren't the same thing, of course, and HTML has a slightly different way of actually assigning the declared classes. All you have to do, basically, is drop the dot at the beginning:

```
<H1 class="class1">This text will be blue.</H1>
<H2 class="class2">This text will be in the Arial
    font.<H2>
```

Redefining Elements

If you think you're stuck with the official definitions of various elements in HTML, you're wrong. With CSS, you can redefine *any* element to have the properties you desire. Don't care for the Arial or Times New Roman fonts? No problem. You can substitute anything else for them if you like.

Take the `H1` (major heading) element for example: Without CSS, it's always going to have a size of 24 points, a black color, and a bold attribute. The `H1` element will also be in Times New Roman font, even though many non-European publishers commonly use Arial for headings and Times New Roman for text. You'll probably want to make such an obvious change, and CSS lets you do just exactly that. Here's how you redefine it:

```
<HEAD>
<STYLE>
H1 {font-family:Arial, Helvetica, sans-serif}
</STYLE>
</HEAD>
```

Henceforth, every `H1` element will have that value.

Contextual Selectors

A *contextual selector,* as you might guess from the apt description, is a selector that works only within a certain context. The context that's referred to is the parent element of another element. Normally, when one element is contained within another — as when a heading contains some kind of emphasis on a particular word (like bolding it) — the contained element inherits the properties of its parent element.

Okay, that's a long-winded way of saying that if you set your H1 elements to be blue and you add <B></B> tags around one word in one H1 element, that bolded word will also be blue. But what if you want all B elements that appear within an H1 element to turn green? You can do that, no problem. And, because you're using contextual selection, no B elements that appear outside an H1 element will be affected. Here's how the code for such a style declaration actually looks:

```
<HEAD>
<STYLE>
H1
{color:blue}
H1 B
{color:green}
</STYLE>
</HEAD>
```

Layers

Okay, not layers, DIVs. This is an old argument going way back to the browser wars between Microsoft's Internet Explorer and Netscape Navigator (the ancestor of both IE and today's Firefox browser). Microsoft, having much more money and clout, clearly won that war and few people today even remember what Netscape was, but the older, more aptly descriptive terminology has stuck despite the fact that the official name for a layer today is a DIV (division of a Web page).

The DIV goes in the BODY element of your Web page. A DIV is defined as a rectangle with a specified width, height, and upper left corner position. That rectangle acts as a kind of miniature Web page within the larger Web page and can contain anything a normal Web page can.

The concept of layers actually goes back further than that, to the days when an overhead projector was the hottest high-tech item on the market. If you're old enough (or recently attended a low-tech school), you probably have memories of your teachers placing one transparency on top of another on an overhead projector, which resulted in the information on the second transparency showing up on the screen on top of the information on the first one. The first transparency was the lower layer; the second was the higher layer; and so forth.

Web pages can be thought of in the same way — as one layer of information superimposed upon another, lower layer. A third, higher layer can then be placed onto it, and so forth, ad infinitum.

Many Web site designers take advantage of this ability to provide distinct types of information on top of one another. This may be a series of maps showing, for example, Europe before, during, and after the Napoleonic Wars, with a user interface that allows a Web site visitor to view them in whatever sequence she desires. This is called an *overlay* in cartographic terminology, which you'll often find in Google Earth. (Shameless plug time: Be sure to see this author's *Google Earth For Dummies* [Wiley Publishing] if it's not already a part of your collection.)

Absolute positioning

Absolute positioning is based upon the upper left corner of the Web page itself, not upon anything that is contained within it. Thus, a DIV that is absolutely positioned at, say, 50 pixels in and down from the upper left corner will be only half as far from the left and top margins as one that's absolutely positioned 100 pixels in and down.

To set a DIV to an absolute position, you simply need to specify that this is what you want and tell how far from the left and top of the Web page you want the upper left corner of your DIV to be. For example, for a rectangle that's 100 pixels by 100 pixels in size, use the following code to set its absolute position to 50 pixels in and 50 pixels down:

```
<BODY>
<DIV
style="position:absolute;top:50;left:50;width:100;
   height:100">
</DIV>
</BODY>
```

Relative positioning

Relative positioning is simple to implement: You simply use the word `rela-tive` instead of the word `absolute` in your HTML code. Otherwise, it works the same as absolute positioning does except for one critical factor — its origin point. It's based, not upon the upper left corner of the Web page, but upon the upper left corner of *the containing element.* You doubtless recall that everything on a Web page is contained by something else — the BODY element is contained within the HTML element and so forth — and this means that, with relative positioning, you have to pay careful attention to this container relationship unless you really, really like dealing with unpredictable results on your Web pages.

If, for example, one DIV is contained within another one, then you have to calculate the second one's positioning relative to its parent DIV element's position, not the Web page as a whole. Let's say that the contained DIV is set to a relative position of 200 pixels in and 200 pixels down. If the parent DIV is set to 100,100, then the position of the child DIV is going to be 300,300 (the position of the upper left corner of the parent DIV plus the position of the child DIV).

Online Sources for CSS

Table 5-1 lists some places on the World Wide Web where you can find more resources like the ones that are covered in this chapter.

Table 5-1	Online Resources for CSS
Web Site Name	*Web Address*
CSS Beauty	www.cssbeauty.com
CSS Standard	www.w3.org/TR/CSS21
CSS Tutorial	www.w3schools.com/css
CSSplay	www.cssplay.co.uk
Dynamic Drive CSS Library	www.dynamicdrive.com/style
Guide to Cascading Style Sheets	http://htmlhelp.com/reference/css

Chapter 6

Designing for Site Navigation

*Y*ou can expect two kinds of visitors to your site: those who want to get what they want fast, and those who want to take the time to explore.

For visitors who want to get somewhere on your site fast, you need to provide a way for them to quickly find what's interesting. A *search engine* is the answer for these people. And I don't mean the kind of search engine that gives them links to the entire World Wide Web, but one that searches only your site (although you can have both).

For visitors who want to leisurely browse your site, you need to provide an easy way to explore it. You can just slap a bunch of plain old links everywhere, but there are a lot of neater and cooler ways to do it.

In this chapter, I show you how to add some glitz and function to your site to make the surfing experience a whole lot easier for your visitors.

Planning Usable Navigation

Usability is an important word for Web designers. It means just what it says — making a site usable. Without usability, nothing else you do matters. What good is it to have wonderful content if nobody can find it? What good is it to have beautiful graphics on a page that is inaccessible except by dumb luck?

Fortunately, designing a usable Web site isn't difficult, and following a few simple rules can set you on your way. As with any set of rules, you may want to break these from time to time, but you do so at your own peril:

- **Keep your navigation system consistent on all the pages in your Web site.** If you have a link to your home page at the top of half your pages and you put that link at the bottom of the rest, you'll confuse your visitors.

- **Put links to your home page and your search function on both the top and bottom of every page.** Too many Web designers put them on only the top or the bottom, forcing users to scroll to find them. Don't make your visitors do extra work.

- **Never use blue, underlined text for anything but a link.** In fact, try to avoid underlining at all. Use bold or italics for emphasis instead; otherwise, you'll fool a lot of people into clicking underlined text to no effect.

- **Don't use too many links in a navigation bar.** Half a dozen is about the most you should add. Remember that a navigation bar is not a site map, but a guide to the major sections within your site.

- **Use words!** Using graphical icons may make your pages prettier, but you should design your navigation bar (or whatever alternative you use) to instantly communicate what it means to someone who has never been to your site before. In this case, a picture is *not* worth a thousand words.

- **If your site is composed of hierarchical pages (and most of them are), consider using *breadcrumb navigation*.** The term comes from the idea of leaving a trail of breadcrumbs as you walk so that you can easily retrace your steps. When applied to a Web site, the metaphor refers to a listing at the top of the page showing the current page's relationship to the hierarchy; most often, these breadcrumbs are links that you can click to go directly back to any place along the trail. The History page on Yahoo!, for example, shows a breadcrumb trail of Directory>Arts>Humanities> History, corresponding exactly to the URL of the page: `http://dir.yahoo.com/Arts/Humanities/History`.

Adding a Search Function

Unless your site consists of just a single Web page, you need a search engine for it. Sites that don't offer search functions are at a real disadvantage compared with those that do have them. Put yourself in a visitor's shoes and ask, "Do I want to spend hours browsing this site in the hope that I may stumble across the information I want? Or do I want to spend a few seconds running a search to get the information I need right away?"

All the search options described in the following sections have their own strengths and weaknesses. Similar programs and services offer varying features. The importance of each feature is a matter for you to decide. I recommend checking out all of them. Because none of them requires much effort to install and use, you may as well road-test every one to see which you like best.

Using Google Site Search

Google Site Search is one of the best of the zillions of valuable tools that Google provides to the Web. You just slap a search box into your Web pages and bam! Your users can search every page in your site — or the whole Web, if you want — using the powerful Google search engine.

Before you can use it, though, you have to get a Google account. No worries — this is a no-obligation situation; you're just getting one more username.

There are lots of Google tools that require this account first, so even if you don't end up using Google Site Search, you'll probably still want to get the account.

Getting the account

To sign up for your Google account, follow these steps:

1. **Go to `www.google.com/accounts/NewAccount` in your Web browser. (See Figure 6-1.)**

2. **Enter your e-mail address.**

3. **Enter your desired password twice (once in each password text box).**

4. **Scroll down and select your location. (See Figure 6-2.)**

5. **Under Word Verification, type the characters that are shown above the text box.**

   This is a measure designed to defeat automated account piracy. Humans can read the graphics characters, while computers can't.

6. **Click the button that says, I Accept. Create My Account.**

   Google will e-mail you a confirmation at the address you entered back in Step 2.

7. **Click the link in that message to complete the account creation process.**

Starting your (site search) engine

Now that you've got your Google account, you're ready to go for your own personal site search engine. Here's how you do it:

1. **Go to `www.google.com/coop/cse` in your Web browser.**

2. **Click the Create a Search Engine button.**

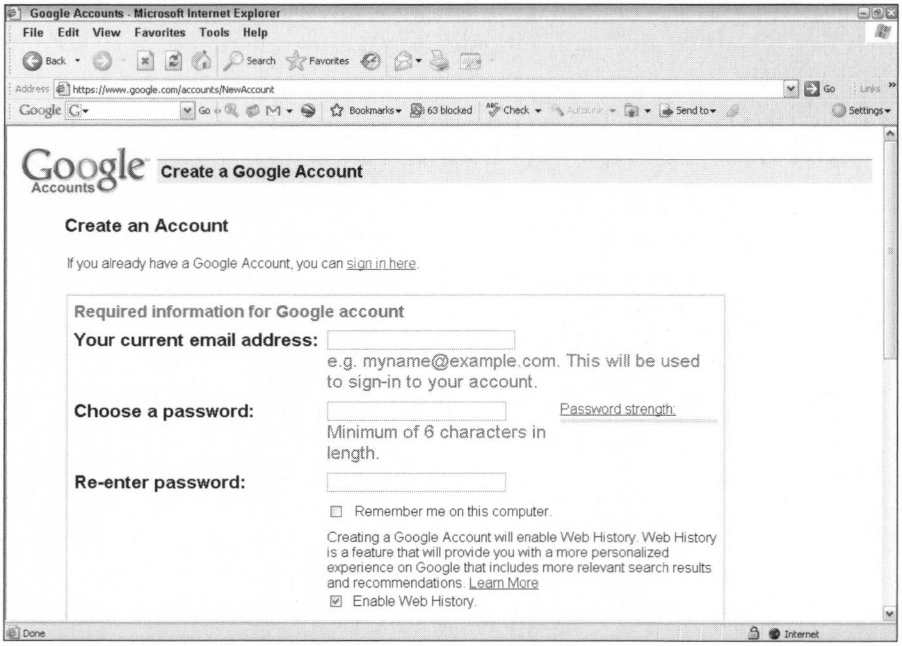

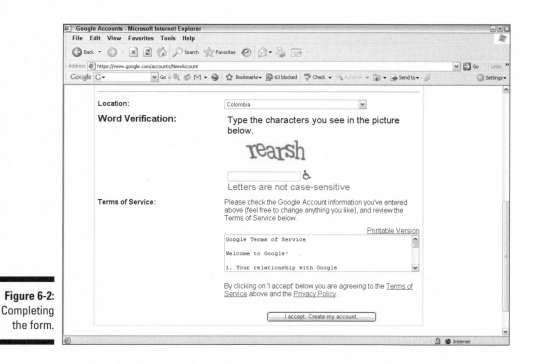

Figure 6-1:
Entering your information.

Figure 6-2:
Completing the form.

3. On the resulting login page, enter your e-mail address and password that you used for your Google account creation.

4. Click the Sign In button.

   If this is a new Google account, you're taken to a page where you need to enter your first and last name before you can continue.

5. On the Create a Custom Search Engine page, shown in Figure 6-3, enter a name and description for your search engine.

6. Next, enter a series of keywords. (See Chapter 17 for some keyword tips.)

7. Select the language for the search engine from the drop-down list.

8. Under What Do You Want to Search? (see Figure 6-4), select one of the options:

   • **Only Sites I Select:** Enables you to limit the search to your own site (or any specific others you want to add).

   • **The Entire Web, But Emphasize Sites I Select:** Searches everything, but puts your sites at the top of the list.

   • **The Entire Web:** Just like using Google from its home page.

9. Scroll down and enter the URLs of the sites you want to search in the text area.

10. If desired, select the check box beneath the text area so that any sites you link to from your Web pages are included in all searches.

11. If you're a nonprofit corporation, a government agency, or a university, you can choose not to show ads on the search results pages. Otherwise, leave the Show Ads on Results Pages radio button selected.

12. Scroll down and select the I Have Read and Agree to the Terms of Service check box.

13. Click the Next button.

14. On the resulting page, click the Finish button.

15. On the next page, click the Control Panel link. (See Figure 6-5.)

16. On the Control Panel page, shown in Figure 6-6, click the Code link.

17. On the next page (see Figure 6-7), select the radio button next to the logo design you like.

18. Click the Save Changes button.

19. Select the HTML code in the text area, copy it, and paste it into your own Web page.

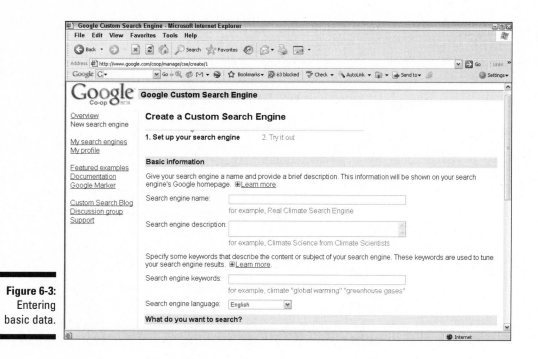

Figure 6-3:
Entering
basic data.

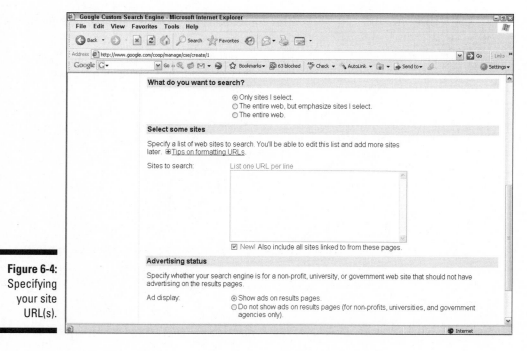

Figure 6-4:
Specifying
your site
URL(s).

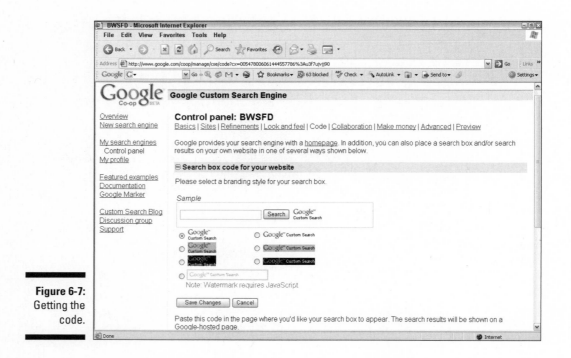

Figure 6-7:
Getting the
code.

Getting a free search engine with FreeFind

After you take a look at the capabilities of FreeFind's search engine (www.
freefind.com), you may not bother to look at anything else (except that I
describe another one that's worth a peek, too). It's a beautifully designed,
full-featured, honey of a search feature that you can add to your site in just a
few minutes. It's customizable, creates a site map for you, keeps an up-to-date
What's New list that shows visitors what you've added lately, gives you extensive reports on what people are looking for, and does pretty near everything
else you can want, except fry your eggs for breakfast. The cost? Nothing.

After you finish drooling over the search engine, you may ask, "What's the
catch?" Advertising supports it, which means that an ad banner appears at
the top of the search page on your site. If your site also has its own advertisers, you can't show any of your ads in competition with FreeFind's ads on
that page.

On most sites, an advertising banner is a pretty small point to consider. Even
if you have your own sponsors, you can still place their ads on every page on
your site that doesn't have FreeFind, and FreeFind helps your visitors get to
all those other pages more easily. FreeFind imposes a site limit of about 2,000
Web pages (32MB), but a polite e-mail message to the FreeFind folks generally
gets them to raise the limit.

You do face one other restriction with FreeFind: FreeFind doesn't allow anyone to use its search engine on adult-only sites, because its advertisers don't want to appear on such sites.

Still with me? Okay, FreeFind's search engine runs on its servers, not on yours, so tons of people can use it simultaneously without tying up all your server resources.

You can set up FreeFind to search just your site, just the World Wide Web outside your site, or both your site and the Web in the same search. You can modify the search form, and FreeFind makes the job extremely easy for you by providing online wizards that help you make custom choices, such as designating link colors (either by name or hexadecimal value).

Joining FreeFind

To sign up for FreeFind, all you need to do is to fill out a simple form, as the following steps describe:

1. **Go to FreeFind's home page (www.freefind.com) and enter your Web site address and your e-mail address in the appropriate text boxes. (See Figure 6-8.)**

   FreeFind keeps your e-mail address confidential, so your address won't be sold to anyone.

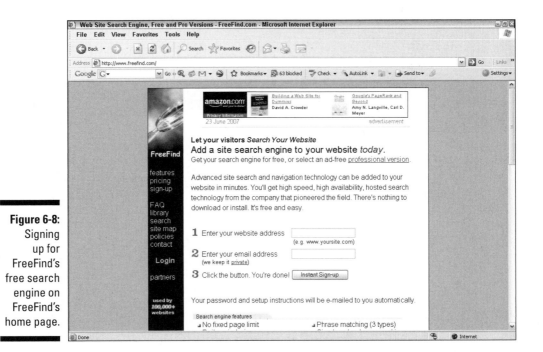

Figure 6-8: Signing up for FreeFind's free search engine on FreeFind's home page.

2. **Click the Instant Sign-Up button.**

   FreeFind sends you an e-mail confirmation message right away. The message contains your password, site ID, and all the links you need to use its service.

3. **Click the link in the e-mail confirmation message to go to the FreeFind Control Center (www.freefind.com/control.html).**

4. **In the form on that page, you need to enter your Web site address, e-mail address, and the password from the e-mail confirmation message; then click the Login button.**

   The Select Account Type page appears.

5. **Click the Select link next to Free Account.**

   Of course, if you're the adventurous type who wants to skip the "try before you buy" approach, you can always click one of the paid service links instead.

   You only have to complete this step the first time you sign in to FreeFind.

6. **On the main Control Center page, click the Build Index tab (shown in Figure 6-9).**

7. **Click the Index Now link.**

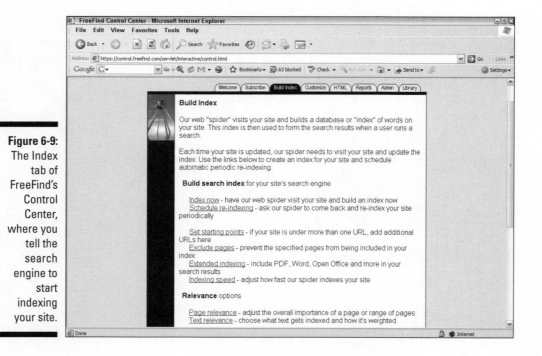

Figure 6-9:
The Index tab of FreeFind's Control Center, where you tell the search engine to start indexing your site.

8. **In the dialog box that appears, click the Finish button to have FreeFind index your site.**

FreeFind starts indexing your site and e-mails you when it's finished. At the same time it does the indexing, FreeFind also creates a site map and a What's New page for your Web site.

Adding the search engine

FreeFind gives you the HTML code for a basic search panel you can add to your pages. All you need to do is copy and paste the version that you want (either from the e-mail message or the attachment) onto the Web page on which you want to use it and then upload the page to your site, and your search engine is fully functional.

You can't use the search engine until FreeFind finishes indexing your site. If you try to use it before FreeFind is finished indexing, you receive an e-mail message saying that the spider's indexing of your site isn't complete, and you get a Web page reminding you to wait.

Here's how to go to the goodies page and get your free code (if you're already in the FreeFind Control Center from the previous steps, you can skip straight to Step 3 here):

1. **Go to the FreeFind Control Center at `www.freefind.com/ control.html`.**

2. **Enter your Web site address, e-mail address, and password, and then click the Login button.**

3. **On the main Control Center page, click the HTML tab (shown in Figure 6-10).**

4. **Scroll down the screen and view the different types of search panels that are available.**

   You can also click the links at the top of the page to jump to particular kinds of panels, such as ones that search your site only, as opposed to those that search the Web and your site.

5. **When you find a search panel you want, click inside the text area underneath it, which contains the HTML code, and select the code.**

6. **Copy the code and paste it into your own Web page code.**

If you want to customize and pretty up the search page, go to the Control Center page and click the Customize tab. You can specify background colors and images, the type of logo that appears, the positioning of the search results, and many other options. The choices that you make there also affect your site map so that both the search page and the site map share the same look.

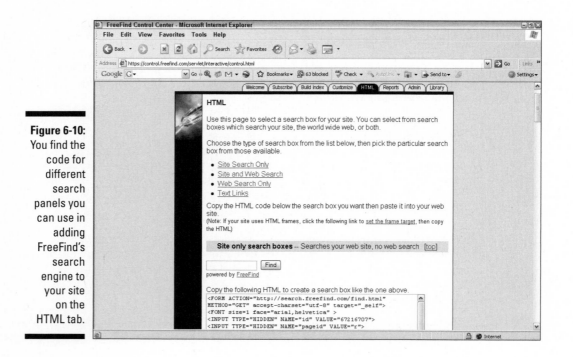

Figure 6-10:
You find the code for different search panels you can use in adding FreeFind's search engine to your site on the HTML tab.

Dropping in Perl CGI scripts with Simple Search

If you're a go-it-alone type who doesn't want to rely on outside servers to process your site searches, you can drop in a Perl CGI script instead. (See Chapter 8 for more on scripts.) It requires a bit more technical skill than some tasks, or a little bit of help from your ISP or network administrator, but it's definitely doable, even if you don't know anything about CGI. One of the best and easiest CGI scripts to use is Simple Search. Written by Matt Wright, one of CGI's greats, Simple Search has been a venerable mainstay of many Web sites. Figure 6-11 shows Simple Search on a Web page.

You can download Simple Search from Matt's Script Archive at `http://worldwidemart.com/scripts/search.shtml`. To add Simple Search to your site, you first need to uncompress (unzip) the main file for the program (`simple.zip`, `simple.tar`, or whatever) and then make a few alterations in the enclosed sample files.

You need to change a few settings in the script to make it work on your site. Make sure that you follow the exact format of what appears in these settings as you replace the sample values in the script with the information for your site, or the script won't work. This mostly means that you must leave all quotation marks and semicolons in place just as they appear in the following examples. Don't replace single quotes with double quotes or vice versa. Keeping a hard copy of the file handy while working on it may help you to remember what to do — and what not to do.

Figure 6-11:
Simple
Search adds
keyword-
searching
capabilities
to your site.

To prepare the Simple Search's Perl script for use, follow these steps:

1. **Go to `http://worldwidemart.com/scripts/search.shtml` and open the file `search.pl` in a text editor.**

2. **Scroll down until you reach the section with the heading `# Define Variables`.**

3. **Replace the `$basedir` value with the base directory path of your own site.**

   For example, in the following script line, the sample value for this variable is `/mnt/web/guide/worldwidemart/scripts/`. Remember to replace only the value itself, not the variable (`$basedir`) or any punctuation marks.

   ```
   $basedir = '/mnt/web/guide/worldwidemart/scripts/';
   ```

   The *base directory path* is the path on your Web server, not your Web site's URL, which you add in the following step. If you don't know this value, ask your ISP or network administrator. Make sure that you include the trailing slash at the end (/).

4. **Replace the `$baseurl` value with the base URL of your site.**

   The value you need to supply for the `$baseurl` variable is the URL of the directory where your site's main page resides. The base URL for Dummies.com, for example, is `http://www.dummies.com/`. And using both `http://` and the trailing slash is important here, too, even if you're not accustomed to using both in Web addresses. In the following lin e from the script, the value you need to replace is `http://worldwidemart.com/scripts/`:

```
$baseurl = 'http://worldwidemart.com/scripts/';
```

5. **Replace the sample values for the `@files` variable with the paths and files that you want Simple Search to process as part of its search.**

   In the following line from the script, the values you need to replace are `*.shtml`, `demos/links/*.html`, and `demos/guest/*.html`:

```
@files = ('*.shtml'.'demos/links/*.html'.
    'demos/guest/*.html');
```

This is one of the easiest places to create a typographical error that keeps the script from working because the `@files` variable can have more than one value. Each value is surrounded by single quotation marks, as usual, but it's also separated from the other values by a comma. If you use more than one value here, pay careful attention to the sample code's syntax.

If you want to search only HTML files in the main directory, for example, you enter the value that the following example shows:

```
@files = ('*.html');
```

To search both HTML and SHTML files in the main directory, you use the following example instead:

```
@files = ('*.html','*.shtml');
```

To search for HTML and SHTML files in a subdirectory called `fauna` as well, you use the following example:

```
@files = ('*.html'.'*.shtml'.'*/fauna.*html'.
    '/fauna/*.shtml');
```

6. **Replace the value of the `$title` variable with the name of your site. In the following line from the script, the sample value you need to replace is `Matt's Script Archive`.**

```
$title = "Matt's Script Archive";
```

This value appears along with the search results, and the next step makes the text into a text link.

7. **Replace the value of the `$titleurl` variable with the Web address of your main page. In the following line from the script, the value you need to replace is `http://worldwidemart.com/scripts/`.**

```
$title_url = 'http://worldwidemart.com/scripts/';
```

This value is usually the same as the `$baseurl` value (see Step 4), although you may want to add the page's filename as well. For example, if your `$baseurl` value is `http://www.mysite.com/` and your main page is `index.html`, you can use either `http://www.mysite.com/` or `http://www.mysite.com/index.html` as the value for `$titleurl`.

8. **Replace the `$searchurl` value with the Web address of your search page. In the following line from the script, the part you need to replace is `http://worldwidemart.com/scripts/demos/search/search. html`.**

```
$search url = 'http://worldwidemart.com/scripts/demos/
    search/search.html';
```

9. **Save the file.**

To prepare the HTML search page for use, follow these steps:

1. **Open the file `search.html` in a text editor.**

2. **Change the `action` attribute of the `FORM` element to the URL where you're locating the Perl script on your Web server.**

   In the following line from the `search.html` file, the value you need to replace is `http://worldwidemart.com/scripts/cgi-bin/demos/search.cgi`.

   ```
   <form method=POST action="http://worldwidemart.com/
       scripts/cgi-bin/demos/search.cgi">
   ```

3. **Save the file.**

Now upload both files to your server. Make sure that you send `search.pl` in ASCII form and that you put it in your `cgi-bin` directory. Send `search. html` in ASCII form and put it in your Web page directory.

You have two options when uploading files. Your FTP program will send a file as either ASCII or binary. ASCII treats the file as text, binary is used for graphics, and so on.

Okay, remember I told you this one took a bit more tech savvy than most? This is where that comes into play. You need to set permissions for the files so they'll work on your Web server. If you don't know what that means, don't worry about it. Just ask your ISP or network administrator to do it for you. Tell them that you need to chmod `search.pl` to 755 and to chmod `search. html` to 744. They'll know what you mean, and they can take care of it in about ten seconds.

There are various opinions on how to pronounce "chmod." Most folks say "chuh-mod," but others say "shmod" or "see-aich-mod."

Showing the Way with Navigational Tools

The more complex your Web site is, the more important it is to use good navigational tools. Although a search engine provides quick answers to specific questions, there's nothing like browsing your way through a site to really get to know what treasures are tucked away. You can help your visitors find their way around your site with some of these handy navigational helpers.

Creating menus with VMaxNav

VMaxNav, a Java applet from Virtual Max, creates an Explorer-style menu that makes site navigation a breeze. As you can see in Figure 6-12, it's attractive, space saving, and useful. It's also easy for Webmasters to work with. You can control the colors and fonts that it uses and even throw in a background image if you want. You can download VMaxNav from `www.geocities.com/ siliconvalley/lakes/8620/vmaxnav.zip`.

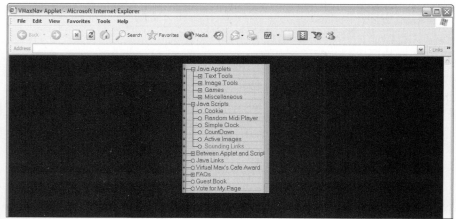

Figure 6-12: VMaxNav creates an attractive site map menu.

The basic code for adding the VMaxNav applet is as follows:

```
<APPLET code="vmaxnav.class" width="200" height="294">
```

You can alter the `width` and `height` attributes, but if you're using a background image, make sure that you use one that either fits the new dimensions or looks good as it tiles. Otherwise, your nice, new navigational tool won't look too good.

The two parameters shown in the following example are required by this applet:

```
<PARAM name="AUTHOR" value="Virtual_Max (http://
   come.to/vmax)">
<PARAM name="KEY" value="Free Version">
```

The AUTHOR parameter is self-explanatory. The KEY parameter value changes only if you register the applet. (The only difference between registered and unregistered versions is that the unregistered one adds a link to Virtual Max's Web site at the end of your links.)

VMaxNav requires one file other than the class file — a text file that lists the links that you want to add. If you want the background image, that's another external file, but the applet doesn't require it. The following examples show you how to specify these files in your code:

```
<PARAM name="URL" value="vmaxnav.txt">
<PARAM name="BGIMAGE" value="vmaxnavbg.gif">
```

I cover the structure of the text file in the "Setting up the external text file" section later in my discussion of the parameters. If you use the name vmax-nav.txt for this file, you don't need to list the URL parameter because that name is *hard-wired* into the applet, meaning that the applet automatically looks for a file with that name, unless you specify otherwise. If you use another name, you do need to specify the URL.

Setting the colors for the navigation tree

You can set the colors for the navigation tree through the TEXTCOLOR, ACTIVECOLOR, and BGCOLOR parameters. You need to enter these values in hexadecimal format. The following code example shows the default color values:

```
<PARAM name="TEXTCOLOR" value="C0C000">
<PARAM name="ACTIVECOLOR" value="80FF00">
<PARAM name="BGCOLOR" value="000080">
```

If these colors suit your design scheme, you don't need to specify them.

Setting the font face, style, and size

You can choose the font face, style, and size by setting the values of the FONT parameter. The font-face options are TimesRoman, Helvetica, Courier, Dialog, or DialogInput.

You must use the exact same capitalization because of the applet's case sensitivity for these font names. Font style values are 0 for normal, 1 for bold, 2 for italics, and 3 for bold italics. Font size values are in pixels.

You put the three values together, separating each by a space. To set Helvetica bold, 20-pixels high, for example, use the following example:

```
<PARAM name="FONT" value="Helvetica 1 20">
```

Specifying how the linked file opens

To specify how the linked file opens, you use the TARGET parameter. The values are the standard _top, _self, _blank, and _parent, or any window name that you've created:

```
<PARAM name="TARGET" value="_blank">
```

Putting it all together

Here's the whole shooting match in one place:

```
<APPLET code="vmaxnav.class" width="200" height="294">
<PARAM name="AUTHOR" value="Virtual_Max (http://
    come.to/vmax)">
<PARAM name="KEY" value="Free Version">
<PARAM name="URL" value="vmaxnav.txt">
<PARAM name="BGIMAGE" value="vmaxnavbg.gif">
<PARAM name="TEXTCOLOR" value="C0C000">
<PARAM name="ACTIVECOLOR" value="80FF00">
<PARAM name="BGCOLOR" value="000080">
<PARAM name="FONT" value="Helvetica 1 20">
<PARAM name="TARGET" value="_blank">
</APPLET>
```

Setting up the external text file

To set up the external text file that VMaxNav draws its information from, you need to follow a strict but simple format. One line in the text file creates one equivalent line in the applet display tree. You specify the level of the line in the tree by the number of blank spaces at the beginning of the line. As the following example shows, a top-level line has no spaces before the text. If it's a second-level line, you add one space before the text; if it's a third-level line, you add two spaces; and so on.

```
Top Level
 Second Level
  Third Level
 Another Second Level
  Third Level
  Another Third Level
Another Top Level
```

Make sure that you save the applet as an unformatted, plain-text ASCII file.

The text on each line has to follow the format `text|URL`, like this:

```
Main Page|index.html
```

When you finish, upload the `.html` file, the `.class` file, the `.txt` file, and the background image file (if you use one). Don't forget that you need to upload the `.html` file and the `.txt` file in ASCII format and the other two as binary files.

Making drop-down lists

Well, I've got just about everything else in this chapter, so it's probably time to throw in a bit of JavaScript, too. The drop-down list shown in Figure 6-13 is easy to add to your site. It's a form that contains a selection menu that helps visitors navigate your site. When a visitor makes a selection from the list, the form calls the JavaScript code and loads the selected page.

Figure 6-13:
A JavaScript
drop-down
list.

To add this JavaScript to your Web page, you first need to put the script into your HEAD element so your code looks like this:

```
<HEAD>
<SCRIPT language="JavaScript">
<!--
// Hide from old browsers
function golinks(where){
self.location = where;
}

// stop hiding -->
</SCRIPT>
</HEAD>
```

Of course, you'll probably have some other stuff in the HEAD element, too, like your title, but I'm focusing on the basics.

Next, put the form into your `BODY` element:

```
<BODY>
<FORM>
<SELECT onchange="golinks(this.options[this.
    selectedIndex].value)">
<OPTION value="http://www.dummies.com/">
    Dummies Press</OPTION>
<OPTION value="http://www.wiley.com/">
    Wiley Publishing</OPTION>
</SELECT>
</FORM>
</BODY>
```

Change the values of the `OPTION` elements to the URLs you want to link to. Of course, you'll want to change the descriptive content, too. To add more links to the list, just add more `OPTION` elements.

Online Sources for Improving Site Navigation

Table 6-1 lists some places on the World Wide Web where you can find more resources like those that are covered in this chapter.

Table 6-1	Online Resources on Site Navigation
Web Site Name	**Web Address**
Bookshelf	www.sakva.orc.ru
FusionBot	www.fusionbot.com
LinkBar	www.consultcom.com/Java/Applets/LinkBar.html
Mondosoft	www.mondosoft.com
siteLevel	http://intra.whatuseek.com

Part III
Adding Sparkle to Your Site

The 5th Wave   By Rich Tennant

"Look into my Web site, Ms. Carruthers.
Look deep into its rotating spiral,
spinning, spinning, pulling you deeper
into its vortex, deeper...deeper..."

In this part . . .

Here, you discover a ton of ways to make your site work, look, and sound great. Chapter 7 tells you where to snag some cool graphics. Chapter 8 talks about the different site add-ins that you can use and shows you how to handle the different kinds that you'll encounter. And Chapter 9 introduces you to the world of Web multimedia.

Chapter 7

Getting Graphic

You can have a perfectly functional Web site without images. But if you compare your site with one that's just as functional but also uses graphics, you'll lose. Most people will go to the other site and leave yours gathering electronic dust.

In this chapter, I take you on a whirlwind tour of places where you can download images by the bushel, I suggest methods for modifying images in fabulous ways, and I share lots of other tips that improve your site's appearance.

Getting Graphics — for Free!

Most of us aren't artists, and even if I know an artist or three, most of them spend their time mucking about with paintbrushes and canvases. Many aren't really comfortable with electronic media. So how do average people who want nice graphics for their Web sites get them? The good news is that excellent graphics are all over the place. Graphics are an integral part of the World Wide Web, and the quality of those graphics has improved tremendously from the early days of the Internet.

Heeding copyrights and credits

Every Web browser is a funnel for graphics. Any image that you can see in it, you can download and put on your site. However, you need to consider a few factors before you use graphics. Yes, you can grab every image file that you find. But you can't necessarily use them all without consequences.

When an artist creates an image, that artist owns the *copyright* to that image. Just like the word says, that gives the artist — and the artist alone — the right to make copies, electronic or otherwise. The artist can give other people permission to make copies of the image — or even sell the copyright to someone — but unless he or she does so, the artist retains total control over the image.

Never take legal advice from anyone who spells copy*right* as copy*write*.

One of the few ways in which someone can lose a copyright is by stating that he's placing a work in the *public domain,* which means that he's surrendering his copyright, and others can do anything that they want with the work. Many people don't understand what public domain means, though, and you sometimes run across a statement on a Web site that says something incredible like, "I retain the copyright to all these images, but I'm placing them in the public domain, so feel free to use them." If you find one of these contradictory disclaimers and you really want to use the images, your best course is to contact the artist for clarification.

Typically, you find five different situations with fine print on an artist's Web site, as the following list describes:

- The artist states that you can't use the images. Just walk away — you can find plenty of others out there.

- The artist states that you can use the images without any conditions. Go ahead and download to your heart's content.

- The artist states that you can use the images if you do certain things, such as include a link back to the page they're on or include a copyright notice under the image. Do what the artist asks and use the images.

- The artist states that you can use the images freely if you run a noncommercial site but that commercial sites must pay. If you're commercial and the work is good, pay up — it's not going to break the bank. After all, you're not buying a Renoir original here.

- The artist provides no information at all about usage. Either walk away or e-mail the artist to find out the policy.

Creating your own images

The easiest way to avoid copyright problems is to make your own images. That way, you own the copyright — unless you're working under contract for someone such as a Web design firm, in which case that company probably owns the copyright. It's impossible for me to cover all that you need to know about copyright in the limited space available here, but the subject is well covered in *Creating Web Graphics For Dummies,* by Bud Smith and Peter Frazier (Wiley Publishing).

Of course, the digital camera revolution also gives you an unprecedented opportunity to create your own Web-ready graphics (check out *Digital Photography For Dummies,* 5th Edition, by Julie Adair King), and programs like Photoshop and Fireworks make it relatively easy for even those of us who aren't very graphically talented to come up with professional-level graphics. Table 7-1 shows the URLs for several popular graphics programs.

Table 7-1	Online Resources for Graphics Programs
Program	*Web Address*
Adobe Fireworks CS3	www.adobe.com/products/fireworks
Adobe Photoshop	www.adobe.com/products/photoshop
Corel Painter	www.corel.com/painter
Corel Paint Shop Pro	www.corel.com/paintshoppro
CorelDRAW	www.corel.com/coreldraw

Differentiating among graphics file formats

Sometimes it seems that there are about as many different graphics file formats as there are people in Manhattan on a Monday afternoon. Every company from Adobe to Kodak has its own way of showing electronic images. When it comes to the Web, though, you really need to consider only three formats — the three that work in all major (and most minor) Web browsers.

GIF

The venerable, old *GIF* (Graphics Interchange Format) file format still sees a lot of use on the Web. Because GIF limits you to 256 colors, it's best to use for images that don't have lots of colors or much in the way of subtle shifts between colors. GIF also has a unique capability — it can contain several images in a single file. These images appear sequentially as you view the GIF file, resulting in a cheap and easy form of animation.

JPEG

The relatively newer *JPEG* (Joint Photographic Experts Group) format, also commonly known as *JPG* because people still have the habit of using DOS 8.3-type filenames, has radically different capabilities. JPEG is a true color format, so you don't need to worry about any color limitations. It also stores image information in a different way, resulting in a highly compressed file that's usually much smaller than a GIF file of the same image.

PNG

The latest puppy in the window is the *PNG* (Portable Network Graphics) format. (You pronounce it *ping.*) PNG does everything that the GIF format does, except create animated images, and does quite a few things much better, such as providing better transparency capabilities. (A more sophisticated format known as *MNG* — Multiple-image Network Graphics — that's currently in the works includes the capability to create animated images, too.)

Putting Your Graphics on a Diet

Fat files are embarrassing. They slow down a page like nothing else, turning a fabulous site into a sluggish turkey. A really good graphics program can trim your overweight files, but such a program will also set you back a pretty penny, and you'll have to work with it for a while in order to get the most out of it. Instead of putting all that money and effort into solving the file size problem, try some of the following Web sites that do the job for you — for free.

GIFWorks

GIFWorks is absolutely one of the best tools you'll find on the Web. Period. You get the idea I like it? A lot? There's a good reason. This is one truly full-featured program, and it's something you may not be familiar with yet — but I think it's the wave of the future on the Web. This program isn't one you download and use on your computer. It stays put, and you use it right on the GIFWorks site.

With GIFWorks, you can do everything to GIF files, from reducing colors to adding special effects. So what does it cost? Nothing, nada, zip. And to top it all off, the same folks have a couple of other sites that do everything from making postcards (MediaBuilder, at www.mediabuilder.com) to letting you get your hands on more than 10,000 high-quality GIF images (the Animation Factory, at www.animfactory.com). I'm not exaggerating when I say *quality*, either. This is some of the best stuff I've seen.

The Animation Factory's images are also free — for noncommercial use. Aha! A catch at last? Nah. If you want to use the images on a commercial site, all you have to do is cough up anywhere from $59.95 for a year's download privileges to the highest rate of $199.95 for a year of the top pro-level service. You don't have to pay any further fees for using the images. The Animation Factory is well worth the price, even if you don't run a commercial Web site, and GIFWorks shows the same attention to quality but costs nothing at all.

Here's how to upload your image to GIFWorks:

1. **Go to www.gifworks.com/image_editor.html.**

2. **Choose File⇨File Open from the GIFWorks menu bar, as shown in Figure 7-1.**

   Come back to this page later and check out the File⇨New 3D Text option. It's a great way to create animated text banners.

3. **On the next page, open a file from the Web by entering its URL and clicking the Fetch Image button. Or upload a file from your local drive by clicking the Browse button, selecting the file, and then clicking the Upload Image button.**

   GIFWorks operates on a *copy* of the image you specify. It doesn't change the original file in any way.

   After the image is uploaded to GIFWorks, you'll be looking at it in the program, as shown in Figure 7-2.

   I'm using a dog from the collection at www.animfactory.com for this example. The dog is animated, which is one of the great strengths of GIFWorks. Many programs can modify and optimize individual GIF images, but an animated GIF is composed of many different images — eight of them, in this case — and GIFWorks can simultaneously modify all of them, thus altering the animated image.

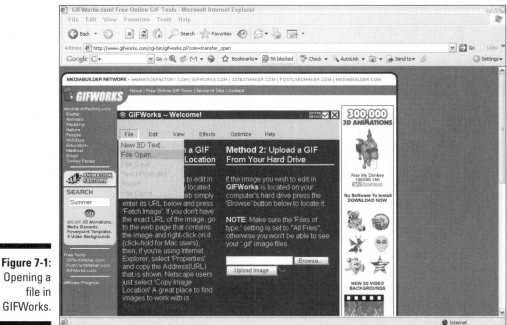

Figure 7-1:
Opening a
file in
GIFWorks.

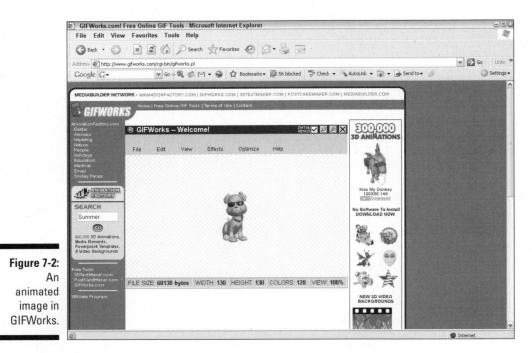

Figure 7-2:
An
animated
image in
GIFWorks.

TIP

Before you begin to work with the image, click the Help menu and take a look at the FAQ.

After your image is at GIFWorks, what you do with the image depends on your situation. Here are some options you can choose from:

✔ **To reduce the file size quickly:** Choose Optimize➪Reduce Colors from the menu bar. You get a whole page full of different versions of the original image, each with fewer colors than the preceding ones. You also get information about the file size, number of remaining colors, and percentage reduction. Scroll down the page, look at each image, and download the one that represents the best compromise between image quality and file size.

✔ **To make a color transparent:** Choose Edit➪Add Transparency from the menu bar. In the pop-up window that appears, click the color you want to become clear. To make a transparent GIF totally opaque, do the same thing, but start by choosing Edit➪Remove Transparency.

✔ **To view information on file size, width, height, and so on:** Choose View➪Image Info.

Okay, that's all the practical stuff that most Webmasters need. Now for the fun part. After you're done being responsible, head for the Effects menu and start playing. You can do so many things to your images that you may have a hard time choosing among them. Unless you're dead set on just trying anything that comes to hand, choose Help➪Effects Gallery to look at some examples.

Figure 7-3 shows what applying some of the effects did to the image shown in Figure 7-2. Enjoy.

Spinwave

Spinwave does just one thing, but it does it very well: It optimizes image files to save space and decrease download time. Spinwave handles not only GIFs but also JPEGs, and each file type has its own *image cruncher*. Both an online version of the program and a version you can run on your own computer are available. The online version, which used to be free, is unfortunately a paid service now. The good news, however, is that it's very reasonably priced if you'll be running your own Web site. You can pay anywhere from $7 for a month of service to $79.95 for a lifetime of service.

Here's how Spinwave works:

1. **Go to `www.spinwave.com/crunchers.html`.**

   JPEG Cruncher is in the middle of the main page (which is shown in Figure 7-4), and beneath it is GIF Cruncher.

2. **Click the Browse button in the cruncher that matches the file type that you want to work with.**

3. **Locate and select the file on your system.**

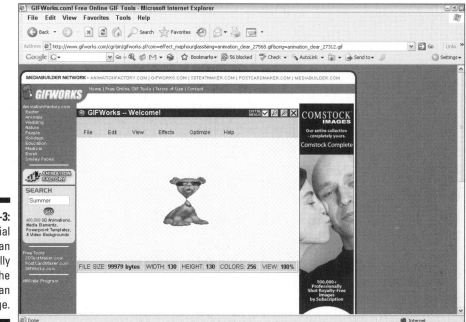

Figure 7-3:
Special effects can radically alter the look of an image.

4. **If you're using JPEG Cruncher, select a JPEG image quality setting from the drop-down list to the right of the Crunch button.**

   GIF files don't have this option.

5. **Click the Crunch button.**

   In a few moments, a new page appears, showing a series of images. The top one is the original image, for comparison purposes. Each successive image is of slightly lesser quality but has a smaller file size.

6. **Scroll down until you find an image that represents a good trade-off between image quality and size, and then download it.**

   If you're not a Spinwave subscriber, the images you can download will have some demo text overlying them. If you want to subscribe, just click one of the Spinwave Member links next to any of the optimized images.

Creating a Logo with CoolText.com

If you want a free logo fast and you don't mind doing it yourself, try CoolText.com at — you guessed it — www.cooltext.com. This Web site generates graphics while you wait, according to the options that you choose. The process is simple and fun, and there's no limit to the number of logos you can experiment with.

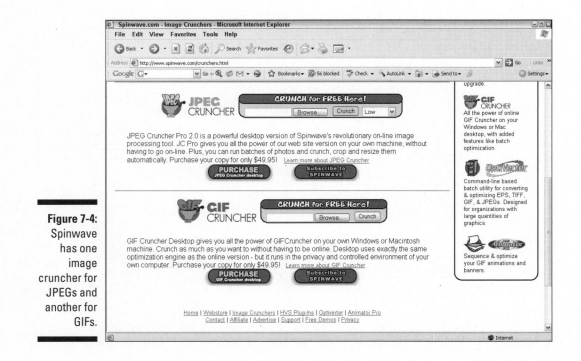

Figure 7-4:
Spinwave has one image cruncher for JPEGs and another for GIFs.

Not only are its logos cool, but so are the site's legal requirements: none, zip, nada. There's no copyright issue to deal with, no ads stuck in the middle of things, and no fine print of any kind. As an act of gratitude for such a great service, you may want to add a link back to this site from yours, but even that's not required.

Although CoolText.com doesn't hold a copyright on the logos you create, you probably do. I'm not a lawyer (and I don't even play one on TV), but it seems to me that the decisions you make during the course of designing the logos qualify them as artistic creations. Don't take my word for it, though. If this point is important for your situation, check with an attorney who really knows copyright law or e-mail the U.S. Copyright Office at `copyinfo@loc.gov`.

To make a custom logo at CoolText.com, follow these steps:

1. **Go to `www.cooltext.com`.**

2. **Scroll down and click any logo style under Choose a Logo Style to Begin, as shown in Figure 7-5.**

   You go to the logo design page, shown in Figure 7-6.

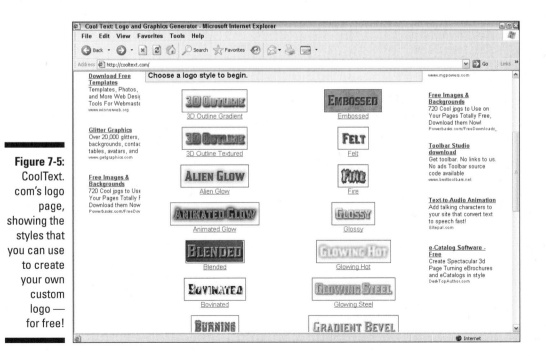

Figure 7-5: CoolText. com's logo page, showing the styles that you can use to create your own custom logo — for free!

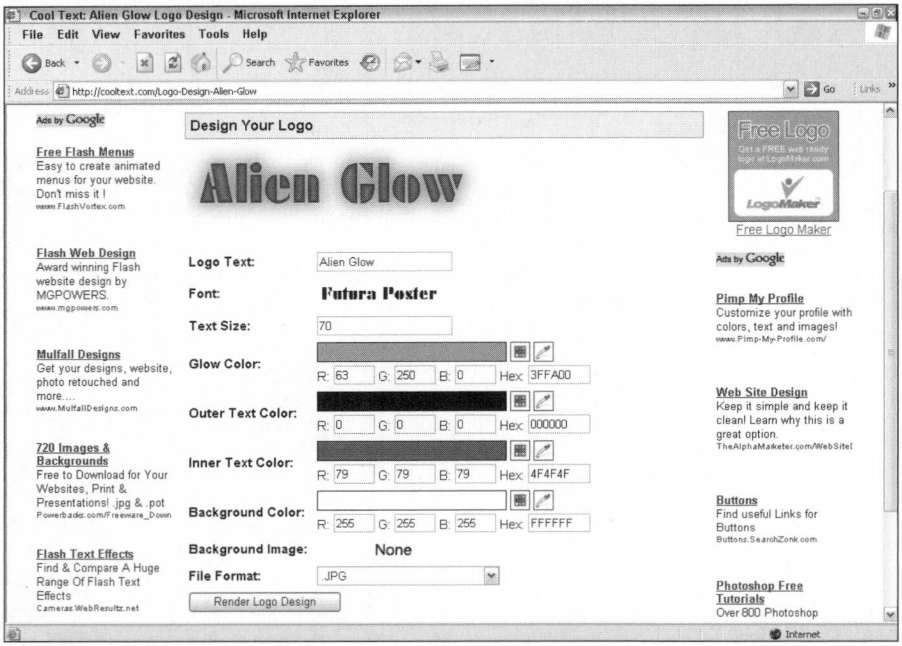

Figure 7-6:
The logo design page, where you choose options for your logo.

Different logo styles offer different options. Depending on the style that you choose, these options may set colors, determine whether text is engraved or raised, and so forth. In this example, I'm using the Alien Glow design.

3. **Type the text for your logo in the Logo Text text box.**

   You usually type your site or company name here, although you can type anything that you want. If you need more than one line, you can put a new line symbol (\n) in the text, as in the following example:

   ```
   First Line\nSecond Line
   ```

4. **Click the font name (in this example, Futura Poster), and then select a font category from the list that's presented. Finally, select the name of a particular font.**

   You're automatically returned to the design page.

5. **Enter a font size in the Text Size text box.**

6. **Click the Predefined Color picker (to the right of the color bar) for the Glow Color category and then select a glow color from the resulting color picker Web page. (See Figure 7-7.)**

   This Web page gives you a long list of named colors, with examples of each color. Just decide which color you like and click it to return to CoolText.com with that color selected. You can specify a glow color either by entering numerical values in the R, G, and B text boxes to indicate the RGB (red, green, and blue) components, or by entering its hexadecimal value to the right.

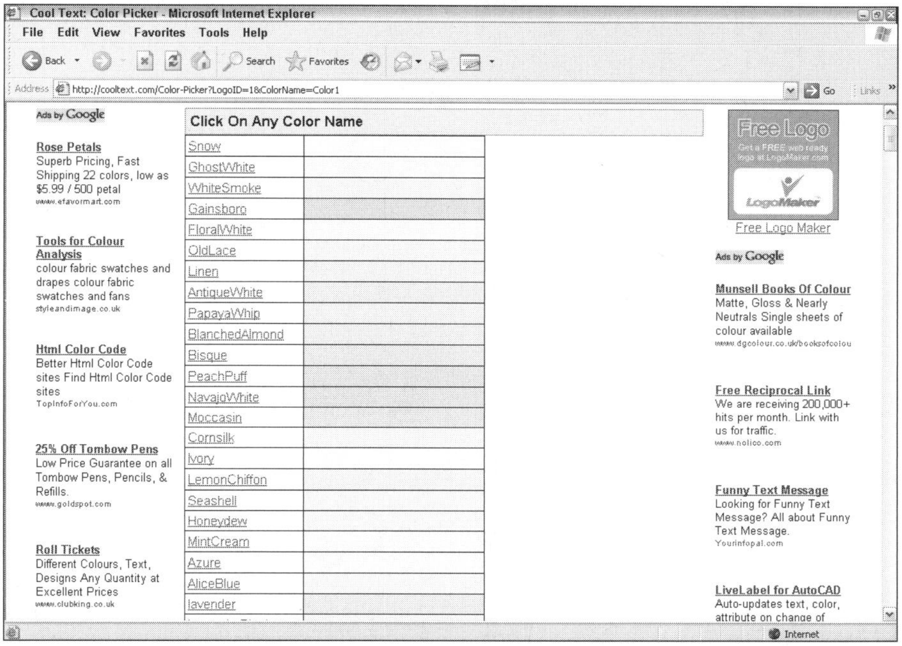

Figure 7-7:
The list of
named
colors lets
you choose
by just
clicking one.

7. **Repeat Step 6 for the other three color settings (Outer Text Color, Inner Text Color, and Background Color).**

8. **Click the current background image in the Background Image category (if one hasn't been chosen, click None), and then click one of the textures on the resulting Web page. (See Figure 7-8.)**

   You're returned to CoolText.com with that texture selected.

   If you need more textures, click the links at the top of the textures page to view more pages.

9. **If you want to specify a file format, click the Edit button for the File Format category and then select one of the file formats in the resulting list.**

10. **After you set all the options for your logo, click the Render Logo Design button.**

Now, all you have to do is sit back and wait until your logo shows up. If you like it, download it right away because it exists on CoolText.com's server for only about an hour. If you don't like it, back up and monkey with the settings until you get what you want.

While you're at CoolText.com, check out the button generator, too. You access it by clicking the Buttons link at the top of the page.

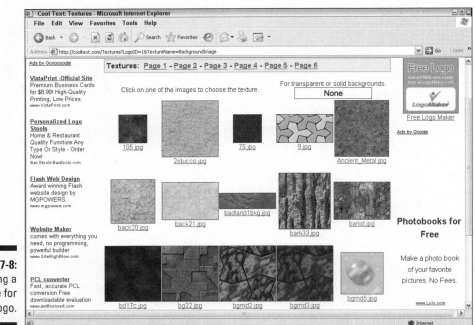

Figure 7-8:
Choosing a
texture for
your logo.

Editing Images

There are plenty of times when you'll need to tweak an image in order to get it "just so" for your site. All graphics programs give you some options for doing this sort of thing, and they all work pretty much the same way. In this section, I show you how to use a handy little graphics editor called IrfanView (www.irfanview.com) to spiff up your Web graphics quickly and easily.

A fully functional copy of IrfanView is included on the CD-ROM that accompanies this book.

Resizing

Although you can make an image appear smaller on a Web page than it really is (see the "Sizing images in HTML" section, later in this chapter), it's usually best to deliberately set the size before it ends up on your site.

This is a simple process, although there are a couple of caveats. When you resize an image, your graphics program has to change the *pixels* — the color dots that make up the image. Obviously, a larger image will take more pixels and a smaller one will take fewer. This means either adding pixels (*interpolation*) or subtracting pixels (*resampling*).

Although graphics interpolation has come a long way, any image resizing process still has to make some compromises. Shrinking an image usually doesn't result in any damage to the ability to view the picture, but it always has to mean some loss of detail. Enlarging an image can add areas of blockiness due to the additional pixels needed to fill the new space.

The best resizing is a minor resizing.

Open the image you want to resize in IrfanView, and then follow these steps:

1. **Choose Image⇨Resize/Resample from the menu.**

   In the Resize/Resample Image dialog box, shown in Figure 7-9, there are three methods of setting the new image size:

   • *To specify a particular physical size,* in the Set New Size panel, select pixels, centimeters, or inches, and then enter the new width and height in the Width and Height text boxes.

   If the Preserve Aspect Ratio check box is selected, you have to enter only one of the values; the other will be automatically entered.

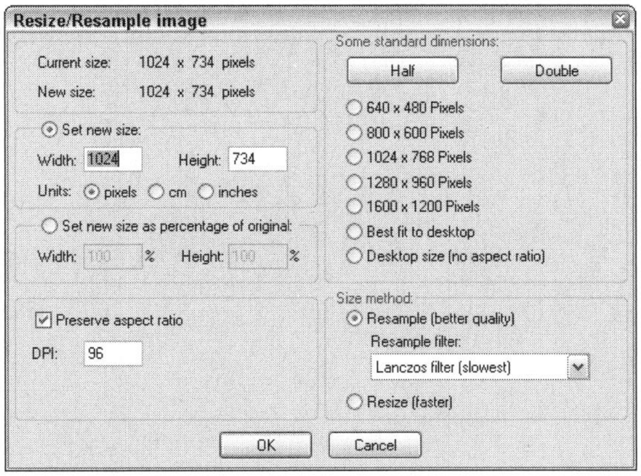

Figure 7-9:
Setting the new image size.

   • *To use a percentage,* select the Set New Size as Percentage of Original radio button, and then enter the appropriate numbers in the Width and Height text boxes.

   • *To use common sizes,* click the appropriate button or select a radio button in the Some Standard Dimensions panel.

2. **Click the OK button.**

3. **Save the image.**

   If you don't save the image after you make your changes, you'll lose it.

Cropping

What if you want part of a picture but not all of it? Get out the scissors — it's croppin' time. You can cut out any rectangular section you want, and, as you'll probably do this a lot, you'll be happy to hear how easy it is.

Open the image you want to crop in IrfanView, and then follow these steps:

1. **Place your mouse pointer at one corner of the area you want to crop and click.**

2. **While holding down the left mouse button, drag the mouse pointer to the opposite corner of your area.**

   As you do so, a guide box shows you the currently selected area. (See Figure 7-10.)

Figure 7-10: Cropping an image.

Photo courtesy of NASA.

3. When you have the area you want selected, release the mouse button.

4. Choose Edit⇨Crop Selection from the menu.

Alternatively, you can press Ctrl+Y.

Rotating and flipping

Just like a picture hanging on a wall, an image on your Web site can some-times look better if it's repositioned. A slight turn to the right, perhaps, or maybe even a complete inversion for a shocking effect. Graphically, I'm talk-ing about rotation and flips.

There are two kinds of rotation in IrfanView. Simple rotation is always by 90 degrees. Four of these in a row returns the image to its original state. Custom rotation allows you to specify an exact number of your choice instead.

To do a simple rotation, just choose Image from the menu, and then click Rotate Right or Rotate Left.

For a custom rotation, do this instead:

1. Choose Image⇨Custom/Fine Rotation from the menu.

The Rotate by Angle dialog box appears.

2. In the dialog box shown in Figure 7-11, enter the degree (up to two decimal points) of rotation. Use a minus sign (-) for leftward rotation.

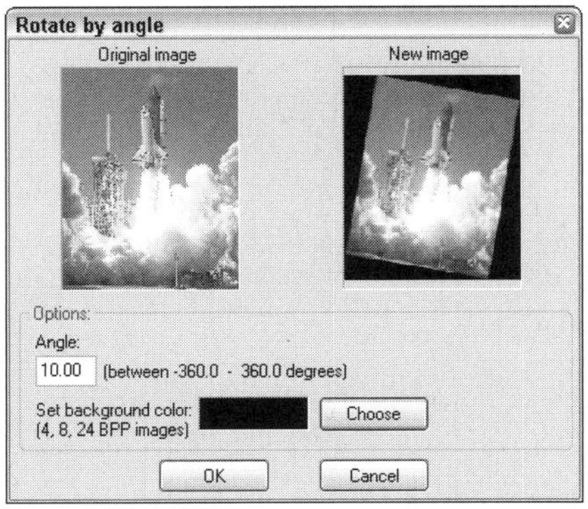

Figure 7-11:
Doing a fine rotation.

Photo courtesy of NASA.

3. **The dialog box displays the original image on the left and the altered one on the right. If you aren't satisfied with the results of your rotation, repeat Step 2 until the altered image suits your needs.**

4. **Click the OK button.**

Flipping an image is done in pretty much the same way as a simple rotation — choose Image⇨Vertical Flip or Image⇨Horizontal Flip from the menu — but it isn't the same thing as rotating an image 180 degrees. Remember that a flip is a mirror image instead of a turned one.

Adjusting color

Color adjustments include a range of possibilities. The most basic are color reduction (for example, making a 256-color image into a 16-color one) or greyscale conversion. The more complex include setting the proportions of red, green, and blue and monkeying with the contrast and brightness.

Gamma correction is a highfalutin' term for fixing an image that's too light or dark. You'll often find this situation when viewing an image on a PC that was done on a Mac.

To do a simple color reduction with IrfanView, follow these steps:

1. **Choose Image⇨Decrease Color Depth from the menu.**

   The Decrease Color Depth dialog box appears.

2. **In the dialog box shown in Figure 7-12, select one of the radio buttons to select a standard color depth.**

   If you select the Custom radio button, be sure to enter another number of colors into the Custom text box.

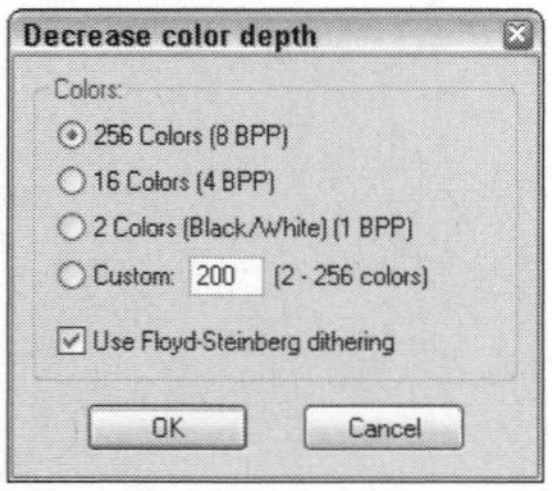

Figure 7-12:
Reducing
colors is
easy.

```
Decrease color depth                    ☒
┌─ Colors: ──────────────────────────────┐
│  ⊙ 256 Colors (8 BPP)                   │
│  ○ 16 Colors (4 BPP)                    │
│  ○ 2 Colors (Black/White) (1 BPP)       │
│  ○ Custom: 200   (2 - 256 colors)       │
│  ☑ Use Floyd-Steinberg dithering        │
└─────────────────────────────────────────┘
        [  OK  ]      [ Cancel ]
```

3. **Click the OK button.**

Greyscale conversion is even easier. Just choose Image⇨Convert to Greyscale from the menu.

Although they're a bit more involved, IrfanView wraps the most complex color adjustments in an easy-to-use package with lots of options. Load up an image and give it a go:

1. **Choose Image⇨Enhance Colors from the menu.**

2. **In the Enhance Colors dialog box (see Figure 7-13), drag the sliders or type values into the text boxes.**

   As you do so, the reference image on the right shows the changes you're making; the original image isn't affected by your experimentation, so feel free to play around with all the settings. You can, at any time, click the Set Default Values button to put everything back to normal.

3. **If the reference image isn't large enough for you, click the Apply to Original button.**

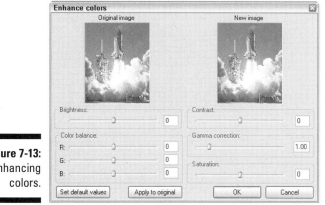

Figure 7-13: Enhancing colors.

Photo courtesy of NASA.

   This adds all your changes to your full-size original image. However, you still haven't actually altered it; all you have to do is click the Cancel button to return to normal.

4. **When you're finished, click the OK button to keep your changes or the Cancel button to abort them.**

Using special effects filters

There's a lot you can do with most of today's graphics programs, but there's always something more that's possible. That's where *filters* come in. A filter is a special effects wizard that automatically alters your images in various ways. You might, for example, apply a filter to a photograph to make the photo look like an oil painting or pencil sketch instead.

IrfanView has its own set of ready-to-use filters. It can also use your Photoshop-compatible filters. The best way to gain a quick understanding of what filters can do is to check out the Effects Browser:

1. **Choose Image⇨Effects from the menu.**

2. **Choose the Effects Browser option from the resulting submenu.**

3. **In the Image Effects dialog box shown in Figure 7-14, select the names of the various built-in effects filters.**

   As you do so, the twin images show you how the original compares to the filtered version.

4. **If required by the filter, enter requested values.**

5. **When you're done, click the OK button to keep your changes or the Cancel button to abort them.**

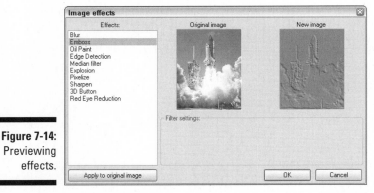

Figure 7-14:
Previewing
effects.

Photo courtesy of NASA.

Basic Design with Images

Getting or creating images is one thing. Knowing the right images to get (or to make) is another, and knowing what to do with them is perhaps most important of all. Misusing graphics — using either too many or too few — can make an otherwise outstanding Web site into an unpleasant mess. This section explores the proper use of images in Web page design.

Placing images for maximum effectiveness

It's easy to overdo any element on a Web page. It's not uncommon to run across sites that are all, or almost all, text, which is fine for some technical material, but pretty dicey if you're trying to appeal to the general public. At the opposite extreme, you'll find pages that are nothing but one image after another, with perhaps a small bit of text that often leaves you more confused than when you started.

Balancing visual elements with text is key to good Web site design. The CNN.com front page illustrates this point well. It's functional, eye catching, and well balanced. Figure 7-15 shows the top portion of the Web page. Note that it's strongly graphical. Even the text and links are all tied in to their attendant graphical background, their colors nicely suiting the overall look of the page.

The major image at the top, a photo and its surrounding frame, is the largest single graphical element on the page, reflecting its importance as showing the latest top story. Farther down (see Figure 7-16), there are smaller photos illustrating other stories, the whole being well balanced by the set of text links leading to various news reports.

This site is particularly interesting in that, except for the news story text links, virtually all the text is either embedded in or otherwise associated with a graphic. And very little of the graphic material is in the form of photos, drawings, or other commonly used image types. You find heavy use of graphical dividers to help structure the visual appeal of the page; however, they're small and don't overpower the other elements nearby.

Figure 7-15:
The top of the CNN.com home page is strongly graphical.

Your own artistic judgment must be the ultimate guide, but these guidelines will help you to create better-designed Web pages:

- ✔ Keep most images relatively small. How small depends upon two factors: the number of images you have on the page and simple visibility.

- ✔ Use your largest picture or artwork as the lead-in to the rest of your material. If it's not the most important image, it probably shouldn't be the biggest one, either.

- ✔ Use small divider images to separate subject areas.

- ✔ Don't allow advertising images to overwhelm the basic material of the Web page.

Sizing images in HTML

Besides file size, you need to consider the physical size of images. Each image, when displayed in a Web browser, takes up a certain amount of real estate on your visitors' screens. Very often, a particular image you want to use just doesn't happen to be the size you want it to be.

Figure 7-16:
The main portion of the page contains smaller graphics and is broken up by text.

You can fire up your favorite graphics program, load the image, resize and resample it, and then resave it. Or you can just let your visitor's Web browser do all the work for you. The ability to alter the size of an image on a Web page is built in to HTML. Although it isn't required, it's good form to specify the width and height of an image, as demonstrated here:

```
<IMG width="100" height="30">
```

Normally, you would use the actual size of the image, of course. But you can use any values you want to. To make the image take up more space on a Web page, just enter larger numbers. To make it smaller — you guessed it — enter smaller values instead.

You have to be careful to proportionally resize the image, unless you're looking for some weird effect. If you want to quadruple the area of the example image, from 3,000 pixels to 12,000 pixels, for example, you set the width to 200 and the height to 60.

See Chapter 3 for details on how to place images.

Online Sources for Quality Graphics

Table 7-2 lists some places on the World Wide Web where you can find lots of high-quality graphics for your site.

Table 7-2	Online Resources for Quality Graphics
Web Site Name	**Web Address**
CoolNotions.com	www.coolnotions.com
Dee's Art Gallery	www.dreslough.com/dee/index.html
All Free Original Clip Art	www.free-graphics.com
Goddess Art of Jonathon Earl Bowser	www.jonathonart.com
Graphics-4free.com	www.graphics-4free.com
Grazia A. Cipresso	www.gcipresso.com
Lindy's Graphics	www.theiowa.net/lindy

I don't list any image repositories in this table. An *image repository* is a Web site that simply provides about a zillion images for download without any regard for where they came from or what kind of legal troubles they may cause for you. They typically involve all sorts of copyright and trademark violations, and the fact that such a repository provides the Donald Duck images that you put on your site doesn't keep Disney's lawyers off your back. Stick with sites like the ones in this table, and you'll keep out of trouble.

Chapter 8

Plugging In Scripts and Applets

● ●

In This Chapter

▶ Checking for CGI access

▶ Implementing CGI scripts

▶ Using JavaScript

▶ Adding Java applets

● ●

This book shows you how to add cool features to your Web site. These features are all programs of one kind or another. Relax, though — you don't have to be a programmer to use them. It's just that HTML has its limitations, and if you want to expand the functionality of your Web site, you have to go just a wee bit beyond it. HTML is mainly focused on the task of displaying text and images, along with the capability to link various files together, and it performs these tasks admirably well.

That's fine if all you want to do is to have a Web site that could be duplicated on paper using only crayons and paste. However, you'll probably want to have many more things, adding capabilities that your average visitor will expect to find on any well-designed site. Here are some of the things that you can do with scripts and applets on your Web site:

✔ Add a search feature that lets visitors find the material they're looking for without having to manually go over every page on your site.

✔ Provide password protection to keep certain areas of your site available only for the initiated.

✔ Enable visitors to communicate with you and with each other through a variety of methods ranging from simple graffiti-like message boards to sophisticated and full-featured chat rooms.

✔ Add timekeeping tools such as clocks and calendars.

✔ Ease site exploration by providing visitors with graphical or hierarchical navigation tools.

✔ Let visitors enjoy games and puzzles on your site.

✔ Link to live information such as news feeds, stock tickers, weather reports, and the like.

Although these programs are written in a variety of programming languages, you don't need to know anything about programming in order to use them. Instead, many of them are hooked up to your Web page by using the *Common Gateway Interface* (CGI). There's nothing mystical or particularly difficult about using CGI, and I give you the basics in the section "Adding CGI Scripts."

Java applets are also popular for adding new capabilities to Web pages. They're programs written in the Java programming language, and plenty of them are free for you to use. Again, to add an applet to your Web page, all you have to do is a little bit of typing — no programming required. The people who wrote the applet have already done all the techy stuff for you, and all you need to do is tell it where to find your Web site in order to use it.

An *applet* is a tiny application, and *application* is just another way of saying *computer program*. So, an applet is a short and (relatively) simple program.

Another common method for adding new functions to your Web pages is with *scripts* (which are short programs) written in the JavaScript programming language. Unlike Perl and Java, JavaScript was designed solely for writing programs for the World Wide Web. You can go all the way and learn to write your own JavaScripts, or you can take advantage of the zillions of existing ones and just plug them in. The code goes right into the same file as your Web page code — it's just a matter of copying and pasting it.

Making Sure That You Have CGI Access

If you're going to use CGI with your Web pages, you have to make sure that you have the capability to do so. This sounds obvious, of course, but you may or may not have CGI access for your Web site. *CGI access* means that you can run programs on your Web server that use the Common Gateway Interface, a method of sending form data from a Web page to an external program for processing.

Nine times out of ten, these programs are kept in a subfolder called `cgi-bin`, so your first step is to look to see if you have such a subfolder on your server. If you do, odds are that you have CGI access, because that subfolder doesn't have any other purpose. If it's there, go ahead and try to use a CGI program. If you follow all the instructions carefully and the program still doesn't work, you may need to have a talk with your network administrator or ISP.

Why your ISP won't help

When your Web site is hosted by the same ISP that you get your Internet access from, you'll probably find that it's not too supportive of your desire to run

CGI scripts. There are a couple of reasons for this, which make good sense to your ISP but don't help you at all:

- ✔ Badly written programs using CGI can represent a security hazard, poking holes in the normal running of things. Because ISPs want everything to run smoothly and under their control instead of someone else's, ISPs tend to frown on this possibility.

- ✔ Most ISPs don't really care about your Web site. They're not bad people, but they're mostly in the business of providing Internet access to their customers, and anything else they have to deal with is just an annoyance that gets in the way of their main job. (See Chapter 16 for more info.)

If your ISP allows you to run CGI scripts, it may be a painful and expensive process on your end. I once had an ISP that wanted to approve the scripts in advance, put them on the server sometime over the next couple of days (it was apparently too much trouble to allow the paying users to access their own files and, therefore, get the job done instantly), and charge me $25 a pop for doing so. From an ISP's point of view, that's reasonable. From my point of view, it was a definite no-go. For starters, I like to do things right away instead of taking days to get around to it. On top of that, you often have to monkey with a CGI script before you get it working just the way you want. Every time I wanted to make a change, it cost another $25 and set me back a couple of more days.

Finding a CGI provider

Fortunately, many Web-space providers do provide you with CGI access. If you live in a city or large town, you can easily shop around and find a new ISP that's on your side, CGI-wise. If not, thanks to the way the Internet works, you don't need to deal with your local ISP at all.

You can go with a virtual server or other commercial remote Web-space provider (see Chapter 16 for details), or you can easily find free Web-space providers by using the search engine at FreeWebspace.net. Go to the main page at www.freewebspace.net and click the Advanced Free Hosting Search link, or just go straight to www.freewebspace.net/search/power.shtml, as shown in Figure 8-1. In the search form, select the CGI check box under Features. Select any other options you desire and click the Search button. My test search, using the default options and the CGI check box, came up with 15 free providers that grant CGI access.

Using remotely hosted CGI scripts

The CGI scripts that you use don't have to reside on the same server that houses your Web pages. This is good, because CGI scripts are run by the Web server on which the script is located and using them puts an added load on your server. If you have lots of visitors, the data processing demands on your server can be pretty strenuous. If you don't have your Web site on a dedicated server with plenty of power, things can get really slow.

When the script is on someone else's server, however, you don't have to worry about the server load. Happily, there are lots of remotely hosted CGI scripts, which means that you can still add their capabilities to your own pages while avoiding the server overload problem. Many of the add-ons in this book are remotely hosted.

Free CGI Resources provides free scripts that work via links to its server. (See Figure 8-2.) Check out some of them at `www.fido7.com/free-cgi`.

Adding CGI Scripts

A CGI script works by taking input from your Web page and sending that input to an external program for processing. Usually, it returns a new Web page that has the results of that processing on it. The input is most often data from a form, but it can sometimes be just a link that a user clicks to activate the program.

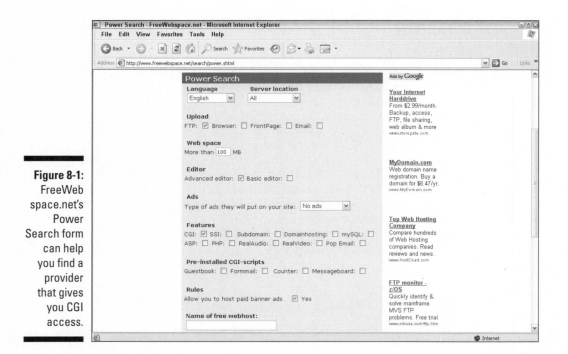

Figure 8-1:
FreeWeb space.net's Power Search form can help you find a provider that gives you CGI access.

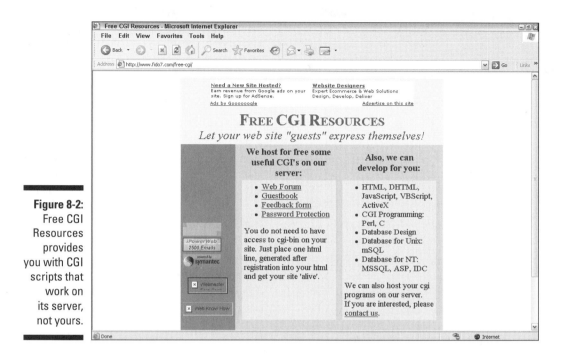

Figure 8-2:
Free CGI
Resources
provides
you with CGI
scripts that
work on
its server,
not yours.

Basic techniques

Before you do anything, you have to get the script. Whenever I describe a script in this book, I provide you with the URL of the site from which you can download the script. After you have the script, follow these basic steps to use it:

1. **Read the instructions for the script. Let me say that again: Read the instructions.**

   After you've worked with a few scripts, it's tempting to just plunge right ahead without looking. After all, most scripts plug in pretty much the same way, and you can often get away with skipping the instructions. That's the cause of about 812 percent of the problems that people have with scripts, though. All it takes is to misunderstand or misinterpret one little setting, and the whole script won't work.

   The instructions are often in the standard ReadMe.txt file. Sometimes, the script doesn't have a ReadMe file, though, and the instructions are embedded in the text of the script itself in the form of comments. (*Comments* are notes the programmer adds to provide information, and they're marked so that they're differentiated from the program code and don't interfere with the running of the program.)

2. **Open the script file in a text editor and make any necessary changes so that it works with your particular setup. After you do this, save the modified script.**

   You may, for example, need to add a list of URLs for a link menu, an e-mail address to send a message to, or the location of your site's main Web page. You don't need to understand the programming in order to do this. Just follow the instructions and replace the sample values in the script with your own values.

   If you use a word processor to make the changes, make sure that the script gets saved as plain text and that the original file extension doesn't get changed either. You don't want a bunch of word processing formatting codes embedded in the script!

3. **Add the HTML code that the script's instructions say to add to your Web page.**

   As with the script, you probably need to change a few sample values to the actual values. The HTML code is usually nothing more than the location of the CGI program, entered as the `action` attribute of a form.

4. **Upload the script and the modified HTML file to your Web server.**

   The HTML file goes in the normal `HTML` folder, and the script goes into the `cgi-bin` folder.

Solving problems

The basic techniques described in the preceding section work in almost all cases, but in some situations, you may need to modify the script a bit more to get everything working just right.

For example, nearly every script you find assumes your `cgi-bin` directory is called `cgi-bin`. Yours may be simply named `cgi`, for example. If that's the case, you need to change the typical folder references in the script to match your folder name.

You may also find that the standard file extensions, like `.pl` for Perl files, aren't allowed in your CGI setup. In that case, you have to change the file extension to whatever your server demands. A file named `search.pl`, for example, may need to be renamed `search.cgi`.

If you try to run the script and nothing happens, here are some troubleshooting options:

✔ **Go back over the instructions and see if you did anything wrong.** Nine times out of ten, it's something simple but so small and insignificant that it's easy to overlook. You may have left out a required comma between two values, or forgotten a quotation mark. Perhaps you misspelled the URL of a Web site. Go over everything you did very carefully, and you'll usually find the problem.

✔ **If the script is fine, make sure that you uploaded all the necessary files.** Some scripts have data files that you need to upload along with them in order for them to work properly.

✔ **Check to see that your `cgi-bin` folder has the correct permissions settings.** If you're not familiar with permissions, ask your ISP to check them for you.

✔ **If all else fails, send an e-mail message to the program's author explaining the nature of the problem and ask for help.** Because most of these programs are free, don't expect too much in the way of technical support. Nobody can afford to both give away programs and spend all their time providing free technical support as well. The best approach is to be polite, perhaps tell the program's author how much you want to use the program (if you don't feel that way about it, you haven't come this far), and make sure that you give all the information you can about the settings you used.

Incorporating JavaScripts

JavaScript has a tremendous advantage over other methods of adding "beyond-HTML" features to your Web pages. It was designed for no other purpose, and it's so tightly integrated with HTML that it's a joy to use. The processing takes place in the visitors' Web browsers, so it's both fast for them and no problem for your Web server. You don't have to understand the language to add other people's scripts to your Web site. In many cases, no alterations to the code are needed. In some cases, you may have to change the filename or add some URLs to a list. Figure 8-3 shows the JavaScript Source at `http://javascript. internet.com`, one of the many places on the Web to get free JavaScript code.

Basic techniques

You need to add two things to your Web pages when you work with JavaScript: the script itself and something that triggers the script.

Figure 8-3:
The
JavaScript
Source
gives you
free
JavaScript
code.

The script

The script has to go in the HEAD element of your Web page, like this skeleton script named whatever:

```
<HEAD>
<Script Language="JavaScript">
/*
You will usually find comments here.
*/


function whatever()
{
Actual code is found here.
}
</Script>
</HEAD>
```

You can place scripts within the BODY element rather than the HEAD element, but that can be risky. A JavaScript needs to be *interpreted* — translated by a Web browser from the human-readable code into something a computer can understand — before it runs. Scripts in the HEAD element are processed before the Web browser processes the elements within the BODY element. That means that these scripts are defined and ready to roll before anything shows up in the Web browser. If the script is in the BODY element, a visitor may possibly attempt to trigger it before it's defined, which begs for a malfunction. It's better to stick with the safer, usual approach.

The trigger

You need to add something to your Web page to trigger the script, which causes it to run. This goes within the BODY element. Many things can trigger a script, but you don't need to be concerned with all the possibilities. The script you add is most likely designed to have a particular trigger, like a rollover image that changes whenever a visitor's mouse pointer is over the image. Or, it may be intended to work after the Web page finishes loading into the browser. You can alter the trigger if you're familiar with JavaScript.

For a script that executes as soon as the Web page loads into the browser, use the onload attribute of the BODY element:

```
<BODY onload="whatever()">
```

For a script that requires the visitor to click an element, use the onClick attribute. This example uses the A element, but onClick is a ubiquitous attribute that you can use with just about anything:

```
<A onClick="whatever()">Click here for whatever.</A>
```

Lots more triggers exist, such as onMouseOver and onMouseOut, which are, respectively, used to execute scripts when a mouse pointer moves onto and away from an element. The documentation for a script normally specifies which trigger(s) it's intended to use. If you want to explore JavaScript, try *JavaScript For Dummies*, 4th Edition, by Emily A. Vander Veer (Wiley Publishing).

Dealing with problems

Fortunately, practically any JavaScript that you pick up is pretty much guaranteed to work — under the right conditions. When it comes to JavaScript, zillions of things can go wrong. The biggest problem is that so many different versions of Web browsers are out there. Not only do Firefox and Internet Explorer handle scripts a little differently, but also different versions of the two major Web browsers don't work the same. That means that a script that works fine in the latest version may not work at all in an older one. Unfortunately, lots of older Web browsers are still out there — not everyone is in a hurry to tie up their systems downloading the newest versions.

If a browser doesn't recognize JavaScript, the script won't run. There's no harm done, just a missed experience for the visitor.

Unless you want to put the time and effort into really mastering the language and doing your own debugging, your best bet is to simply try out the script you want to use. Test it in Firefox, Internet Explorer, and any other Web browser you think your target audience uses. If the script works well in all the browsers, you're home free. If it causes problems in any of them, you need to decide how important that segment of the audience is to you. For example, if your site is dedicated to Microsoft products and your script won't work in Firefox, you're probably pretty safe in going ahead with it anyway, because the vast majority of your visitors are likely to use Microsoft's Internet Explorer.

Dropping In Java Applets

Java applets run the gamut from the trivial and useless to the fabulous. Many Java applets perform some type of image modification, like the popular Lake applet). Others add rotating banner ads or scrolling ticker-tape-style messages. The really nice thing about Java applets is that, like JavaScript, they run on the visitor's machine, which reduces the load on your Web server. Some drawbacks, however, are the length of time that they take to download to the visitor and the slight delay on the visitor's end while Java starts up (if it isn't already running). Figure 8-4 shows the main Java page for Sun Microsystems (`www.java.sun.com`), the company that invented the language.

Major programs are called *applications*. Your word processor or spreadsheet program, for example, is an application. Although Java is indeed used to write applications, the Java programs that are written for the Web tend to be very small, so they're known by the diminutive name *applet*.

Figure 8-4:
The java.
sun.com
main page
is the home
for the Java
language.

Despite the similarity in their names, Java and JavaScript are only vaguely similar, and they work quite differently. But they do have one important thing in common: They're both executed on your visitors' computers, which takes the load off your server.

Basic techniques

Java applets are composed of .class files (rarely, you see a .cls extension instead). The file may be downloaded by itself, but you often find it in a .zip or other compressed file along with some other supporting files — documentation and perhaps graphics or sound files as well, depending on the applet's function.

After you have the files, you need to add code to your HTML file to activate the applet. You do this with the APPLET element, and many different attributes may or may not come into play, depending on the particular applet involved. Almost invariably, the applet's documentation provides the HTML code you need, and all you have to do is to cut and paste it, changing only a few items, such as the names of image files, to make it fit your site. No applet included in this book does it any other way.

Sometimes, an applet's author doesn't include a documentation file but has all the necessary information on the Web page from which you download the applet. Make sure that you print a copy of that page. Better yet, save the page to your system so you can easily cut and paste the HTML code and refer to the instructions if you have any problems.

You can never count on any Web site being operational all the time. If you don't make a copy of the Web page that shows the instructions, you'll be out of luck if the Web server is down the next time you try to go back.

At its most basic, you add a Java applet contained in a file called bongo. class like this:

```
<APPLET code="bongo.class">This would have been
        drumming.</APPLET>
```

The content between the start and end tags is phrased this way because that content is ignored by any Web browsers that support Java and won't show up on them. It's displayed only by browsers that aren't Java-capable (or that have Java turned off). It's not necessary to add any content between the start and end tags, but it's a nice gesture because it lets visitors know to turn on Java or upgrade their browsers if they want to get the full benefit of your site.

The applet may also have some additional attributes, as described in the next few sections.

Name attributes

The applet may have a `name` attribute. This is used when you have multiple interacting Java applets, and one of the applets needs to send information to another one. Naming applets lets them identify each other. In the following example, the `name` attribute tells other applets that any task belonging to `"HitIt"` should be processed by this applet:

```
<APPLET code="bongo.class" name="HitIt"></APPLET>
```

Width and height attributes

You also need to specify the `width` and `height` attributes for the applet. These values are found in the accompanying documentation:

```
<APPLET code="bongo.class" width="200"
        height="100"></APPLET>
```

Codebase attributes

If the `.class` file isn't in the same folder as the `.html` file that calls it, you need to use the `codebase` attribute. It tells the Web browser where to find the Java applet. If the example file were in the `drumming` subfolder, the HTML code would look like this:

```
<APPLET code="bongo.class" codebase="/drumming"
        width="200" height="100"></APPLET>
```

 Unlike most URLs in HTML, the `codebase` location must be within either the same folder as the `.html` file or a subfolder of it. This means that you can't access a Java applet on another server with it.

Parameters

In most cases, the applet also requires that you add some other information to the HTML code. This information, called a *parameter,* is added via the `PARAM` element. The following example adds a particular sound file to the bongo applet:

```
<APPLET code="bongo.class" width="200" height="100">
<PARAM name="CurrentSound" value="quickroll.au">
</APPLET>
```

The parameter is usually the name of an image or sound file, the URL of a Web page, or the text of a message. There can be lots more in the way of parameters, depending on what the particular applet does. The parameters may set font size, background color, speed of change, or just about anything else. Some parameters are optional; others are required. As with everything else, read the documentation carefully.

Troubleshooting applets

When you upload the `.class` file and any supporting files to your Web server, make sure that you have carefully checked the documentation to see where the files should go. Many Webmasters carefully separate different file types into different folders. For example, it's a good and useful technique to keep your image files in a different folder from your `.html` files. If nothing else, doing so makes it easier to read the file listings and helps you avoid using the wrong file-type settings when uploading files.

This approach can cause problems, however. For example, say that you're using an applet that manipulates images. If the Java applet expects to find the `.html` file that it's called from, the image files, and itself all in the same folder, you need to make an exception to your usual filing technique and keep all the necessary files in the same place.

Another common problem that may occur during the uploading of the files is that you upload the `.class` files as ASCII instead of binaries. If you upload them as ASCII, they won't work. Also make sure that you upload any image or sound files as binaries and that you upload any text files — and, of course, the `.html` file — as ASCII.

Even if you upload an image file correctly, you can still have trouble. First, check the documentation to see if the applet works with that file type. If everything is okay, it's possible that the file itself is the problem. Not all graphics programs create files that all other graphics programs can read. UMAX scanner software, for example, makes TIFF files that some graphics programs can't read. JPEGs created with Photoshop 4 won't work with all Java applets. The solution? Load the image into another program — you may have to try a couple of them — and save it again from the second program. Upload it again, and the new file may work.

Online Sources for Scripts and Applets

Table 8-1 lists some places on the World Wide Web where you can find more information on the topics covered in this chapter.

Table 8-1	Online Resources for Scripts and Applets
Web Site Name	*Web Address*
CGI Resource Index	`www.cgi-resources.com`
CGI: Why Things Don't Work	`www.raingod.com/raingod/` `resources/Programming/Perl/` `Notes/CGIDebugging.html`
Freewarejava.com	`www.freewarejava.com`
Intro to CGI	`www.mattkruse.com/info/cgi`
Java Boutique	`www.javaboutique.internet.com`
JavaScript Kit	`www.javascriptkit.com`
Perl Primer	`www.webdesigns1.com/perl`
WDVL: The Perl You Need to Know	`www.wdvl.com/Authoring/` `Languages/Perl/PerlfortheWeb`

Chapter 9

Web Sights and Sounds

· ·

· ·

*W*eb pages don't just sit there any more. They've come a long way since the early stages of just displaying text on your computer screen. New forms of multimedia experiences crop up all the time. Television and radio stations, for example, have broadcast on the Web for a long time, but most of them target only individual users; few of these broadcasters have realized the importance of allying with Webmasters to get more exposure for their signals. I dug up a few sites for you that are Web-based themselves, existing only on the Web instead of being traditional broadcast or cable stations, and they do understand how much you, the Webmaster, mean to them.

I also point you to plenty of sources for sound files that you can use on your Web site. Of course, as with any innovation, there's a certain amount of debate about the use of sound on Web pages. Aside from the carping of die-hard traditionalists who just plain insist that you shouldn't use it, there are some serious considerations. Sound doesn't necessarily go with every site. If you decide to use it, you need to match the mood of the music with the page's theme. The right song can add a new dimension; the wrong one can sound ridiculous — and maybe even make your site a bit of a joke.

If you use sound, make sure that you give your visitors the ability to turn it off. Embedded sound with no controls is an annoyance to many visitors. You may as well give them the option because they can simply turn off their speakers to get rid of the sound. (Either that, or they just leave your site in disgust, never to return.)

Getting Music and Video

First things first: You gotta get the music or whatever media before you can add it to your Web site. Okay, grabbing music off the Web, off a newsgroup, through FTP, or just about any other way that data moves on the Internet is a pretty easy thing to do. However, you face two problems with taking just any old song that you can get your hands on, and the same goes for video. First, if you can snag it with no trouble, so can everyone else — and you presumably want your site to stand out from the crowd. Second, you face the question of copyright. The odds are pretty good that you have no idea who owns the copyright to a song or video that you snag from some Web site or if it's in the *public domain* (for everyone to use) instead of under copyright.

You can avoid this copyright mess by following these few simple suggestions:

✔ Get your own custom music or video by hiring professionals to create it for you — totally new and completely unencumbered. That way, you won't have any legal hassles, and nobody else can use it on another site.

✔ Buy or download royalty-free music and video collections.

✔ Use public-domain music and video (if you don't mind everyone else using the same music or video on countless other Web sites, too).

✔ Create your own music or video.

The following sections describe how to get these different types of files for your site.

Finding music houses

Professional music suppliers can accommodate your desires to play unique music on your site, either by selling you custom compositions that they design to serve your particular needs or by providing you with music that they already have on hand for you to buy or license. The exact deal you strike depends on the company's policy and how much money you're willing to part with. Some companies license you to use the music only in certain ways (sort of like the way software licenses say things like you can use a program on only a single computer). So when you talk to them, be sure to specify that the music will be used on Web pages. You shouldn't, however, have to pay any royalties — fees for every time you play the music — just the flat fee when you get the music.

LicenseMusic.com (shown in Figure 9-1) is one good source that sports a useful database of what's available. Table 9-1 lists some other good Web sites where you can find or order royalty-free music.

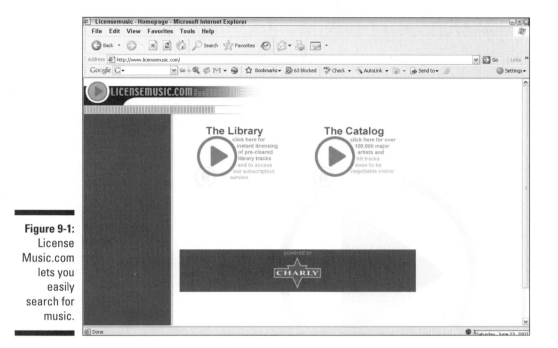

Figure 9-1:
License
Music.com
lets you
easily
search for
music.

Table 9-1	Royalty-Free Music Suppliers
Web Site Name	*Web Address*
Catovah Arts	www.catovah.com
Fresh Music Library	www.freshmusic.com
LicenseMusic	www.licensemusic.com
Music 2 Hues	www.music2hues.com
Music Bakery	www.musicbakery.com
Nash Music Library	www.nash.co.jp/sod/nml
Partners In Rhyme	www.partnersinrhyme.com
PBTM Library	www.pbtm.com
SONOTON	www.productionmusic.com
Royalty Free Music	www.royaltyfree.com

Finding public-domain music and video

Not all music or video is currently under copyright. Music has been around a long time, and most of it's in the public domain — meaning that nobody holds the copyright to it. The reverse is true of video. Video is a more recent technology, and the massive proliferation of compact, lightweight video cameras means that most moving pictures have been created within the past few years.

Copyright can prove to be a tricky issue. If you make a mistake, you can end up in federal court, paying hundreds of thousands of dollars in fines. Rest assured, however, that very few copyright infringers ever go to prison, although the law provides for that eventuality. On the other hand, some of these copyright infringers find themselves spending all their time talking to lawyers. And paying lawyers. So before you add some public-domain music or video to your Web site, make absolutely sure that it *is* in the public domain.

Table 9-2 lists some good public-domain music and video sources.

Table 9-2	Public-Domain Music Sources
Web Site Name	*Web Address*
Classical Piano Free Downloads	`www.sheetmusic1.com/new.great.music.html`
Musopen	`www.musopen.com`
PD Info	`www.pdinfo.com`
Public Domain Music	`http://pdmusic.org`
U.S. National Archives	`www.archives.gov/research/index.html`
Virtual Sheet Music	`www.virtualsheetmusic.com/Downloads.html`
Web-Helper.net: Public Domain Music	`www.web-helper.net/PDMusic`

Some public domain music sites provide copies of sheet music that you can use to create new recordings of your own. Others have music files that you can download and use right away. There's a catch, however; a recording of a public domain song is not in the public domain. The written music is, but the recording isn't. Yes, I'm repeating myself, but it's critical for you to remember that. The legal reasons are so convoluted that any two lawyers have three opinions about why it's so, but it's a fact. So, unless the site specifically states that it's releasing its music files into the public domain, you probably have to pay for the download. Some sites that charge commercial sites to use their recordings are willing to let noncommercial sites use them for free.

Picking a File Format

Your main concern when choosing a file format for either Web audio or Web video is download time — the length of time it takes for a Web site visitor to be able to experience the music or movie. Most people won't be willing to go make a sandwich to pass the time waiting to hear your favorite song, and even your dearest friends may not be happy about spending all afternoon trying to see the video of your vacation.

Three main factors affect download time: the speed of the network connection, the file size, and whether the file has to completely download in order to start playing. No matter how fast your Web server's connection is, you have no control over the speed of your visitors' connections. Thus, the only thing you can really do is modify either the file size or the manner in which the file is displayed.

I deal with file compression in the following section, so now I want to take a look at streaming versus regular files. With a regular file, such as the MP3 format that is so popular for reproducing music, the entire file must be downloaded and then played. With a streaming file, such as Real Audio, the user can hear the first part of the music while the rest of it is still on the way.

In theory, it sounds like a great idea. Sometimes, though, streaming files (whether with video or audio content) can be jerky and aesthetically deficient, especially with slower connections. So you have to decide whether speed of display is more important to you than smoothness of presentation.

Tables 9-3 and 9-4 show some commonly used video and audio file formats, a description of each, and whether the format is streamable.

Table 9-3	Video File Formats	
File Extension	*Description*	*Streamable*
.avi	Microsoft's Audio Video Interleave format can be problematic. Although it achieves good quality, various factors can yield a large file size, and it can't support full-screen movies.	Yes
.mov, .qt	The Apple movie format for QuickTime is excellent and has great file compression.	Yes

(continued)

Table 9-3 *(continued)*

File Extension	Description	Streamable
.mpeg	The Motion Picture Experts Group format is as popular for video as its MP3 cousin is for audio. With both high file compression and excellent reproduction quality, this is the vehicle of choice for many Webmasters.	Yes
.ram	The Real Audio Movie format was the most common form of streaming video, but it lost popularity because it requires the use of a proprietary program, RealPlayer, which is often criticized for carrying too much advertising and being somewhat difficult to use.	Yes
.wmv	Windows Media Video tends to produce small files of good quality.	Yes

Table 9-4   Audio File Formats

File Extension	Description	Streamable
.aiff, .au	These files are mainly used on Macintosh systems. Because the majority of computer users don't own Macs, think twice before committing to it because your other visitors may or may not be able to use it. File sizes tend to be large.	No
.midi	The Musical Instrument Digital Interface is a venerable old music format. So many MIDI files are online that it is impossible to count them, and this format is supported by the vast majority of all music creation programs. Nonetheless, it's mainly biased toward non-vocal music and thus may have limited utility for Webmasters despite its small file size.	No
.mp3	This is the king of the audio files. Everybody has heard of — and probably has — songs in MP3 format. Although people may argue that other formats have technical advantages, MP3s are widely supported and are probably instantly playable on almost all your visitors' systems.	Yes

File Extension	Description	Streamable
`.ra`	The Real Audio format (from the same folks who brought you streaming video) can create smaller files than many of the others, but at a serious cost in sound quality.	Yes
`.wav`	Waveform Audio files are good in that any computer with sound capabilities can play them, but they're notorious for their large file sizes.	No
`.wma`	Windows Media Audio files are often smaller than MP3s and have very good quality.	Yes

Compressing Files

Windows Movie Maker is a quick and painless way to familiarize yourself with the various factors that affect file size and the ways these factors can create a good or bad Web experience for your visitors. A full exploration of video preparation is outside the scope of this book, so if you're interested in delving more deeply into working with Web video, check out *Digital Video For Dummies,* 4th Edition, by Keith Underdahl (Wiley Publishing).

To experiment with various settings and see how they affect file size, follow these steps:

1. **In Windows Movie Maker, select a movie by clicking its icon. (See Figure 9-2.)**

2. **Click the Save to My Computer link on the left side of the screen.**

   The Save Movie Wizard appears, shown in Figure 9-3.

3. **Enter a filename for your movie in the first text box.**

4. **If you don't want to save your videos in the My Videos folder, the default setting in the second text box, click the Browse button and choose a different location.**

5. **Click the Next button.**

   On the next page, the default setting Best Quality for Playback on My Computer is selected, as shown in Figure 9-4.

6. **Before checking out the other options, take a moment to look over the values in Setting Details and note the estimated file size those settings generate.**

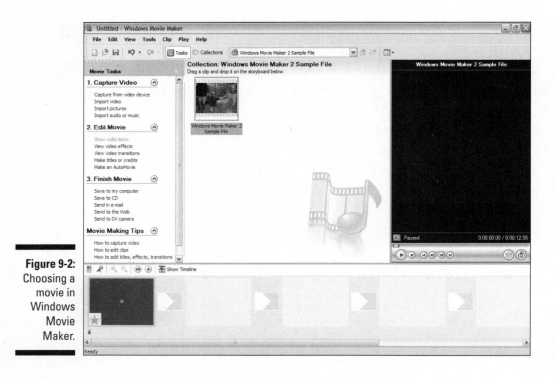

Figure 9-2:
Choosing a movie in Windows Movie Maker.

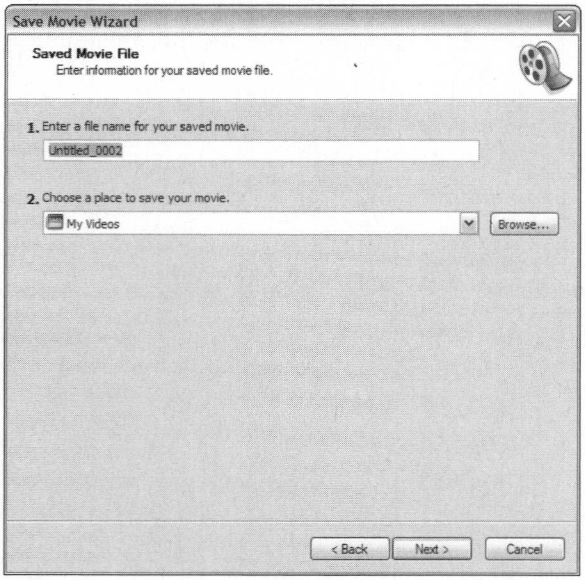

Figure 9-3:
The Save Movie Wizard guides you through the process.

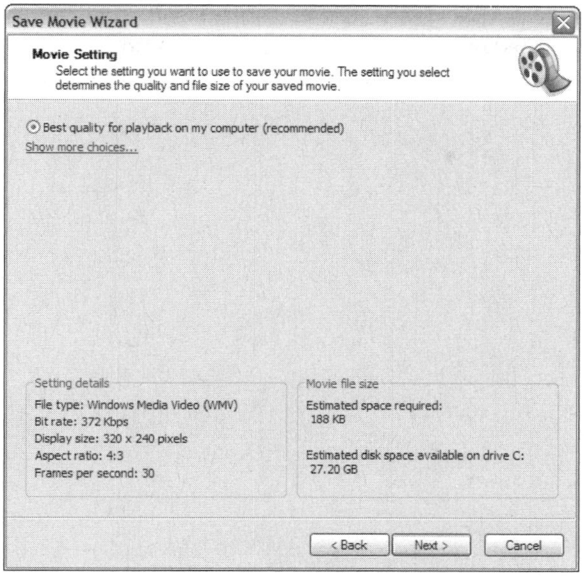

Figure 9-4:
The settings
determine
the file size.

7. **If you want to go with the default setting, skip ahead to Step 10. Otherwise, click the Show More Choices link to see additional options.**

8. **If you have a particular file size in mind as your target, select the Best Fit to File Size option button and then either enter the value or scroll up or down until you find it. You can set the target file size in either K (kilobytes) or MB (megabytes).**

   As you set different values for the target size, only one of the values in Setting Details changes: Bit Rate. This setting determines the amount of information that's included in the file. A lower bit rate means a lower quality of video and a smaller file size, whereas a higher bit rate means the reverse.

9. **Select the Other Settings option button, as shown in Figure 9-5. From the drop-down list next to it, select various settings and observe the impact on the values in Setting Details.**

   The Video for Broadband option, for example, sets a bit rate of 512 Kbps, a display size of 320 x 240 pixels, and a replay rate of 30 frames per second, generating a 260K file. The Video for Dial-Up Access option, on the other hand, sets a bit rate of only 38 Kbps, a display size of 160 x 120 pixels, and a replay rate of 15 frames per second, resulting in a file only 20K in size.

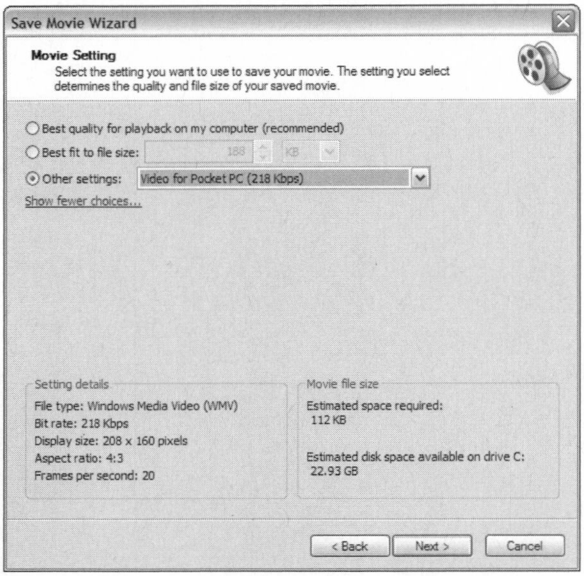

Figure 9-5:
Selecting
the Video
for Pocket
PC option.

10. **After you've arranged the settings to your satisfaction, click the Next button.**

    The file is saved.

11. **Click the Finish button to close the Save Movie Wizard.**

Adding Audio and Video Files to Your Site

You put both audio and video files on your Web page in the same way — or ways, rather. The simplest way to do it is the same way you connect any file to a Web page. Just put in a link for visitors to click, something like this one:

```
<a href="videofile.mpg">Click here to see the
    vacation video.</a>
```

Depending upon a particular visitor's system and configuration, the link to the video or sound file will cause different responses when clicked. It may work right in the browser. It may have to launch an external application to play the file. It may prompt the visitor to download the file. And so on. The one thing that won't happen is that the file will be a seamless part of your Web page.

If you'd like to make it so, you need to use the EMBED element. Here's the basic setup:

```
<embed src="musicfile.mid" width="300" height="100">
</embed>
```

You may want to pay attention to a few other attributes besides `width` and `height`. The most important of these is `autostart`, which, just like it sounds, starts the music or video playing automatically. Just alter the code so it reads like this:

```
<embed src="musicfile.mid" width="300" height="100"
    autostart="true">
</embed>
```

The other useful attribute is `loop`, which sets whether the file will play more than once and, if so, how many times. To set it to play over and over again forever, just do this:

```
<embed src="musicfile.mid" width="300" height="100"
    autostart="true" loop="true">
</embed>
```

To specify how many times to loop, just use the number instead of the word `true`. Here's an example:

```
<embed src="musicfile.mid" width="300" height="100"
    autostart="true" loop="3">
</embed>
```

Of course, Web authoring tools provide easy ways to add embedded objects to your Web pages. Dreamweaver, for example, uses a generic approach for adding both sound and video files. Here's how it goes:

1. **Open Dreamweaver and make sure the Common toolbar icons are showing. (See Figure 9-6.)**

2. **Click the arrow on the right side of the Media icon (shown in Figure 9-6) and choose Plugin from the menu that appears.**

   Alternatively, you can choose Insert⇨Media⇨Plugin from the main menu.

3. **Navigate to the media file you want to embed and select it.**

   You now have a plug-in symbol on your Web page, as shown in Figure 9-7.

4. **With the Properties Inspector (displayed at the bottom of the window), about all you can do is set the `width` and `height` attributes. If you want to do more, click the Parameters button in the Properties Inspector.**

   After you click the Parameters button, the Parameters dialog box appears, shown in Figure 9-8.

The Media icon

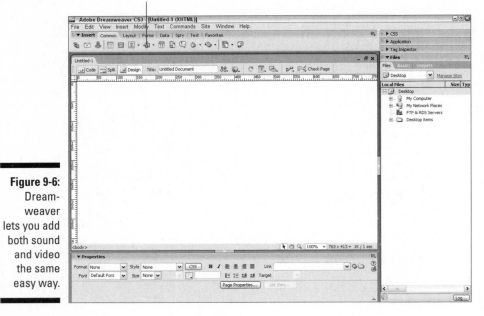

Figure 9-6:
Dream-
weaver
lets you add
both sound
and video
the same
easy way.

5. In the Parameters dialog box, set the values you want for different parameters (attributes).

For example, to set the autostart attribute to a value of true, type **autostart** under Parameter and **true** under Value.

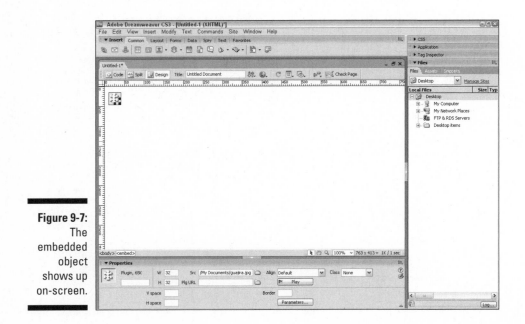

Figure 9-7:
The
embedded
object
shows up
on-screen.

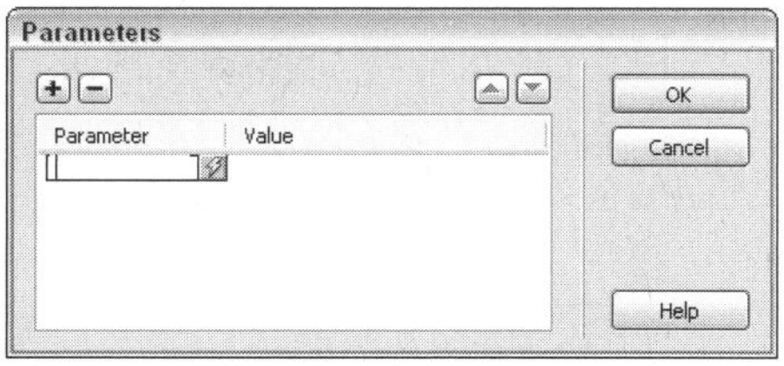

Figure 9-8:
You enter
attributes as
parameters.

6. **When you're finished setting parameter/attribute values, click the OK button.**

    The Parameters dialog box closes. You've completed adding the file to your Web page.

Adding a Flash music player

When it comes to adding sound, you can get a lot more sophisticated than plain old HTML. Sound players based in Adobe Flash, for example, let you seamlessly integrate everything from your MP3s to your own recordings into your Web site.

What if you aren't a Flash wizard or you just don't want to spend that kind of money to get started? No problem — lots of programs let you create your own Flash-based players with little effort or investment.

One of the tops on my list is the Fun SoundPlayer Maker (www.funsound player.com). Here's how easy it is to use:

1. **Go to www.funsoundplayer.com, download the Fun SoundPlayer Maker, and install it.**

2. **In the Template tab, shown in Figure 9-9, select the template with the design and features you want for your Web page.**

    If none of the basic templates are suitable, you can download more at www.funsoundplayer.com/player-templates.php.

3. **Click the Settings tab. (See Figure 9-10.)**

4. **Under Player Size, you can change the Width and Height settings, either by using the scroll arrows or by directly typing the values into the text boxes.**

5. **Choose the source of the sound you want to play under Sound Location.**

    Depending upon the template you selected, the Sound Location setting will present different choices, such as Include to Player (embedded) or External File(s).

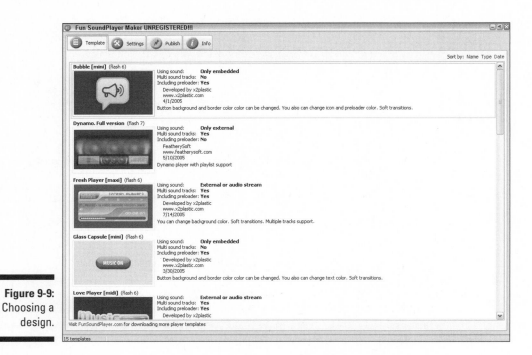

Figure 9-9:
Choosing a
design.

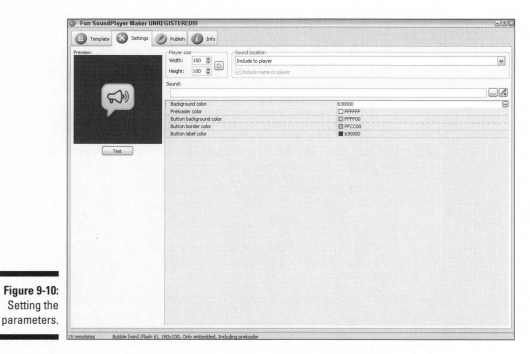

Figure 9-10:
Setting the
parameters.

6. **Under the Sound heading, click the "..." button to browse for a file.**

7. **Under Web Site Sound Folder, enter the location of the folder where you store your sound files on your Web site.**

8. **Set Play Default to Yes for autoplay; otherwise, set it to No.**

   This setting is available with only some of the templates.

9. **To customize the colors of the player, click in the color box next to the appropriate setting.**

   These will vary depending upon the template.

10. **Either type the hexadecimal color code or click on the "..." button that appears on the right side.**

    In the latter case, you get the system color picker (shown in Figure 9-11). Simply click on the color you want and then click the OK button.

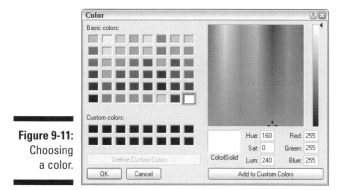

Figure 9-11: Choosing a color.

11. **If desired, click the Test button to open a pop-up window with the functional player.**

12. **Click the Publish tab. (See Figure 9-12.)**

13. **Select which of the three save options you prefer:**

    • **Save as Template HTML Page:** This creates not only the player, but a basic Web page that includes it as well.

    • **Save SWF and Copy the Template HTML Code to the Clipboard:** Use this if you already have a Web page that you want to embed the player in. Paste the HTML from the clipboard into your own Web page.

    Material on the clipboard isn't permanent! If you don't paste it right away, you could lose it and would have to start over.

    • **Save SWF Only:** For those who don't need any help.

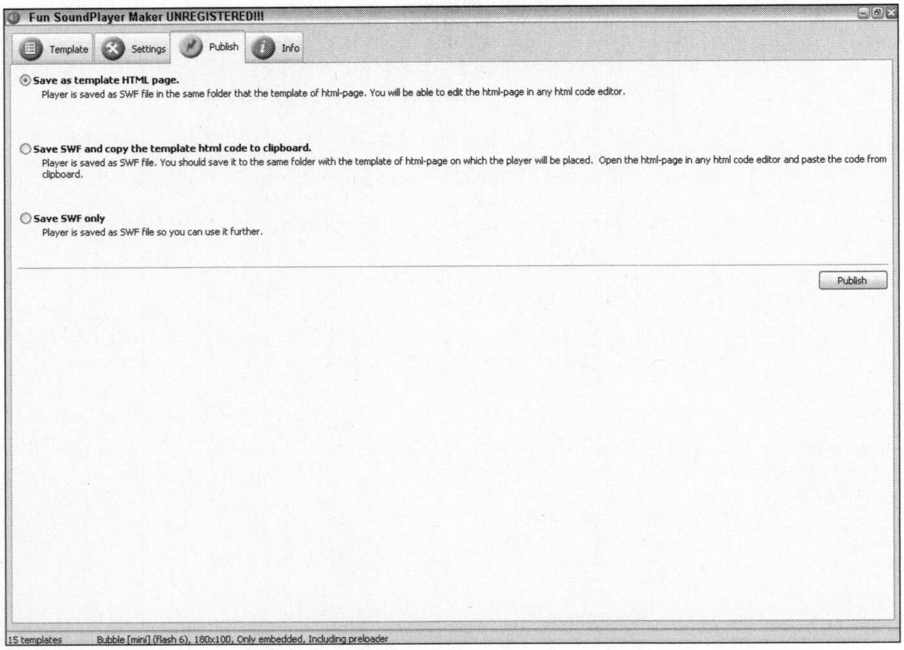

Figure 9-12:
Saving
the sound
player.

14. Click the Publish button.

Table 9-5 gives the URLs of some other Flash sound player utilities.

Table 9-5	Flash Sound Player Utilities
Web Site Name	**Web Address**
Chameleon Flash Sound Player	www.lucidflash.com
Making a Simple Player	www.lukamaras.com/tutorials/sound/ simple-mp3-loop-tune-player.html
Oven Fresh Audio Player Maker	www.ovenfreshweb.com/audio- player-maker.htm
soundPlayer Component	www.hotscripts.com/Detailed/ 53816.html
soundPlayer Pro	www.flashloaded.com/flash components/soundplayer
xmp3Player	http://allwebcodesign.com/setup/ addons-xmp3Player.htm

Importing YouTube video

YouTube (www.youtube.com) is one of the hottest sources of videos on the Web. Unlike many video sources, however, you can't just download the file and use it. You have to either link to it or embed it. To link to it, simply copy the address in the URL text box and add it as a link in your site. (See the code samples in the "Adding Audio and Video Files to Your Site" section, earlier in this chapter.)

Fortunately, the embedding process is about as easy as it can possibly get. YouTube gives you the source code for it right next to every video. (See Figure 9-13.) All you have to do is click in the Embed text box, which automatically selects the whole thing, and then copy the code and paste it into your own Web page.

YouTube uses both the `<object>` and the `<embed>` elements for embedding video. This makes sure that the video will display in any Web browser.

Online Sources for Web Audio and Video

Table 9-6 lists some places on the World Wide Web where you can find more resources like the ones that are covered in this chapter.

Figure 9-13: The Embed text box contains the code you need.

Table 9-6	Online Resources for Web Audio and Video
Web Site Name	*Web Address*
Adobe Audition	www.adobe.com/products/audition
Anvil Studio	www.anvilstudio.com
Cakewalk	www.cakewalk.com
FinaleMusic	www.finalemusic.com
GoldWave Digital Audio Editor	www.goldwave.com
MAGIX	www.magix.net
PG Music	www.pgmusic.com/products_bb.htm
SimpleServer:Shout	www.analogx.com/contents/download/ network/ssshout.htm
SoftStep	www.geneticmusic.com/softstep.htm
Sonic Spot: Audio File Formats	www.sonicspot.com/guide/ fileformatlist.html

Part IV
From Blogs to Toons — Good Content Makes Contented Visitors

In this part . . .

This part is about getting your visitors involved in your site so that they keep coming back for more. Chapter 10 views this topic from a special perspective — the add-ins here put the visitor in control. Chapter 11 covers the latest wrinkle in generated content: blogging. And Chapter 12 shows you where to go to get fresh content — from news to quotation applets — for your site.

Chapter 10

Letting 'Em Have Their Say

* *

In This Chapter

▶ Providing guestbooks

▶ Constructing message boards

▶ Creating chat rooms with ParaChat

* *

*I*n Chapter 19, I give you the lowdown on polls and forms and how they can add value to your Web site by attracting more users and making your site *stickier,* meaning people tend to come back more often. The add-ins in this chapter (guestbooks, message boards, and the like) are similar to the polls and forms in Chapter 19 but have one important difference. With polls and forms, you have total control over the topics and possible responses. But with guestbooks, message boards, and chat rooms, you give up some control over your Web site's content. You turn that control over to your visitors by providing them with a forum where they can express themselves.

Censorship and your Web site

Censorship is an ugly word to most people, especially in connection with the Internet. Unfortunately, in running your own Web site, you sometimes find that you need to limit in some way what others can post to your site. In extreme cases, you may even need to bar a particularly disruptive person from posting in your chat room, for example. Is this act — and that of setting up filters — a form of censorship? The answer to this question depends on why you're doing it. If your intention is simply to keep someone from voicing an opinion, you're engaging in censorship, plain and simple. If your intention is to defend the free speech rights of the rest of the members against someone who's interfering with them, that's another matter entirely.

This topic isn't an idle philosophical matter but a very real consideration that you'll likely face as a Webmaster. It's a sad fact that someone, sometime, will probably jump into the middle of your nice, happy online community and try to mess it up. Although you may expect a certain amount of disagreement and even heated discussion in any group, personal attacks and deliberate disruption of discussions are different matters. As a Webmaster, your responsibility is to act for the benefit of your peaceful visitors. And at times, that may mean you have to ban a troublemaker from your site.

Providing Guestbooks

Guestbooks are the digital equivalent of a graffiti wall, which doesn't necessarily mean that they're going to contain limericks or dirty words. But they *are* designed so that people can leave short messages for all to see.

Many guestbooks offer an additional option that allows users to create messages that only the guestbook owner — the Webmaster — can view. This enables people to leave private comments for you.

The guestbook stacks the posted messages one after the other, with the vast majority of guestbooks putting the newest message on top and moving all the others down. A few guestbooks work the other way around, but I don't recommend that type because you have to scroll too much to get to the most recent message.

You may want to use a couple of e-mail features built in to most guest books:

- ✓ **Thank-you note:** This feature sends a nice note to each visitor who leaves a message.

- ✓ **Message copies via e-mail:** This feature e-mails the Webmaster a copy of each message posted. This is a nice timesaver; otherwise, you have to constantly go to the guestbook to see what new messages have been posted.

GuestCity (www.guestcity.com) is one of the easiest guestbooks in the world to set up. It's free, and the only catch is that an unobtrusive advertising banner appears at the top of your Web page. GuestCity remotely hosts the guestbook on its site, so you don't have to have any knowledge of CGI scripts to run the guestbook.

To set up your GuestCity guestbook, follow these steps:

1. **Go to www.guestcity.com and click the Get Your Own Guestbook Now link near the bottom of the page.**

   Alternatively, you can click the Create link in the top of the yellow box on the left side of the page.

2. **On the subsequent page, shown in Figure 10-1, enter a username and password.**

3. **Scroll down and enter a title and description for your guestbook. Then select a category and primary language for it from the drop-down lists, and select the Public or Private option button (private means that the guestbook is only for your site's visitors).**

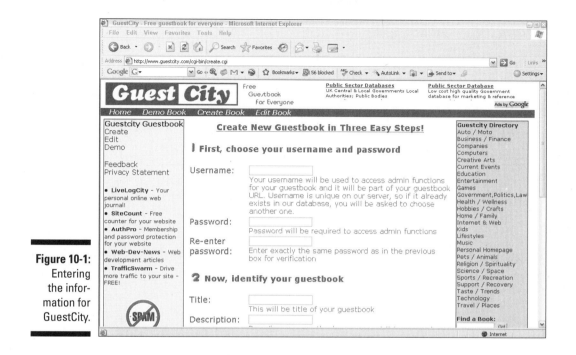

Figure 10-1:
Entering
the infor-
mation for
GuestCity.

4. **Scroll down again and enter your name and e-mail address in the appropriate text boxes, followed by the URL and title of your Web page.**

5. **Click the Create Guestbook button at the bottom of the page.**

6. **Copy the HTML code from the resulting page (shown in Figure 10-2), paste it into your Web page, and upload your page to your server.**

   You now have a guestbook.

If you want to customize the guestbook, you have a full range of options. Here's how to get to them:

1. **Go to www.guestcity.com and click the Edit link in the yellow box on the left side of the page.**

2. **On the next page, enter your username and password under Manage Your Guestbook and then click the Login button.**

   The Guestbook Manager appears, as shown in Figure 10-3.

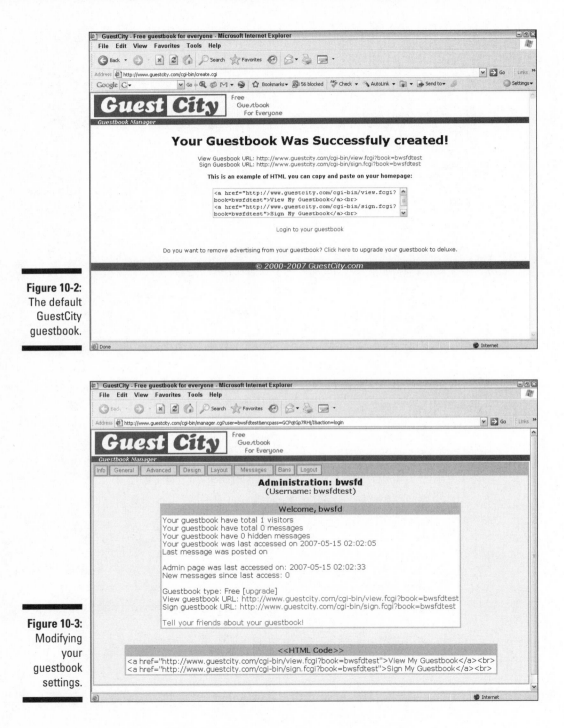

Figure 10-2:
The default
GuestCity
guestbook.

Figure 10-3:
Modifying
your
guestbook
settings.

3. **Click the buttons across the top of the Guestbook Manager to access the various settings, detailed in the following list:**

   - *Info:* This is the default page for the Guestbook Manager. It shows information on message activity and gives you an extra copy of the HTML code for your guestbook.

   - *General:* This is the same information you entered when you signed up — your name, guestbook title, and the like.

   - *Advanced:* This isn't really advanced, but it's beyond the default settings, anyway. You can choose details like whether to send acknowledgments of guestbook entries and what order to put the messages in.

   - *Design:* This is where you specify the colors you want to use in your guestbook.

   - *Layout:* This allows you to choose how much information to reveal about each visitor who uses the guestbook.

   - *Messages:* This is the control center where you delete old messages and, in the case of bad posts, may elect to ban a visitor from posting another time.

   - *Bans:* If you're feeling lenient, you can go here to remove the ban you put on a poster with the Messages button.

   - *Logout:* This enables you to quit the Guestbook Manager.

Creating Message Boards

Message boards provide the structure that simple guestbooks lack. Most of the messages that people post on message boards are fairly short, but unlike a guestbook, messages aren't just listed in a simple top-down or bottom-up order that's based on when they're posted. Instead, a message board lists its postings by topic. In fact, the whole purpose of a message board is different from that of a guestbook. Both guestbooks and message boards let people leave messages, but message boards also let people interact with one another.

Before a new message is posted, the poster chooses a subject or *topic line* for it. As other people respond to the message, that topic automatically carries over, and the reply is connected to the original message. Usually, the board lists these postings in a *hierarchy,* where each response is indented beneath the message it replies to, and the series of messages on one topic is called a *thread.* Visitors to your site can follow a thread from beginning to end, jump in and reply to any message in the thread, or start an entirely new discussion by posting a new message.

Message boards almost always deal with a particular field of interest that visitors to a Web site have in common. Here are some common examples:

- Professional discussions
- Political issues
- Regional concerns
- Hobbies
- Current events
- Technical support

Obviously, a publicly available forum on controversial topics gives people who are less than polite an opening to be disruptive. A worthwhile message board program includes a filter feature where you can specify any terms you want to prohibit. (For example, if you run a board for wild turkeys, you may not want them to have to see words like *stuffing* or *Thanksgiving*.) Filters prevent messages containing the terms you list from going onto your message board.

Setting up a message board with Brandon Fisher

Brandon Fisher (www.brandonfisher.com/msgboards) gives you a place to host your message boards. Although the company remotely hosts the boards it provides, the boards are customizable so that you can mimic the look and feel of your Web site. You get a well-designed message board with all the bells and whistles.

Brandon Fisher has a whole mess of nice features, including one that lets you add your own background image to all the board's pages or set password-protected access so that you can hold private discussions.

To create a free message board with Brandon Fisher, follow these steps:

1. **Go to www.brandonfisher.com/msgboards/yourmsgboard.asp.**

2. **Under Administration (see Figure 10-4), select a category.**

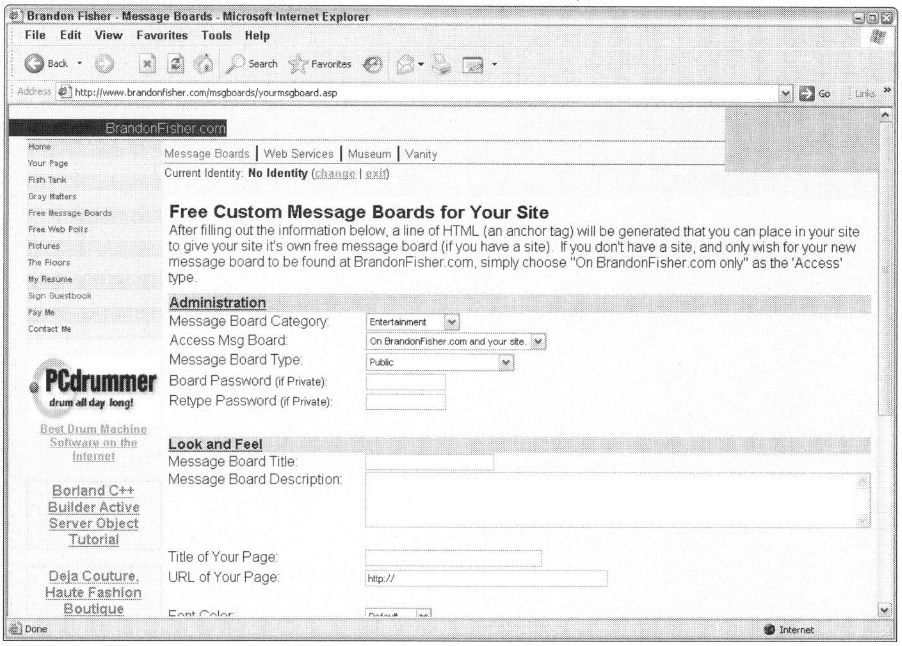

Figure 10-4:
Creating
your
message
board.

3. **Select whether you want your users to access the message board on just your site, on just Brandon Fisher's site, or on both.**

4. **Select either a public or a private board.**

5. **If you decide to run a private board, enter the password twice.**

6. **Under Look and Feel, type a title and a description for your message board.**

7. **Next, type the title and URL of your Web page.**

8. **Select a font color from the drop-down list.**

9. **Either select a background color from its drop-down list or enter the URL of an image you want to use for the background.**

10. **Under Contact/Login Information, type your name and e-mail address.**

11. **Enter a password for accessing your message board.**

12. **Click the Edit/Create Message Board button.**

13. **On the resulting page, shown in Figure 10-5, copy the HTML code and paste it into your own Web page code.**

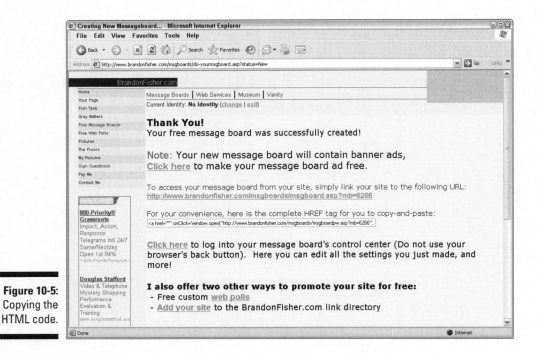

Figure 10-5:
Copying the
HTML code.

Giving Visitors the Gift of Gab

Chat rooms provide a way for visitors to your site to engage in live, real-time communication. Like message boards, chat rooms enable lots of users to leave messages on the same topic, but these messages don't appear in topic-related threads. Instead, the messages appear as they're sent, and the various conversation threads run together in the same area. You may think that this sounds a bit chaotic, and I can't agree more. Chat room discussions are totally unstructured, and the more people that are in a chat room, the more confusing it is to try to follow a conversation.

But chat rooms are fun and popular, and even chat novices quickly get used to picking out the specific conversation they're a part of. Still, carrying on a conversation in a chat room is kind of like talking to one or two people in the middle of a large party. This isn't your problem as a Webmaster, though, except that you may want to recommend these rooms mainly for smaller gatherings. People who regularly hang out in chat rooms understand and accept their peculiarities, and if your visitors really want chat rooms, providing them is easy enough. Several sources on the Web offer their services to help you add a chat room to your site. In this section, I cover ParaChat, but other chat room source sites are listed in Table 10-1 at the end of this chapter.

ParaChat (www.parachat.com) is one source that gives you a fast way to slap a Java chat room onto your Web site. To add ParaChat to your site, follow these steps:

1. **Go to www.parachat.com/basic/get-yours.html (shown in Figure 10-6).**

2. **Enter values for the width and height of the chat room in the first two text boxes.**

   The default values are 600 pixels wide and 400 pixels high, but you should choose whatever size best fits the design of the Web page on which you intend to place the chat room.

3. **Enter a name for your chat room.**

   In general, the name should reflect either the theme or the name of your site.

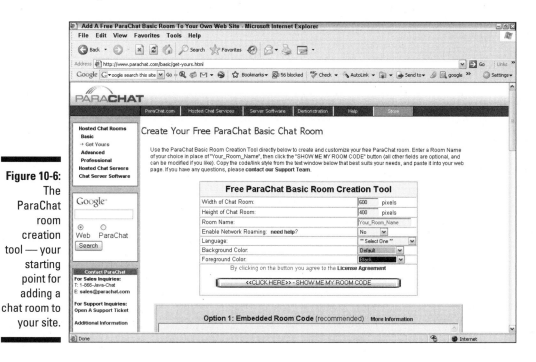

Figure 10-6: The ParaChat room creation tool — your starting point for adding a chat room to your site.

4. **The next option relates to a special service provided by ParaChat. The default value is No. If you want to use this service, choose Yes.**

   Network roaming, although it sounds as if it has something to do with cell phones, means that you make your new chat room available to everyone using ParaChat, and that your site visitors can likewise visit all ParaChat chat rooms that have this option selected.

5. **Select the language in which you want the chat room to appear.**

   Current choices are English, Spanish, Portuguese, French, German, and Italian, with English being the default option. Note that this doesn't restrict in any way which language your visitors can use when talking with each other in the chat room; it simply affects the display on-screen. For example, the Spanish version says that a username is *requerido* rather than saying it is *required* and the Connect button says *Conectar*.

6. **Select the background and foreground colors that you want for your chat room from the last two drop-down lists.**

7. **Click the Click Here – Show Me My Room Code button.**

8. **Scroll down to copy and paste the resulting code (shown in Figure 10-7) into your Web page and then upload the page to your site.**

   The simplest way to do this is to click inside the code listing, press Ctrl+A to select all the code, and then press Ctrl+C to copy it. Go into your Web page creation program, place your cursor where you want to insert the code, and then press Ctrl+V to paste it into place.

   Of course, you can also use the menu options for this — choosing Edit➪ Select All, Edit➪Copy, then Edit➪Paste — but the old keyboard method (which goes all the way back to CP/M, for those of you who have been around computers for a while) is a lot faster.

9. **Save the Web page.**

After you fire up the Web page in which you pasted the chat room code, all that you — or any of your visitors — must do is to wait for the chat applet to load, enter a nickname in the appropriate text box, and click the Connect button.

After you connect to the chat room, you go to the chat screen. The people currently in the chat room are shown in the area on the left side. Enter your messages in the long text box at the bottom of the chat window. Click in the color box at the bottom to set a color for your text to appear in. Click B to make the text bold or I to italicize it. Click the Send button to send your message. Your message then appears in the top area of the screen, along with all the other participants' messages.

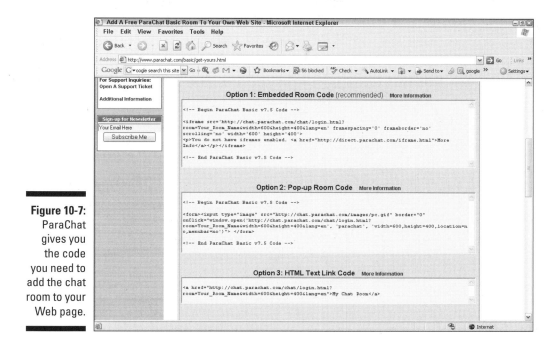

Figure 10-7:
ParaChat
gives you
the code
you need to
add the chat
room to your
Web page.

Online Sources for Adding Community to Your Site

Table 10-1 lists some places on the World Wide Web where you can find more resources like those that are covered in this chapter.

Table 10-1	Online Resources for Adding Community
Web Site Name	*Web Address*
Boards2Go	www.boards2go.com
Bravenet	www.bravenet.com
Chat-Forum.com	http://chat-forum.com/freechat
Dreambook	www.dreambook.com
HTML Gear	http://htmlgear.lycos.com
Pliner.Net	www.pliner.net/chat
QuickChat	www.quickchat.org
Website Free Stuff	www.websitefreestuff.com/chat_rooms.html

Chapter 11

Bloggin' the Night Away

In This Chapter

▶ Constructing blogs with Blogger

▶ Building a blog on a hosted site

*B*logs (or 'blogs, if you want to get technical) are Web logs — essentially, a way for you to alter the content of your Web site at will. Blogs cover a wide range of content, from daily diaries to professional journalism, and their popularity seems to know no bounds.

You can use blogging technology to keep your site updated without having to get into coding, and you can make changes while you're on the road, away from your design computer. Just drop into an Internet café and fill out a form, and your site is updated right away.

Adding Blogger to Your Site

Blogger — another Google Web service — is perhaps the most popular Web log provider and one of the easiest to use. To get started, follow these steps:

1. **Go to www.blogger.com and click the Create Your Blog Now button.**

2. **Enter your e-mail address, password, and the Word Verification; select the I Accept the Terms of Service check box, and click the Contine button.**

3. **On the resulting page, scroll down and click the Advanced Blog Setup link.**

   You can, of course, simply fill in the information on this form, but all that does is create a blog on Blogger, not on your site. You can put in a link to it, but it's just not the same.

4. **On the Advanced Blog Setup page, shown in Figure 11-1, enter a title for your blog under Blog Details.**

5. **Select the appropriate radio button to either list your blog at Blogger or not.**

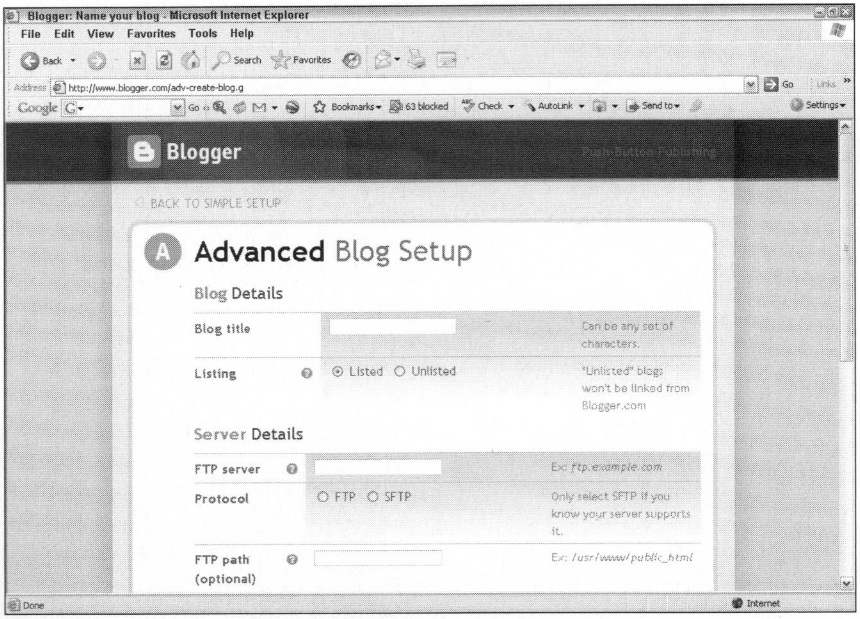

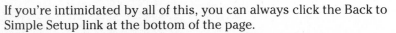

Figure 11-1:
Using
Advanced
Blog Setup.

6. **Under Server Details (see Figure 11-2), enter the required information (FTP server address, your username, and so on).**

   If you don't know this information, ask your Web provider for it.

   If you're intimidated by all of this, you can always click the Back to Simple Setup link at the bottom of the page.

7. **Type the letters that you see under Word Verification.**

8. **Click the Continue button.**

   The template page appears, as shown in Figure 11-3.

9. **Select the option button next to the design you like best.**

   You can scroll down to see more examples than are shown in the figure.

10. **Click the Continue button.**

    Your new blog is created, and you go to a page where you click the Start Posting arrow.

11. **On the Create New Post page (see Figure 11-4), enter either some prepared material or just any old thing that comes to mind.**

12. **Click the Preview link.**

13. **If you don't like what you see, you can click the Hide Preview link and go back to the drawing board. If you're satisfied, click the Publish Post button instead.**

    You're done.

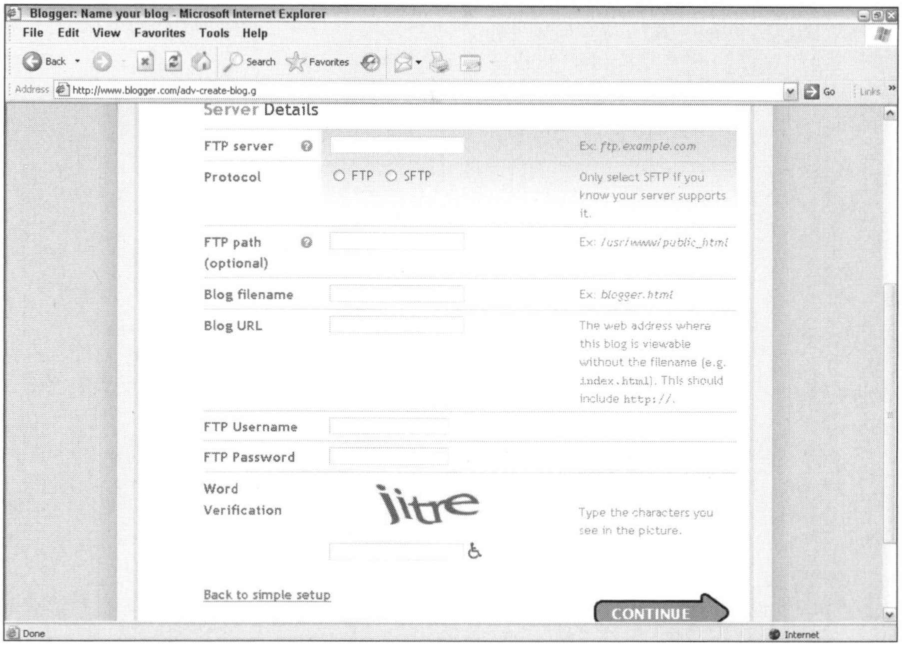

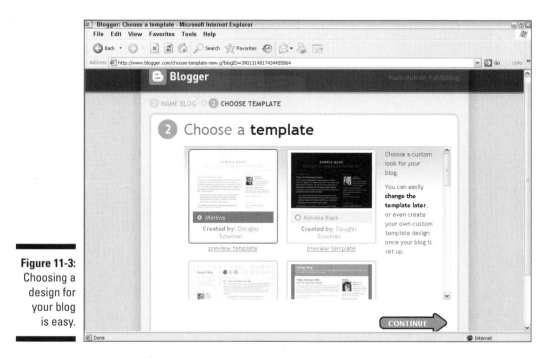

Figure 11-2: Providing FTP details.

Figure 11-3: Choosing a design for your blog is easy.

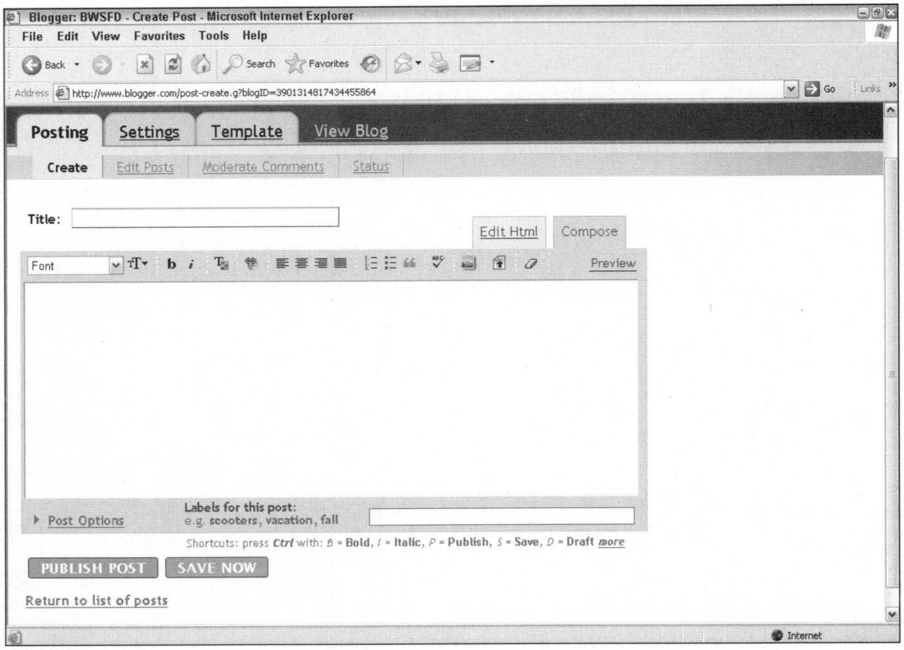

Figure 11-4:
You can
create,
preview,
and publish
a new post
from here.

Bloggin' on Bravenet

On top of using outside services like Blogger, you may be able to set up a blog provided by your own Web host. (See Chapter 16 for more information on Web hosting.) Depending upon your Web service account, you may already have a ready-to-go blog that's easy to set up, perhaps even via a simple control panel.

Although the exact details may vary from one provider to the next, the general process is often very similar. The following sections show you how it works on a Bravenet account (www.bravenet.com).

Adding a blog

Before you can do anything, you need to add a blog to your Bravenet site, of course. Once you're done with that, you can start playing with the settings and getting your message out to the world.

To add the blog, follow these steps:

1. **In the Bravenet Account Manager, click the Web Tools tab. (See Figure 11-5.)**

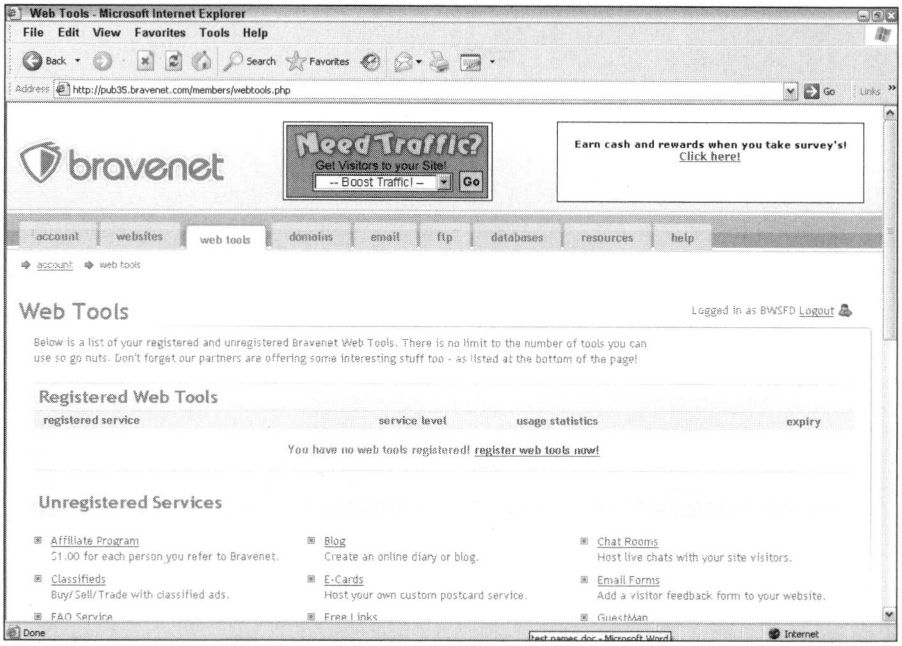

Figure 11-5:
The Web
Tools tab.

2. **Click the Blog link.**

3. **On the resulting page, click the Get Your Blog button.**

4. **On the next page, scroll down and click the Continue button.**

   You select the button on the left for free service or the one on the right for paid service, which gives you a few more options. In this example, I've selected the free service. You can always upgrade to the paid version later if you'd like.

5. **In the Service Startup Wizard, shown in Figure 11-6, enter a title and subtitle for your blog in the appropriate text boxes.**

6. **Select one of the themes (templates).**

   If you're not thrilled with any of the three, you can change it later; there are more themes available, just not at this stage.

7. **Select the radio button to either receive or not receive an e-mail message every time someone comments on your blog.**

8. **Click the Save and Continue button.**

   This returns you to the Blog Service Manager.

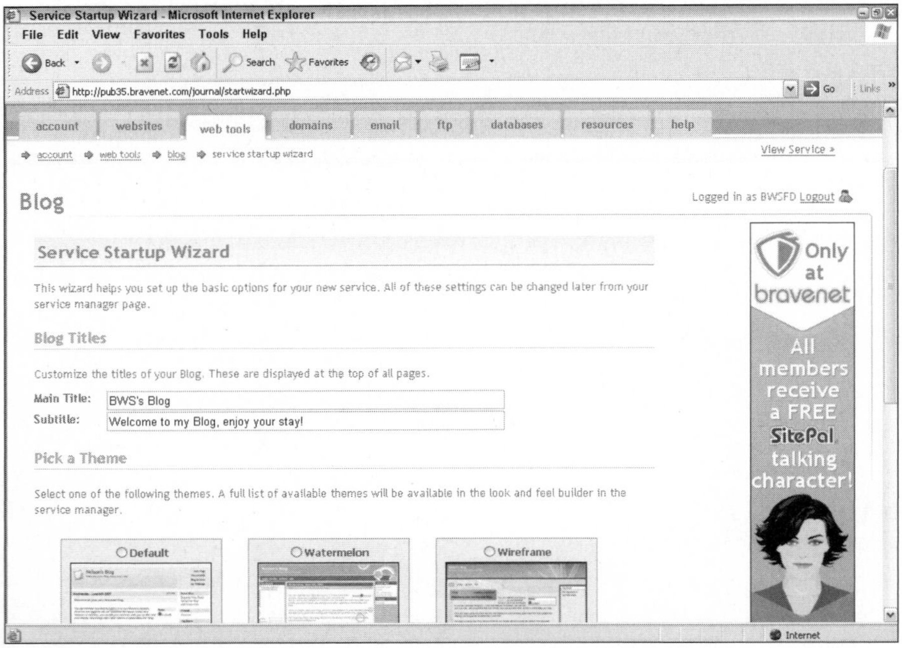

Figure 11-6:
Making the
initial
choices.

Customizing your blog

Now that you're a blogger, you'll probably want to tinker with a few of the settings. I mention in Step 6 of the preceding section that you can choose more themes. Here's how it's done, starting from exactly where the previous steps left off:

1. **In the Blog Service Manager (see Figure 11-7), click the Look and Feel link.**

2. **At the bottom of the Look and Feel Editor, shown in Figure 11-8, click the Select a Theme link.**

   Do this first, ignoring the tabs at the top of the editor. Those tabs enable you to specify each part of your own theme design. This means that selecting one of the prepared themes will automatically wipe out any custom theme you've created. Unless you're really good at graphic design, go with the installed themes first.

3. **Scroll down to view the available themes (see Figure 11-9) and click the one you want.**

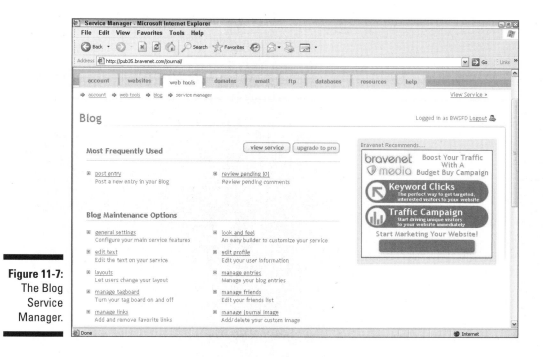

Figure 11-7:
The Blog
Service
Manager.

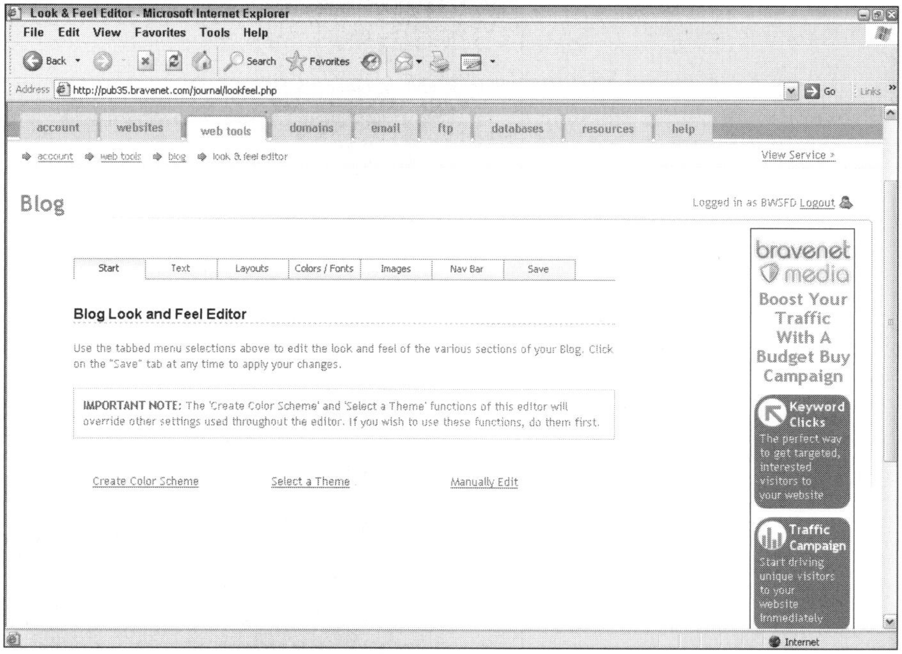

Figure 11-8:
The Look
and Feel
Editor.

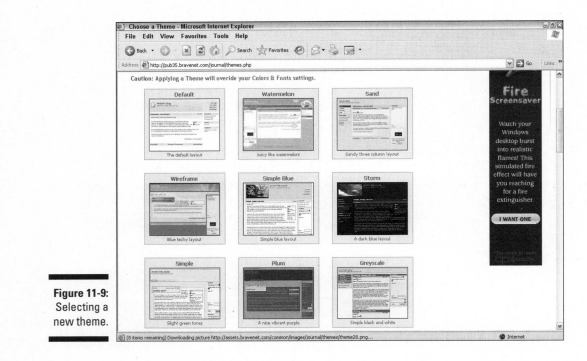

4. **You get a dialog box reminding you that you're about to override any existing theme or settings. Click the OK button to proceed or the Cancel button to abort.**

5. **Click the Save tab in the Look and Feel Editor, and then click the Save All Changes button that appears.**

Making a post

Now it's time to get some use out of that blog of yours. After all, what's a blog without blogging? Here's how you do it:

1. **If you've been following along with the example in the previous section, click the Service Manager link.**

2. **Click the Post Entry link.**

3. **On the resulting page, shown in Figure 11-10, enter a title for your post in the text box.**

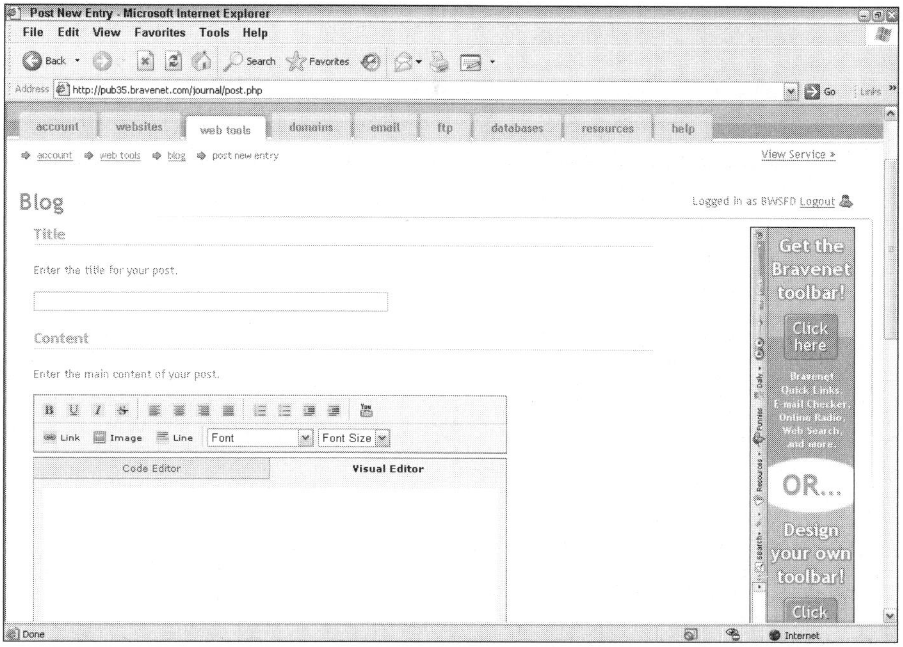

Figure 11-10:
Posting an
entry.

4. **Scroll down and type your message in the text editor. (See Figure 11-11.)**

   You can click the Code Editor tab to directly type HTML. Click the Visual Editor tab to type like you do in a word processor.

   In addition to the sort of buttons common to all word processors (bold, center, add image, and so on), the button on the far top right is a nice touch — it adds YouTube videos to your blog. (See Chapter 9 for more information on YouTube.) There's also a row of smileys at the bottom that you can add by just clicking them.

5. **Scroll down and, if desired, click the Add Emoticon/Smiley link next to the Mood and/or Music text boxes. (See Figure 11-12.)**

6. **Under Blog Entry Options, you can specify three sets of options:**

   • **Date and time of the message:** If you don't set the time and date, they'll be set automatically.

   • **Privacy settings for the post:** Controls comment access/approval and publicity on Bravenet.

   • **Abbreviation parsing:** Settings for automatically adding pop-up tooltips to explain abbreviations used in the post.

7. **Click the Post Entry button.**

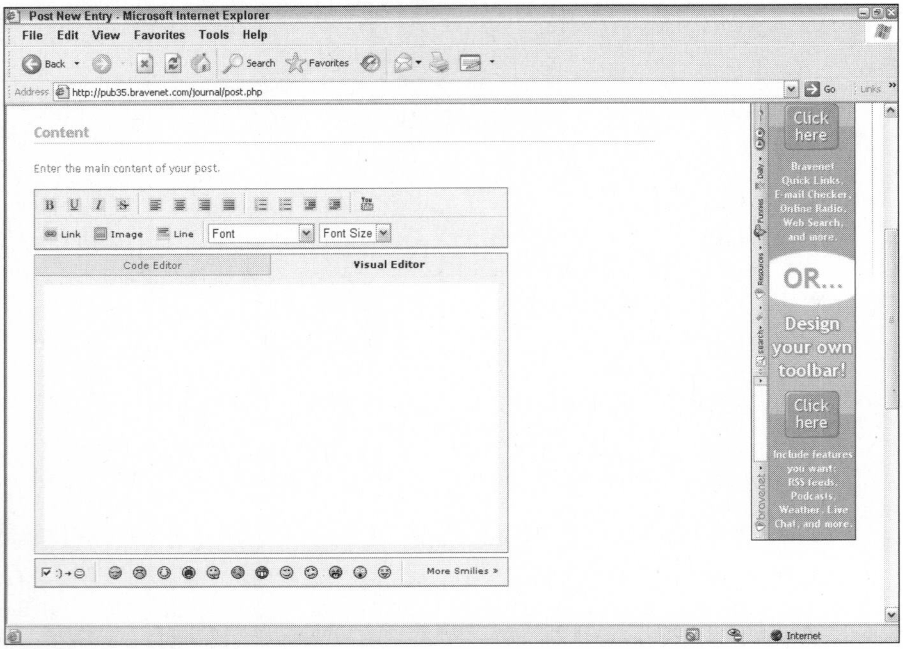

Figure 11-11:
The Text Editor.

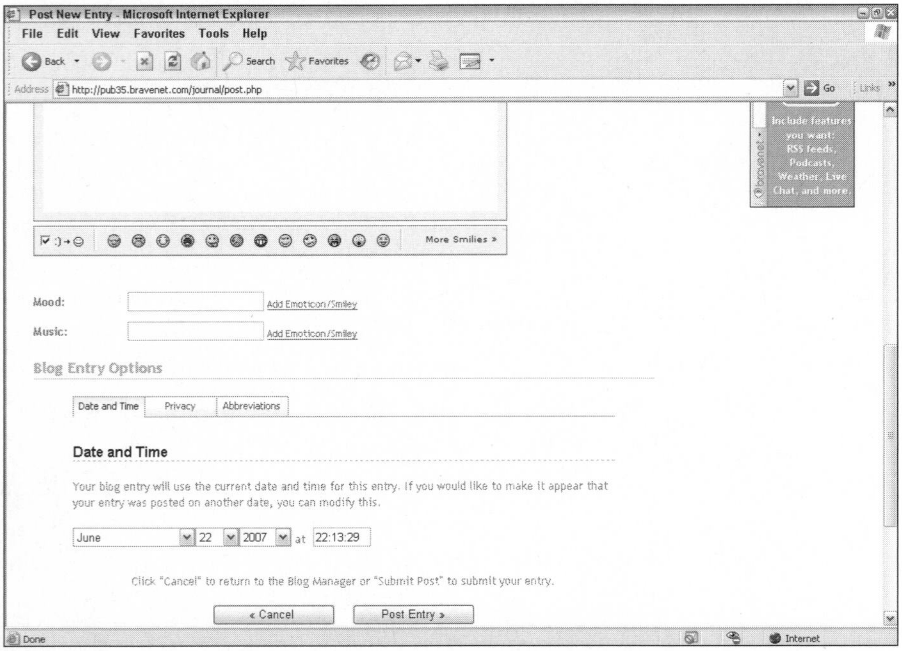

Figure 11-12:
Filling out the bottom portion.

Online Sources for Blogs

Table 11-1 lists some places on the World Wide Web where you can find more resources like the ones that are covered in this chapter. All of the sites in the following table allow you to create your own blog for free.

Table 11-1	Online Sources for Blogs
Web Site Name	*Web Address*
Blogger	www.blogger.com
Blogging.com	www.blogging.com
Introduction to Blogging	http://codex.wordpress.org/ Introduction_to_Blogging
LiveJournal	www.livejournal.com
TypePad	www.typepad.com
WordPress	www.wordpress.com

Chapter 12

Using Content Providers

*F*resh content keeps people coming back to a Web site. No matter how great your site, how wonderful your prose, and how fabulous your graphics, few people will visit your site over and over again just to see something they've already seen.

If your Web site provides a repeatable service, like automated translations or HTML validation, you can get away with leaving your site alone. For the vast majority of sites, though, if you can't give your visitors new material from time to time, you'll lose 'em.

It's a treadmill that you can never get off of; you've got to keep updating your site's material, or your site dies. All Webmasters want high-quality content for their Web sites, but generating that content isn't easy. Fortunately, plenty of people crank out all sorts of stuff that you can use.

Whether you know it or not, you're already familiar with this sort of material. Your daily newspaper typically consists of some locally produced material and lots of items from content providers. The comics, most columns, horoscopes, and many of the articles in the newspaper come from people who don't work for that paper. The news and information companies that do this sort of thing are latching onto the Web as the newest and best market for such canned content.

Still, life can be a bit too serious at times — people like to kick back and have fun once in a while. If you're looking for fun things that you can add to your site, however, it almost seems like the Web just doesn't get it. Everything's so darned functional. Where's the stuff that doesn't actually do anything? Where's the stuff that's a completely delightful waste of time?

It's my job to keep you up-to-date on the latest and greatest of everything Web-related, so I also went out looking for Web site add-ins that take a step away from the serious side of things — extras like riddles, games, and cartoons.

 If you need to justify the fun things to your boss, point out that they attract people to your site, and they make your site *stickier* so that visitors come back for more.

The prices for canned content range from absolutely free to somewhere between "Oh, no!" and "You've got to be kidding!" But you can find plenty of high-quality, free material out there. So if you're running a small Web site, you don't need to break open your piggy bank to get the good stuff.

Running RiddleNut.com's Random Riddles

Ever wonder how seven batters from one baseball team can come up in the same inning, but nobody scores a run? Oh, and the team didn't use any substitutions either. Got you wondering? Good.

How about this one?

> One of us falls and never breaks.
>
> One of us breaks but never falls.
>
> What are we?

The answer to the first riddle is that, of the first five batters, two are out, while three get on base. Now the bases are loaded with two outs. The sixth batter hits a grand slam. Wait a minute — here are four runs! Didn't the riddle say that nobody scores? Yes, but the guy who hits the grand slam fails to touch first base. That means that he's the third out and the grand slam never happened. All right, so what about the seventh batter? Well, the player who hit the grand slam isn't called out until the pitcher protests to the umpire that he missed the base, and the pitcher's not allowed to protest until the next batter comes up.

The answer to the second riddle is *night and day.* There can be nightfall and daybreak but never nightbreak and dayfall.

If you like riddles, the Random Riddle from RiddleNut.com (at, of course, www.riddlenut.com) is a gold mine. More important, if your visitors like riddles, you can hook them by adding these Random Riddles to your pages. You don't even need to sign up or anything.

These riddles are okay for all ages.

The people at RiddleNut.com honestly appreciate riddles as an art form. And they want you to help spread the word by adding riddles to your Web page — for free. Here's how you go about it:

1. **Go to www.riddlenut.com/build.php.**

   The Random Riddle for Your Website page appears, as shown in Figure 12-1.

2. **From the first three drop-down lists, select a text color, link color, and background color.**

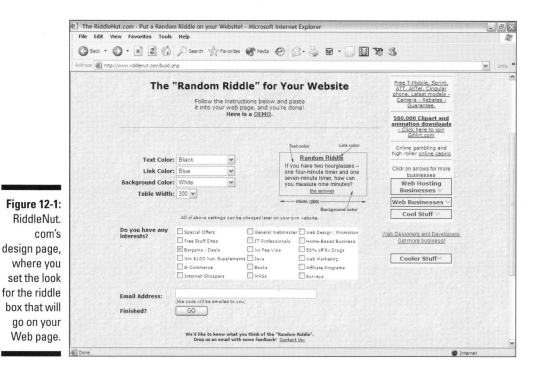

Figure 12-1:
RiddleNut.
com's
design page,
where you
set the look
for the riddle
box that will
go on your
Web page.

3. **In the Table Width drop-down list, select a width (in pixels) for the table that holds the riddle.**

4. **In the Do You Have Any Interests section, select any check boxes for topics you want to receive e-mail about. If you don't want any e-mail, make sure all the check boxes are deselected.**

5. **Type your e-mail address into the text box.**

6. **Click the Go button.**

   You receive an e-mail message containing HTML code.

7. **Copy the HTML code from the e-mail, paste it into your Web page within the BODY element, and then upload the Web page to your site.**

Yes, I know that I say in Chapter 4 not to put JavaScript code in the body of your page because somebody may activate it too soon. But this one is different. Really. No visitor can do that with this JavaScript because it doesn't appear until it's ready to use.

The resulting code is like the following example, allowing for differences in color and table-width choices:

```
<CENTER>
<SCRIPT LANGUAGE="JavaScript1.1"
SRC="http://www.riddlenut.com/include/riddle.php?
    fontcolor=Black&linkcolor=Blue&backcolor=
    White&tabwid=300">
</SCRIPT>
</CENTER>
```

The Random Riddle on your page looks something like the one shown in Figure 12-2.

Unlike some remotely hosted Web site add-ins, this one has no control center where you can adjust your settings. However, you can manually adjust the settings in your own page's source code. The key items here are the `fontcolor`, `linkcolor`, `backcolor`, and `tabwid` attributes. Each attribute corresponds to the color and table-width choices that you make on the RiddleNut.com design page. By changing the values of the three color attributes on your site, you can alter the riddle box without going back to the RiddleNut.com site. You can enter either named colors or hexadecimal values, as in the following example:

```
SRC="http://www.riddlenut.com/include/riddle.php?
    fontcolor=Green&linkcolor=0000FF&backcolor=
    White&tabwid=300">
```

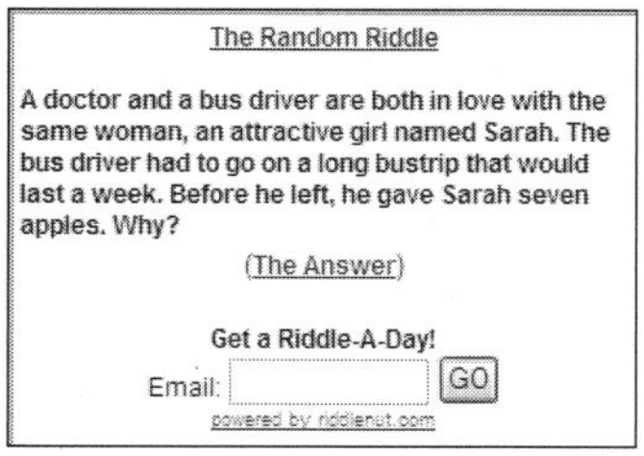

Figure 12-2:
The Random
Riddle
script as it
appears on
your Web
page.

> The Random Riddle
>
> A doctor and a bus driver are both in love with the
> same woman, an attractive girl named Sarah. The
> bus driver had to go on a long bustrip that would
> last a week. Before he left, he gave Sarah seven
> apples. Why?
>
> (The Answer)
>
> Get a Riddle-A-Day!
>
> Email: [   ] GO
>
> powered by riddlenut.com

Don't alter the RiddleNut.com code's punctuation. You may feel that you
need to place quotation marks (" ") around the attributes' values or add a
hash mark (#) in front of a hexadecimal number. If you do any of these things,
you mess up the table's size and color characteristics. In one test where I
played around with the punctuation by adding single quotes (' ') around
the attributes, I managed to make the entire riddle box disappear. If the preci-
sion needed to alter the source code makes you uncomfortable, you can go
back to the RiddleNut.com design page, redo your settings, and repaste the
code with the new values into your own page. That's the safest way to do it.

The minimum table width in the RiddleNut.com drop-down list is 200 pixels,
but it appears to create a riddle box 220 pixels wide in actual practice. No
matter how small a number you put in the code as the value for `tabwid`, it
reverts to this default minimum. The maximum width, however, can go well
beyond the 450-pixel mark, which is the highest one on the riddle setup page.
I lost interest after pushing it to 800 pixels, which is a good deal wider than
you need for this add-in on any normally designed page, but you're welcome
to see how far it will go.

Adding Bogglers to Your Web Page

Do you like a good brainteaser? Bogglers.com (at — you guessed it —
`www.bogglers.com`) comes from the same folks who brought you the
RiddleNut.com site. Like riddles, brainteasers are cool additions to any site.
But brainteasers offer a different sort of amusing exercise than riddles do.
Riddles, after all, come in a particular form in which the answer is usually
disguised in the way the question is phrased. Bogglers, on the other hand,
are word games, plain and simple, and they mostly depend on the graphical
placement of words or the arrangement of letters. Often, the answer is a won-
derfully terrible pun.

What, for example, is the meaning of PODIVEOL or UGOME? If you can't figure them out, drop in to the Bogglers.com Web site and run through the brain-teasers until you find the answers — I'd never spoil your fun by telling you. (What's that? You say that I told you the answers to the riddles, so why not give you these answers, too? Oh, all right. Here they are: "dive in pool" and "you go before me." Still, it's worth your while to go to the site and browse through the tons of brain food that you'll find.)

Better yet, slap a Boggler on your own site and play with it there. You'll see what a blast it is, and appreciate how much your visitors will like it. Adding Bogglers to your site is even simpler than adding a riddle — just follow these steps:

1. **Go to www.bogglers.com/getcode.php.**

   The Random Brain Boggler for Your Site page appears, as shown in Figure 12-3.

2. **Select a frame color from the first drop-down list.**

3. **Optionally, select a background color from the second drop-down list.**

   You probably want to leave it at the default setting of Invisible (no color) because some of the word games rely on the color of the lettering. Because you don't know what that is in advance, you're best off covering all future bets by sticking with the default. If you must pick a color, go with White.

4. **Type your e-mail address into the text box.**

5. **In the Do You Have Any Interests section, select any check boxes for topics you want to receive e-mail about. If you want don't want any e-mail, make sure all the check boxes are deselected.**

6. **Click the Go button.**

   Boggler then sends you an e-mail message containing the HTML code.

7. **Copy the HTML code from the e-mail, paste it into your Web page's body, and then upload the page to your Web site.**

   Yes, paste it in the BODY element. (See the Technical Stuff note in the "Running RiddleNut.com's Random Riddles" section if you don't trust me. Sniff.)

Here's the code that you get if you go with the default choices:

```
<CENTER>
<SCRIPT LANGUAGE="JavaScript1.1"
SRC="http://www.bogglers.com/bogglers.php?color=
    blue&tbcolor=">
</SCRIPT>
</CENTER>
```

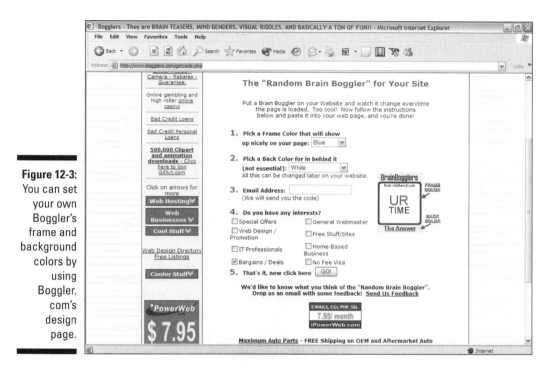

Figure 12-3:
You can set your own Boggler's frame and background colors by using Boggler. com's design page.

You can alter the values of the attributes just by typing in new ones. This time, you have two attributes: `color`, meaning the border color, and `tbcolor`, meaning the background color. And I can't repeat this warning enough: *Don't* mess with the syntax. Don't add anything to the source code that Bogglers generates. Just enter new color names without quotation marks or enter hexadecimal values without hash marks.

Figure 12-4 shows a Boggler that's on a Web page and ready to be enjoyed.

Figure 12-4:
A Boggler on your Web site, ready to . . . well, boggle your visitors' minds.

Placing Quotations on Your Site

Quotations, *bon mots,* and memorable lines — the world is full of them, and we're all fond of spouting them on occasion: Benjamin Franklin's simple wisdom, "When you're finished changing, you're finished." The Duc de La Rochefoucauld's famous, "One is never as unhappy as one thinks, nor as happy as one hopes." And who can forget the immortal line of President Richard Nixon, "I have often thought that if there had been a good rap group in those days, I might have chosen a career in music instead of politics."

Quoting with the Quote Machine

The Quote Machine (`www.insanityideas.com/quotemachine/`
`remotequote.html`) is incredibly simple to add to your site. You just have to fill out one little form. The following steps describe the process:

1. **Go to www.insanityideas.com/quotemachine/remotequote.
html.**

   The Quote Machine – Remote Quote page appears, as shown in Figure 12-5.

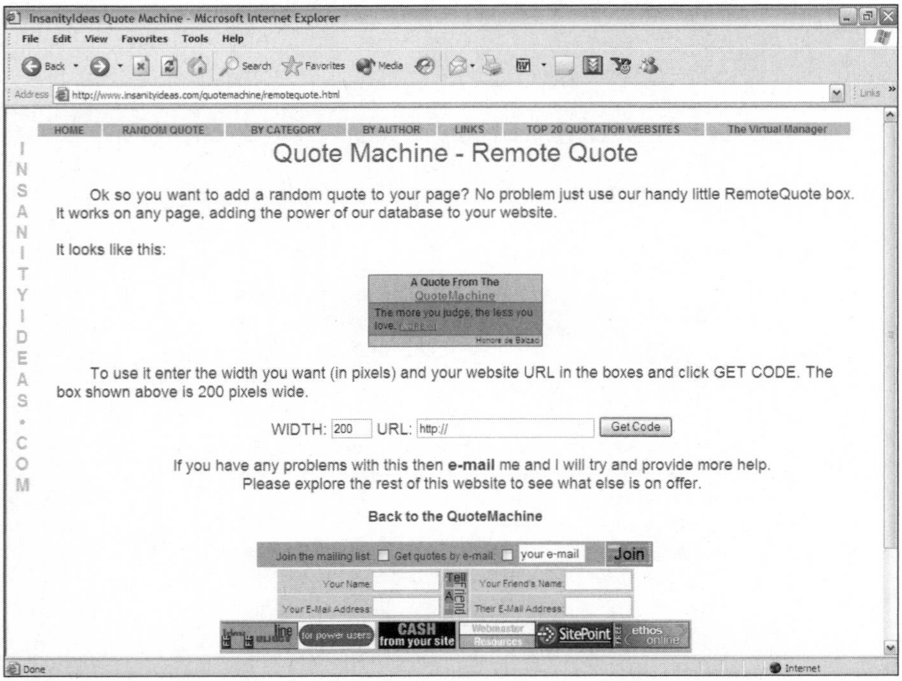

Figure 12-5:
Filling out the form for the Quote Machine.

2. **If you want to set a different width than the default value of 200, type the desired value into the Width text box.**

3. **In the URL box, type the Web address of the Web page to which you want to add the quotations.**

4. **Click the Get Code button.**

5. **Copy the HTML code from the text area on the resulting page.**

6. **Paste the code into your own Web page where you want the quotation to appear and upload the page to your site.**

Figure 12-6 shows the Quote Machine as it appears on your Web site.

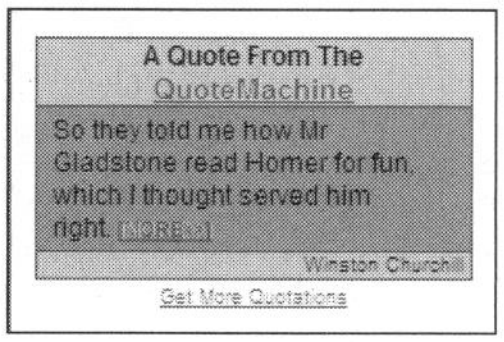

Figure 12-6:
A quote
from the
Quote
Machine as
it appears
on your
Web site.

Quoting with Quoter

Quoter, a Java applet by Paul Lutus, is simple and versatile. It's a stand-alone, not connected to any service, so it's considerably stickier than the Quote Machine because nothing about Quoter can lead people away from your site. It's also a freebie that its creator distributes under a *CareWare* license. (What's CareWare? Check out `www.arachnoid.com/careware` for details.)

To add Quoter to your site, follow these steps:

1. **Go to `www.arachnoid.com/quoter`, where you can see the applet in action.**

2. **Scroll down to the bottom of the page and click the word Quoter in the sentence that says Download Quoter code/CSS elements (16K).**

3. **After you've downloaded the file `quoter.zip`, unzip it into the directory that contains the Web page you plan to add it to.**

4. **Add the following code to your Web page where you want the quotation box to appear:**

```
<div align="center">
<div class="quotebox quotefont" id="quotebox"></div>
</div>
```

5. **Add this code inside the HEAD element of your Web page:**

```
<link rel="stylesheet" type="text/css" href=
    "quoter.css"/>
<script type="text/javascript" src=
    "quotes.js"></script>
<script type="text/javascript" src=
    "quoter.js"></script>
```

6. **Upload your Web page and the `quoter.js`, `quotes.js`, and `quoter.css` files.**

   You now have the basic setup, as shown in Figure 12-7.

Now comes the fun part. If you want more than just the plain vanilla installation, there's plenty of room for more control. All three of those files you uploaded are editable, which means that you can feel free to jump in and alter any of the settings in the Cascading Style Sheets (`.css`) or JavaScript (`.js`) files.

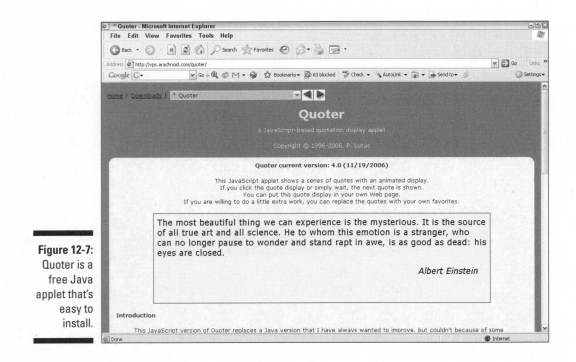

Figure 12-7: Quoter is a free Java applet that's easy to install.

Want to add more quotations? Just open up `quotes.js` (it's a plain text file) and type and delete to your heart's content. Each quotation must be within quotation marks, the whole followed by a comma:

```
"Man is the only animal that blushes -- or needs to.
      Mark Twain",
```

Don't like the size of the font? Go into `quoter.css`, where you'll find all the visual variables to monkey with. Each setting is well-named and easy to spot, so when you see the part that says:

```
.quotefont {
   font-size: 14pt;
}
```

. . . you know you're in the right place. Even without knowing anything about CSS (see Chapter 5), you can easily see where to change the font size. Just make the 14 into whatever other size you want.

The other file, `quoter.js`, should best be left alone unless you're skilled at JavaScript programming. The only things you might want to change in it are the speed variables for the quotations. The `var char_pause` variable sets the time between each character being "typed" on the screen. It's set to 60 milliseconds by default. The `var quote_pause` variable tells how long to let the quotation remain on screen. Its default is 8000 milliseconds.

Because Quoter simply displays text from a file that you create, you don't have to use it for quotations. You can also use it for displaying one-liner jokes, for example. You can put anything that you want in the box, as long as it fits.

Setting Up MyPostCards.com on Your Site

We all send cards to other people — birthday cards, Christmas cards, Hug An Australian Day cards, or whatever. But instead of trotting down to the local Hallmark store or drugstore, you can now send them from different Web sites. Why not make your site one of them?

MyPostCards.com is a free service that lets you set up a page where visitors can design their own e-postcards. They can choose different images, backgrounds, and songs and then type a personal message. When they're done,

MyPostCards.com sends the recipients an e-mail message telling them where to view the card. The recipients click the link in the message, and their Web browsers load the page that holds the card.

To set up MyPostCards.com's service on your site, follow these steps:

1. **Go to `http://mypostcards.com/bas`.**

2. **Scroll down to the bottom of the page and click the Free Service Terms and Conditions link.**

3. **Read the terms and conditions and then click the I Agree to These Terms link at the bottom of the page.**

   The next page contains general information about how the system works.

4. **Scroll down to the bottom of the page and click the Sign-Up Form link.**

   The Free Service Application page appears, as shown in Figure 12-8.

5. **Enter your name and e-mail address in the appropriate text boxes along with your desired username and the URL of your Web page.**

6. **If you want to receive the newsletters that MyPostCards.com offers, leave the check boxes selected. If not, deselect them.**

7. **Click the Submit button.**

   MyPostCards.com then sends you an e-mail containing your password.

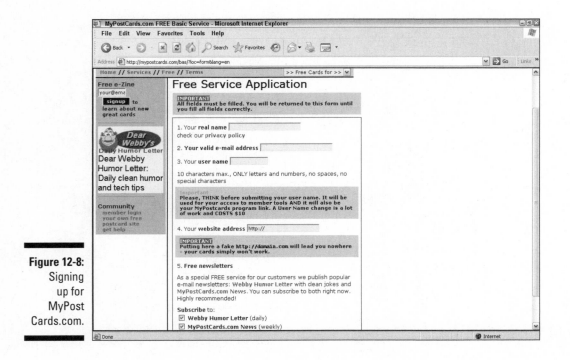

Figure 12-8:
Signing up for MyPost Cards.com.

8. After you receive the e-mail, go to `http://mypostcards.com/ members` and enter your username and the password that was in the e-mail message; then click the Submit button.

9. On the following page, scroll down to Checklist for New Users and click the Profile Editor link.

   The Global Account Settings page appears, as shown in Figure 12-9.

10. Enter the title and URL of your Web page and the URLs for your image and sound files.

11. Scroll down the page and enter a title in the Card Page Title text box, shown in Figure 12-10.

12. Enter values for the background, text, and link colors.

   You can use either color names or hexadecimal values.

13. Enter the URL for any background image you want to use.

14. Type any custom text you want added to your postcards and any message you want included on the notification e-mail that is sent to your users.

   You can use a maximum of 1,200 characters for each of these messages. If you're unsure of how many characters you're using, just click the Check Size button.

15. If you want, you can enter a new password.

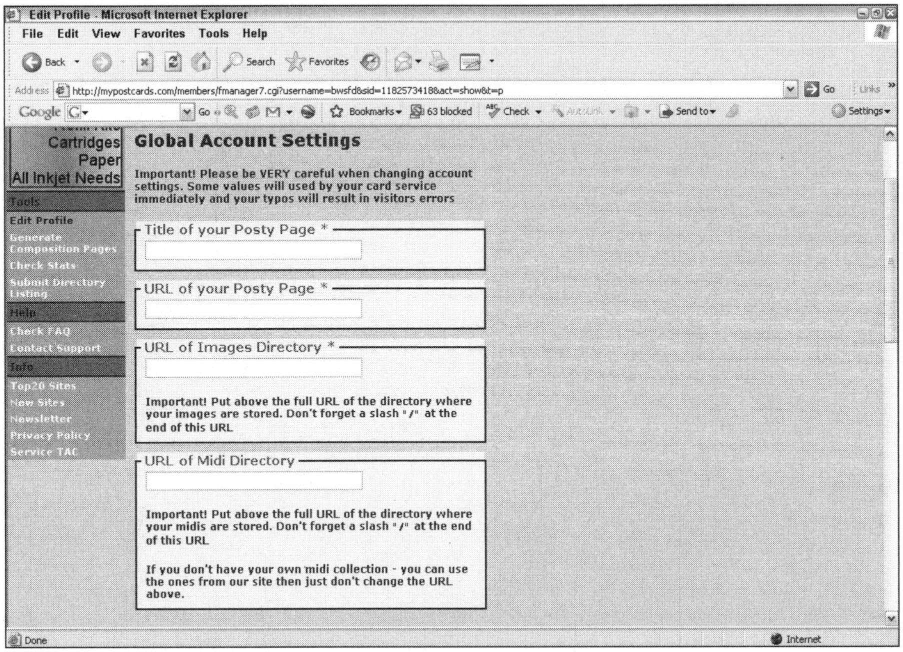

Figure 12-9:
Using the
Profile
Editor.

16. **Click the Submit button.**

    The Global Account Settings page reappears.

17. **In the Checklist for New Users area, click the Generate HTML for Card Page link.**

    The Generate Composition Pages page appears, as shown in Figure 12-11. You have two options here: the simple or advanced design. The advanced design is a template for HTML wizards so that they can play with a variety of official W3C CSS designs.

18. **For the simple design, select the appropriate option buttons to indicate whether you'll be using music and/or enhanced text. Set the border width the same way.**

19. **Click the Generate button.**

    The generated postcard page appears, as shown in Figure 12-12. Of course, the images you specified back in Step 10 will appear instead of the samples shown in this figure.

20. **Choose View➪Source from your browser's menu bar.**

    The source code for the page is displayed.

21. **Save the source code to your hard drive and then upload the file to your Web server.**

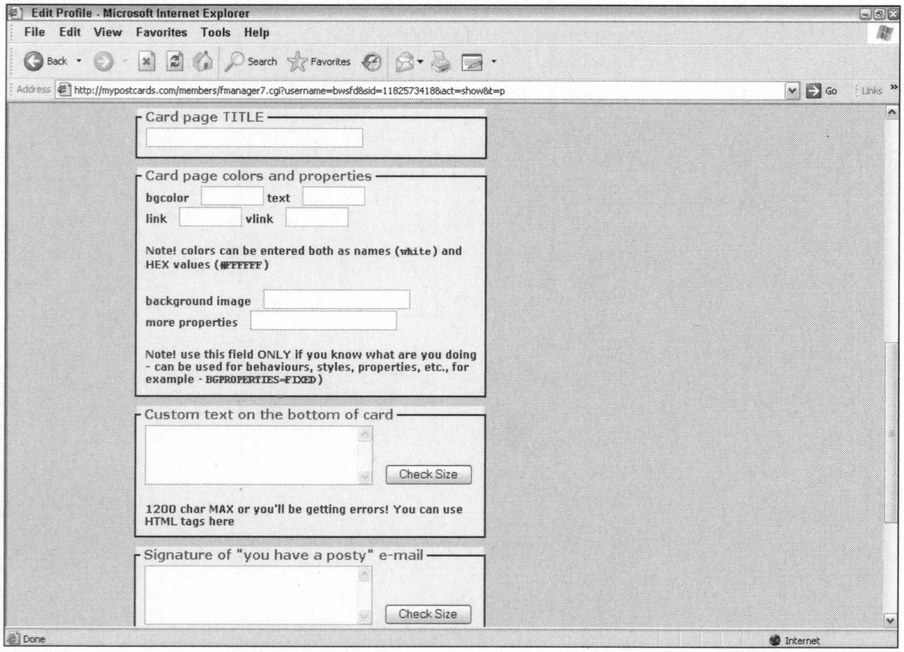

Figure 12-10:
Entering card page values.

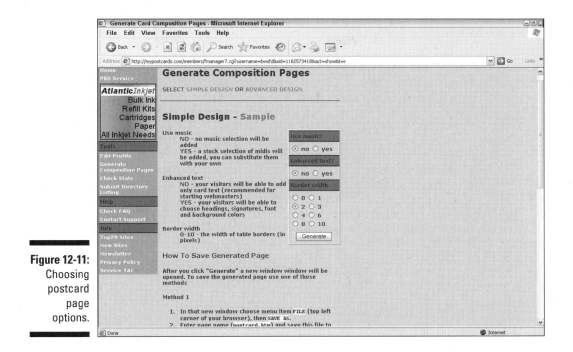

Figure 12-11:
Choosing
postcard
page
options.

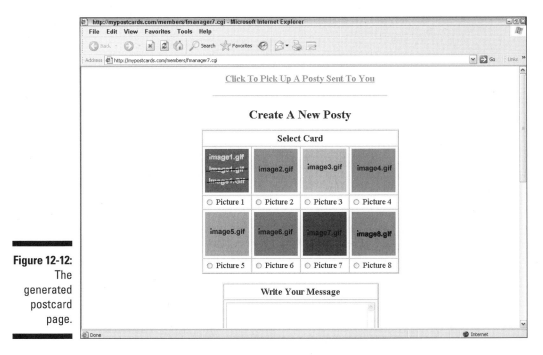

Figure 12-12:
The
generated
postcard
page.

Providing Weather Forecasts on Your Site

I figure that most of the people on the Net spend almost all their free time indoors, but amazingly, they still maintain a fascination with what's happening outside. Okay, I admit that I have to drive through the outside world sometimes, and the guys from marketing often take their laptops and cell phones to the beach to "work." But all you really need to know is whether a thunderstorm is coming your way, right? And if that bright flash and the sudden puff of smoke from your modem don't tell you that, what can? Still, you just can't please some folks, and if your visitors want to check out the latest weather conditions and forecasts, who am I to stand in their way?

Weather.com (at `www.weather.com`, of course) is the online version of the Weather Channel. If you're not familiar with that channel, you obviously don't get cable TV. It offers some really nice weather graphics that you can put on your Web site.

To add all this wonderful weather wizardry to your site, follow these steps:

1. **Go to the Weather on Your Website page at `www.weather.com/services/oap.html`.**

2. **Scroll down the page and click the Get It Today button.**

3. **On the resulting page, shown in Figure 12-13, click the Sign Up link in the upper right corner.**

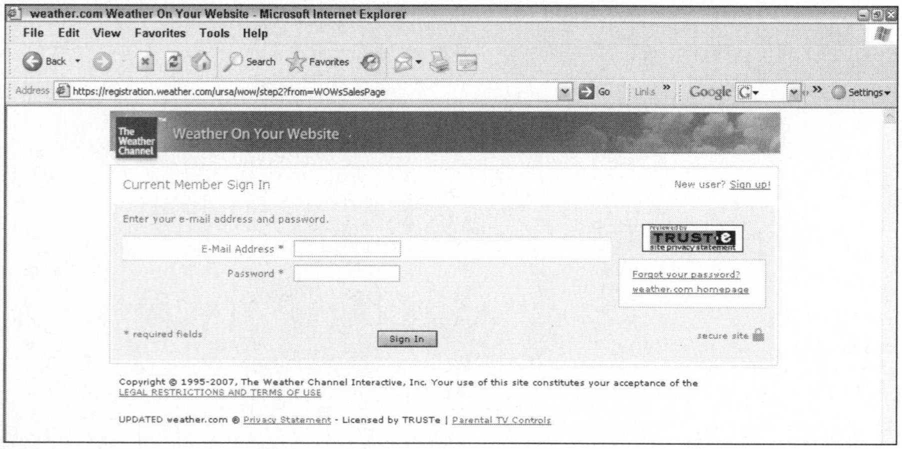

Figure 12-13: Click the Sign Up link for new users.

4. **On the Set User Profile page, shown in Figure 12-14, enter all the required information (such as your e-mail address) in the appropriate text boxes.**

5. **Unless you want to receive weather-related e-mail offers, deselect the Subscriptions check box.**

   Agreeing to this means that you're giving up your privacy, and the site can share your name, address, and other information you provide with other companies.

6. **Click the Save and Continue button.**

7. **On the Settings page (see Figure 12-15), type your company name.**

8. **Select your industry from the drop-down list.**

9. **Enter your phone number and the URL of your Web site in the appropriate text boxes.**

10. **Select the I Accept check box for the legal agreement.**

11. **Click the Save and Continue button.**

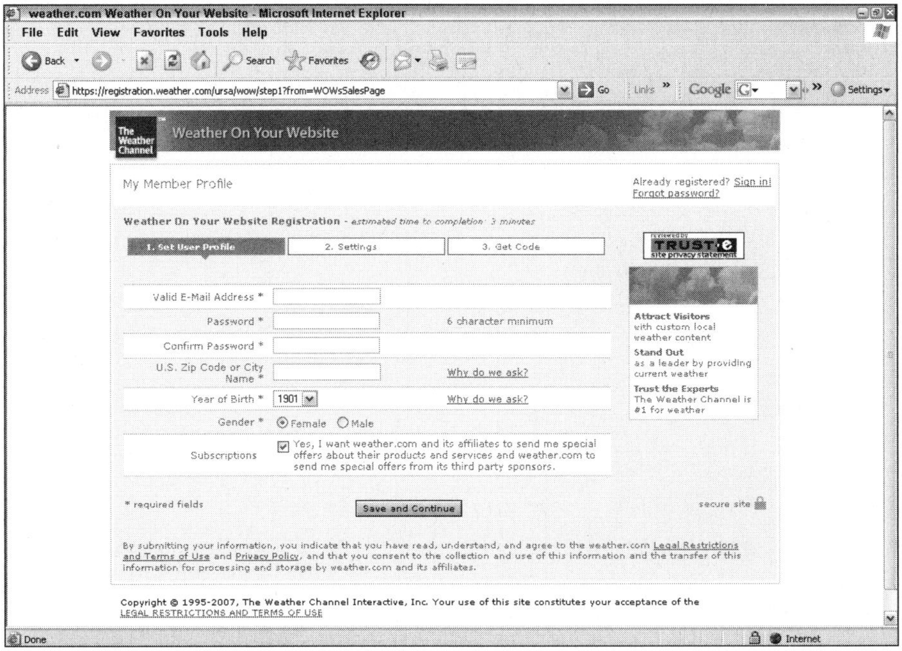

Figure 12-14:
The Set
User Profile
page.

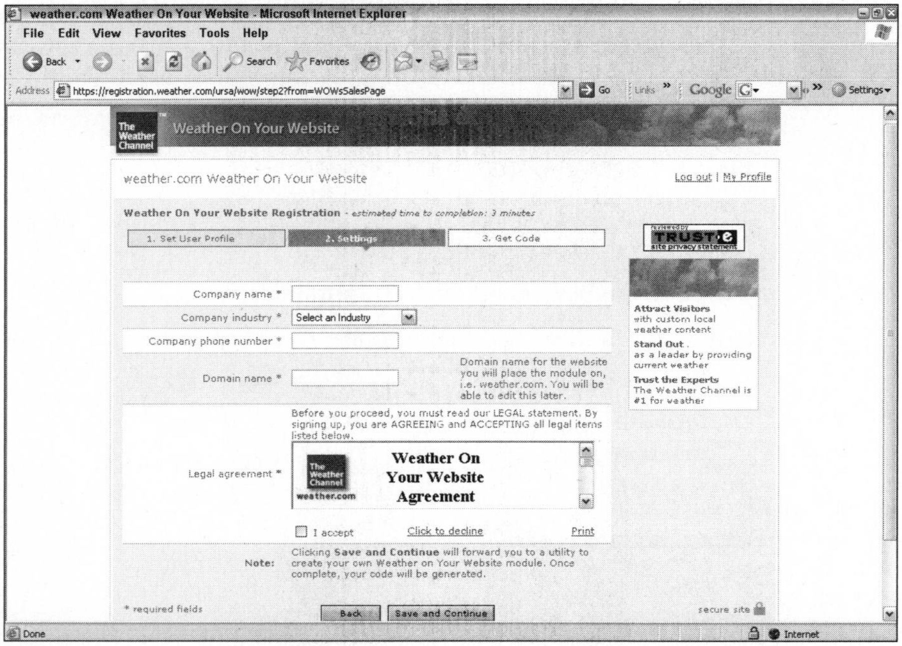

Figure 12-15:
The Settings page.

12. **On the Website Builder page, shown in Figure 12-16, you can click the Customize button to choose such items as background images if you desire. The resulting options are:**

 • **Basics:** Size, city name (or zip code if you're in the U.S.), unit of measurement (English or metric), and your domain name.

 • **Background:** Background photos or colors.

 • **@weather.com Links:** To display news about seasons, lifestyles, travel, and so on.

 • **Weather Info:** Choose up to three specialized items of weather info, such as humidity, dewpoint, or UV index.

13. **Click the Finish and Generate Code button.**

14. **Copy the HTML code from the page that appears (see Figure 12-17) and paste it into the source code for your Web page.**

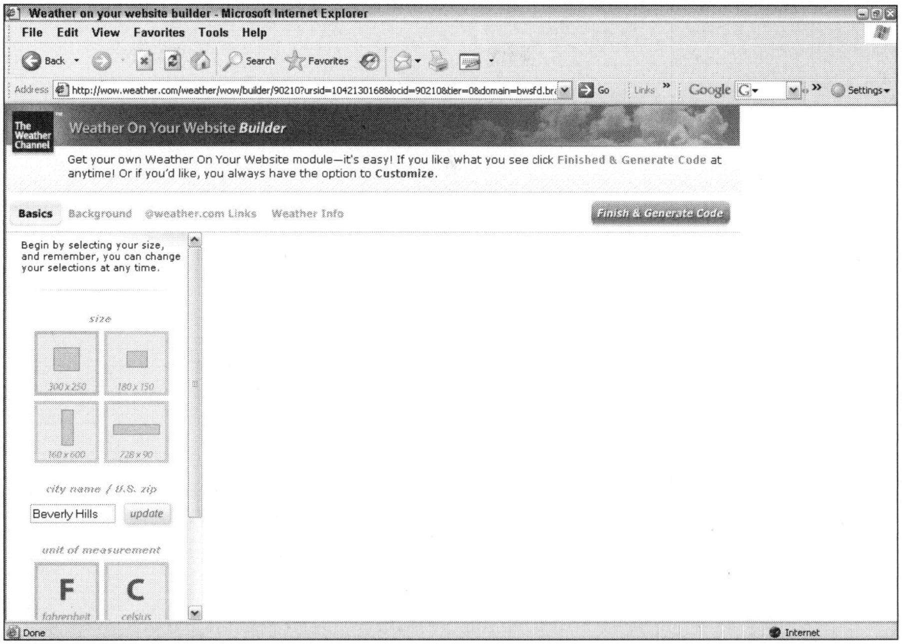

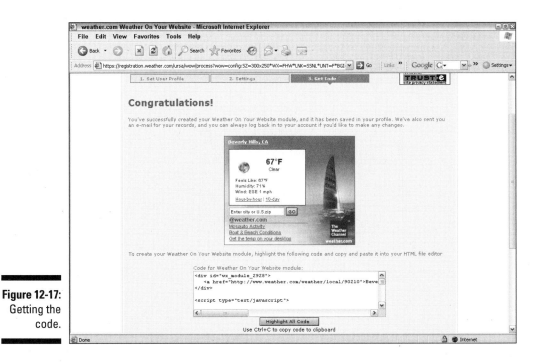

Figure 12-16:
The Website
Builder.

Figure 12-17:
Getting the
code.

Chowing Down at Feedroll.com

More and more these days, people turn to the Web for the latest news. It sure beats waiting for the 11 o'clock news on TV to get caught up on the day's events. Unless you want your visitors surfing other sites to get their news, you need to add it to your Web site. But you don't need to connect with a bunch of reporters or spend all your time collating tons of reports from distant parts of the world to provide your visitors with the latest news. Just plug in a ready-to-use news service that uses RSS.

RSS is short for *Really Simple Syndication,* and it's just as good as it sounds. You just hook your Web page up to a *feed* that automatically updates the material on your site for you — 24 hours a day, 7 days a week — freeing you up to go do whatever else you need to do instead.

All RSS files are required to be XML compliant. The good news is that you don't have to be an XML wizard to get the job done. In fact, you don't even have to know what that means to add an RSS feed, and an XML feed can be seamlessly added to your site using just plain old HTML.

There's an ever-increasing number of RSS news sources available to you, ranging from personal blogs (see Chapter 11) to the heavy hitters of journalism. Table 12-1 gives some examples.

Table 12-1	RSS Content and Info
Web Site Name	*Web Address*
Ask Dave Taylor	`www.askdavetaylor.com/how_can_i_add_the_ask_dave_taylor_rss_feed_on_my_web_site.html`
BusinessWeek	`www.businessweek.com/rss`
Feed Digest	`www.feeddigest.com`
Fortune	`www.timeinc.net/fortune/information/rss`
Free Website Content	`www.thefreedictionary.com/lookup.htm`
Humor Feed	`www.humorfeed.com/feed.php`
New York Times	`www.nytimes.com/services/xml/rss`
PC World	`www.pcworld.com/resource/rss.html`
Salon	`www.salon.com/plus/rss`
USA Today	`http://asp.usatoday.com/marketing/rss/index.aspx`

Just as Web pages are meant to be seen in Web browsers, RSS feeds are intended to go to programs called *RSS feed readers,* and not every feed source provides the code to flow their content directly onto your Web site. What you need in a case like that is an intermediary service that gets the feed for you, repackages it in a Web-friendly form, and funnels it to your own Web site as finished content.

Sound complicated? Well, it may be for them, but it isn't for you. Feedroll.com offers a service that'll take all the sweat out of using RSS. They have both free and paid services. The free version is for incoming RSS to your site. The paid version ($14.95 per month) adds the ability to specify URLs from other sources, but is mainly for syndicating your own content to others.

If you'd like to turn things around and become the content provider, check out the book *Syndicating Web Sites with RSS Feeds For Dummies,* by Ellen Finkelstein (Wiley Publishing).

Here's how to set up a news feed to your site:

1. **Go to `www.feedroll.com` and click the RSS Viewer icon. (See Figure 12-18.)**

   Ignore the FEED Combiner icon, but keep it in mind for later. It's a method for — you guessed it — combining the feeds from various sources into one input for your site. For now, though, stick with the simpler version.

Figure 12-18: The main Feedroll. com page.

2. **Scroll down the resulting page, shown in Figure 12-19, and click in the Source Title drop-down list under Select Your Source.**

   Figure 12-20 shows some of the options you have available. The paid version allows you to specify an RSS URL that isn't on the list.

3. **If you can't find what you're looking for, click the Click Here to Add Free News Feeds link.**

   This opens a pop-up window with several other RSS sources that you can choose from.

4. **If you prefer to do your own CSS programming (see Chapter 5), select the Use My Own CSS check box.**

5. **Under Width, enter the value (in pixels) for how wide you want your RSS results to be.**

6. **Click the Text Align drop-down list and select Left, Center, or Right.**

7. **Click the Text Font drop-down list and select which font you want to use.**

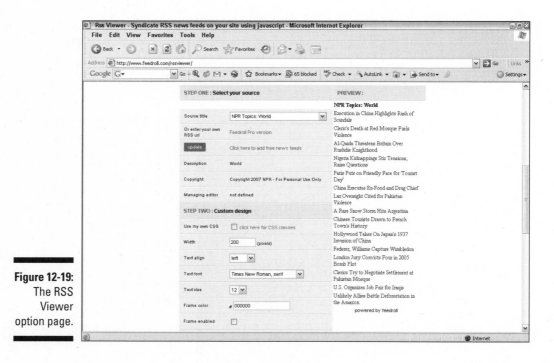

Figure 12-19:
The RSS
Viewer
option page.

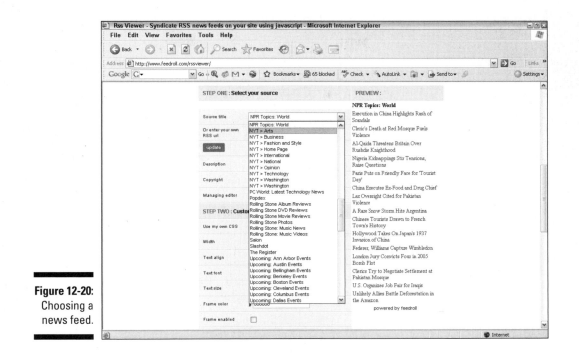

Figure 12-20:
Choosing a
news feed.

8. **Select a Text Size from the drop-down list of that name.**

9. **The next two options deal with the border around your RSS results. To set its color, enter the value (in hexadecimal numbers) in the Frame Color text box.**

If you're not familiar with hexadecimal color codes, just check out an online color chart like the one at `www.webmonkey.com/reference/color_codes` or the one at `www.w3schools.com/html/html_colornames.asp`.

10. **To turn the border on, select the Frame Enabled check box. To leave it out, leave the check box deselected.**

11. **To set the spacing between RSS sources, enter a value (in pixels) in the Feed Table Spacing text box. (See Figure 12-21.)**

12. **Enter hexadecimal values for the colors you want to use in the Title Text Color, Title Background, Box Text Color, and Box Background text boxes.**

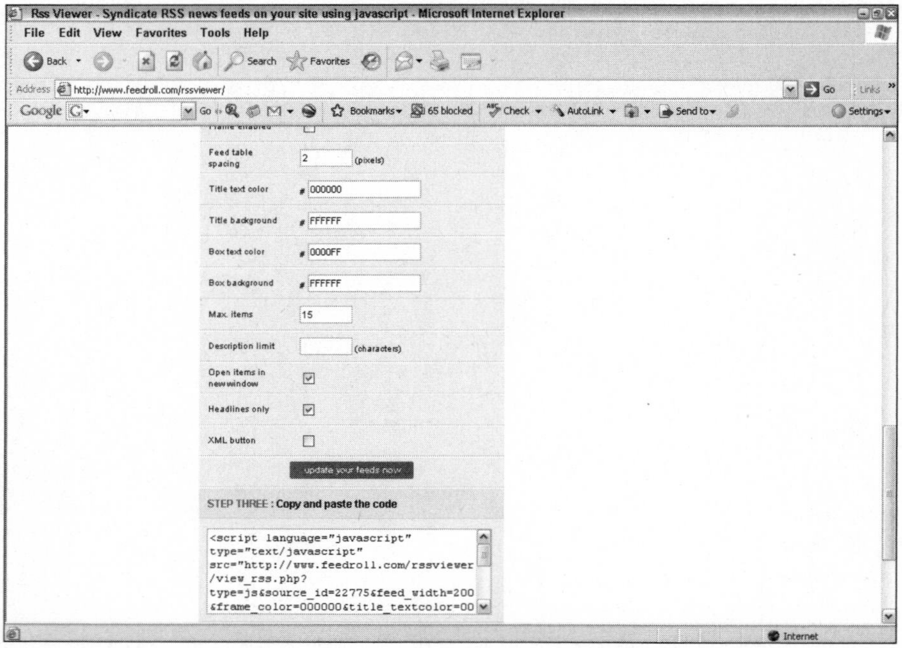

Figure 12-21:
Finishing the
bottom of
the form.

13. **To set a limit on the number of articles shown, enter a value in the Max. Items text box.**

14. **To set the length (number of characters) of displayed descriptions, type the value into the Description Limit text box.**

15. **If you don't want to send your visitors away from your site when they click an RSS link, make sure the Open Items in New Window check box is selected.**

16. **To display headlines only, select the — you guessed it again — Headlines Only check box.**

17. **To add an *XML button* (a standard icon indicating an RSS feed), select the XML Button check box.**

18. **Click the Update Your Feeds Now button.**

19. **Copy the resulting code from the text area at the bottom of the page and paste it into your own Web page.**

Table 12-2 gives the URLs of several services similar to Feedroll.com.

Table 12-2	RSS Feed Providers
Web Site Name	*Web Address*
Feeddesk	www.feeddesk.com
Feedzilla	www.feedzilla.com
Fresh Content.net	www.freshcontent.net
RSS Builder	http://netshaq.com/rssfeedbuilder
RSS Content Builder	http://rsscontentbuilder.com
RSSFeedBox	http://rssfeedbox.com
RSS Feed Reader	http://rssfeedreader.com

Online Sources for Content

Table 12-3 lists some places on the World Wide Web where you can find more resources like the ones that are covered in this chapter.

If you sign up with a service that supplies jokes or quotations, you have no control over the content of the material. Make sure that you check out samples from the content provider before you commit, because some of the topics may not fit your site's theme.

Table 12-3	Online Resources for Fun Add-ins
Web Site Name	*Web Address*
AAA Postcards	www.aaapostcards.com/linkus.phtml
Bpath	www.bpath.com
CartoonStock	www.cartoonstock.com/daily.asp
ComicExchange	www.comicexchange.com
EzineArticles.com	www.ezinearticles.com
FreeSticky	www.freesticky.com

(continued)

Table 12-3 *(continued)*

Web Site Name	Web Address
Internet.com RSS Newsfeeds	`www.webreference.com/services/news`
Nave Humor	`http://navehumor.com/php/feed.php`
On Your Site! The Daily Laugh!	`www.onyoursite.com/jokes`
On Your Site! Quotables	`www.onyoursite.com/quotes`
ThinkExist.com	`http://en.thinkexist.com/DailyQuotation/stepsize.asp`

Part V
Raking In the Bucks

The 5th Wave   By Rich Tennant

"Oh, we're doing just great. Philip and I are selling decorative jelly jars on the Web. I run the Web site and Philip sort of controls the inventory."

In this part . . .

In this part, I take a look at how you can make money from your site. Chapter 13 explodes the myths about Internet income and shows you how to really make a profit. Chapter 14 tells you how to set up a credit-card merchant account. And Chapter 15 shows how to work both ends of the affiliates game.

Chapter 13

Stalking the Wild Dollar: Internet Commerce

More pure bull hockey is floating around about Internet commerce than about practically any other topic in the world. If you haven't found thousands of e-commerce Web sites promising you the moon — and a moon made of gold and platinum at that — you aren't looking.

According to these self-proclaimed gurus of e-commerce, all you need to do is put up a Web page — not even a site, just a page — and the money comes rolling in. You can vacation in Acapulco this weekend and sun yourself on the Riviera by Monday. The secret to this success? Well, of course, they can't just *tell* you what it is. That kind of information is worth some real money, you know.

This "get-rich-quick-over-the-Internet" scheme reminds me of an ad that used to run in the backs of cheap magazines many, many years ago. For 25¢, the ad promised, you could discover how to make a fortune fast. After you sent in your quarter, you got back a pamphlet that, boiled down to its basics, told you to put an ad in a magazine asking people to send you a quarter. Today's get-rich-quick schemes are no more solid than that one, even if they're draped in the latest finery of high technology.

So is there any truth at all to the glowing promise of Internet commerce? Yes, there is. The Internet represents the greatest market that's ever existed, and the opportunity is very real. You *can* make a fortune in e-commerce, just as you can make a fortune in any other kind of commerce. But success takes a combination of brains, toughness, marketing savvy, luck, and — most of all — determination to succeed. In this chapter, I show you how to become a real Internet marketer.

Learning the Real Secret to Internet Success

Are you ready for the real secret of success in any business? Here it is:

Put the right product or service in front of the right audience at the right time for the right price.

There ya go. That's all you need to do to succeed. Well, okay, implementing this advice isn't always easy. And when it comes to e-commerce, there are some special considerations.

Developing the right attitude

If you go into Internet commerce figuring that you don't need to do any real work — that it's just something that you can dabble in between football games or pay attention to if you happen to feel like it — you're better off going fishing. At least that way, you may end up with food on your table.

To win in any kind of business, you need a different attitude than you need to hold down a job. Let's face it; the whole point of most jobs is merely to keep a paycheck coming in. Most people work in jobs they don't care about — even jobs that they hate. They stick with their jobs solely because they have bills to pay. (Honestly, would you show up for work if you won the lottery? No? Neither would most people.)

If you run your own business, though, work is different. If you're sick and tired of rush hour, wearing suits and ties or high heels, and having bosses stand over your shoulder demanding that you work harder than they do, the Internet may be your ticket to financial independence. But you must pay a certain price. To run your own business, you must work harder than you ever have before. And you need to take a good, hard look at who you really are.

Notice that I'm not saying "what you really want" but "who you really are." There's a good reason for that. If you're going to win in business, you win, not because you're doing something, but because you're being yourself. In my own case, if I won the lottery, I'd take a few days off to meet with my attorneys and accountants and get everything in order, but I'd go back to work as soon as possible. I can't help it because I'm a book person. Winning enough money to afford even more books can't change that fact.

What do you love most in the world? Whatever is your true passion is also your natural business. If you do anything else with your life, you can't give it the same kind of energy. That's plain old human nature. Who can give 100 percent all the time if they don't care about the outcome? If you're stuck in a job at a desk in a cubicle and the company you work for experiences a crisis, what you do usually doesn't matter. The situation isn't your doing, and you're not in charge anyway. Even if you do manage, by superhuman effort, to overcome the situation and save the day, you know you probably won't even get a raise out of it. After all, you're just doing your duty.

If you want to make a break from the traditional working world, you must make a clean break from the employee attitude, too. An Internet business is different — it's yours. It's a part of you, and if you listen to your inner voice, it's a natural extension of yourself. It's not what you do — it's who you are.

Focusing on your business

Many people believe that you can sell anything on the Internet. After all, zillions of people are on it, so anything that you create is sure to appeal to someone. Well, that belief is more or less true, but it doesn't mean that you can make money from your creation.

If you're serious about making money, you must remember the key factor in Web site appeal: focus, focus, focus. If you run your site as a hobby or a public service, you can afford to drift a bit, but if you depend on it for your living, you must stay on target. Any drifting off the mark costs you money.

What I'm talking about here is *specialization*. When it comes to general merchandise, the Internet is pretty much already lost to you. Why? Because it's got JCPenney and Kmart and Wal-Mart (see Figure 13-1) and all those other well-established companies with very deep pockets. You're not going to put those companies out of business in a physical shopping mall, and you're not going to take them out on the Internet either. They already enjoy the kind of name recognition that takes a long time to build. And they can spend more money on one ad than the average online business has in its annual budget.

Even if you do have the kind of bucks that going up against the big outfits takes, I advise you to put your money into specialized stores. The future of e-commerce lies in smaller companies that can focus all their energies on a relatively small market. Here's where the size of the Internet really comes into play for you — a relatively small market on the Internet is much larger than it would be even in a large city.

Figure 13-1:
The major general retailers effectively dominate their markets, on and off the Internet.

Reaching customers all over the globe is the Internet's greatest strength. Like the telephone and air travel before it, the Net is making the world — especially the world of commerce — much smaller than it was even ten years ago. By targeting a particular submarket, you can tightly focus your business efforts and still reach more people than you ever could reach by running a local business. And a functional Web site is much cheaper than even a small physical store. You can indeed start successful businesses on a shoestring if you use the Net.

Even if you do need some kind of physical facilities for your operation, such as storage space for your products, you don't need to concern yourself with the appearance and attractiveness of those facilities. For most online businesses, a small warehouse space does just as well as a fancy, glitzy store in a major shopping mall. In many cases, you can start with a spare room in your house. If you end up needing more room to handle all the merchandise that people are ordering . . . well, we should all have such problems, right?

Getting supplies flowing

Okay, so now you know what your online business is all about. If you choose wisely, you probably already know plenty about the field. You know all the major suppliers, your competition, and all sorts of little tidbits that outsiders know nothing about. You know what other companies in the industry have tried, what worked and what didn't, and how your potential customers feel about it all.

Depending on your field, you need to either create your product or line up some good, low-cost suppliers. If you create your own product or market your own service, you're already there. If you rely on outsiders, though, you must do some research. Even if you already have a supplier in mind, you'll probably be able to find a better deal or get more or better services if you ask around.

Identifying potential suppliers

Track down everyone who makes what you want to sell. Use search engines to find their Web sites and then print out some of those companies' Web pages. Make folders for each company (the manila kind, not the hard-drive kind) and arrange the hard copies neatly so that you can refer to them at a moment's notice.

If a site you're researching offers a Contacts link, follow it to see whether its information is useful to you. Different companies provide different amounts of contact data. Some companies have confusing and relatively worthless listings or nothing significant at all. Others provide fully detailed breakdowns of their operations by department and by significant personnel, including everything from phone numbers, to e-mail and snail-mail addresses, to descriptions of people's job functions. You're looking for the director of sales and marketing. In the unlikely event that one isn't listed, go for the shipping manager.

The Contacts link may say something different, such as About Our Company or Regional Offices. Be creative and explore the site exhaustively when you're looking for contact info.

If you can't find the information you're looking for on the company's Web site, you can turn to one of the many business-phone-number databases on the Web. I list some for you in Table 13-1.

Table 13-1	Business Phone Number Sources
Web Site Name	*Web Address*
AT&T AnyWho Online Directory	`www.tollfree.att.net/tf.html`
BigBook	`www.bigbook.com`
Infobel World Telephone Directories	`www.infobel.com`
InfoSpace Yellow Pages	`www.infospace.com/home/yellow-pages`
Switchboard.com	`www.switchboard.com`
Yahoo! Local Yellow Pages	`http://yp.yahoo.com`

Try the AT&T AnyWho Online Directory that's listed in Table 13-1 before you spend any money on long-distance calls. This directory is a source of toll-free business phone numbers. Even if the company you're looking at doesn't list a toll-free number on its own site, it may still have one that shows up in the AT&T listings.

After you get a phone number and/or e-mail address, check with the supplier to find out whether it uses drop shipping. (*Drop shipping* is an arrangement in which you gather the orders and submit them to the supplier; the supplier then sends the merchandise directly to the customer and puts your return address on it. You, of course, must pay the supplier for the merchandise, but you pay a wholesale rate and keep the rest for your profit.)

If the supplier doesn't drop ship, find out the minimum order that you can place and what kind of discount you get for different sizes of orders, if any. In either case, make sure that you find out how long the company normally takes to fulfill your orders. You need to know this information so you can quote an expected delivery time to your customers. (Now you know why so many order forms say something like "Takes 4 to 6 weeks for delivery.")

Choosing a shipping company

If you get stuck with delivering the product to your customers yourself, you need to establish a business account with at least one shipping company. Most companies traditionally use UPS for shipping merchandise, although offering several alternatives to your customers doesn't hurt. You can also use the U.S. Postal Service, and FedEx is making a serious effort to compete with UPS these days on its own turf. Table 13-2 lists the URLs for some of the major shipping companies' Web sites.

Table 13-2	Major Shipping Companies
Web Site Name	*Web Address*
DHL	www.dhl.com
FedEx	www.fedex.com
Purolator Courier Ltd.	www.purolator.com
United Parcel Service	www.ups.com
United States Postal Service	www.usps.com

Make sure that you find out from your shipping company if you can get discounts for volume shipping.

Designing for E-Commerce

You may understand Web site design in general, but designing an online store requires some special considerations. Face the fact — if you're building a shopping mall in the real world, do you want an architect who specializes in houses or an architect who's built stores all his life?

Yes, your Web site must display a pretty face. Yes, it must perform all the functions you need to show your wares and process orders. But the key point to Web design is this one rule:

It must be simple to use.

If customers face any kind of hitch in the process, you're going to lose money. That's guaranteed — 100 percent. As you plan the site design for an e-commerce store, you must approach it from the buyer's viewpoint and concentrate on making the store easy to navigate and the buying process painless. Regardless of what you sell, here are some ways to satisfy your potential buyers' needs:

- ✔ **Include a picture of the product.** If you sell some type of merchandise, make sure that you include at least one picture.

    Use thumbnail images instead of full-sized ones so that the basic product page doesn't take too long to load. (Customers may lose interest if they must wait too long for the site to load.)

- ✔ **Give detailed information, if appropriate.** How much information you give depends on what you're selling. With many products, you can easily fit all the necessary information about the product into the product's description. However, providing additional information gives you an opportunity to sing the product's praises at length, even if it's not totally necessary.

- ✔ **Clearly state the cost.** Put the price right out in the open where everyone can see it. You'd be surprised how often you can follow link after link on e-commerce sites without ever finding the price clearly stated.

- ✔ **Make it easy for customers to buy the product.** If you're using shopping-cart software for multiple products, make sure that it's easy to use and doesn't require a bunch of back-and-forth steps to work. If you sell a single product or service, make sure that your site can quickly accommodate the customer's decision to buy. Here are a few ways to do that:

    - *Put a Buy This Now link at the top of the page — and put one at the bottom, too.*

    - *Don't ask a bunch of extra questions on the order form. Stick with the basics, such as name, address, payment method, and shipping options.*

    - *If you want to add a survey, add it after the entire sales process is complete, not as an impediment to the ongoing sale.*

Online Sources for Internet Commerce

Table 13-3 lists some places on the World Wide Web where you can find more information about the topics that are covered in this chapter.

Table 13-3	Online Resources for Internet Commerce
Web Site Name	*Web Address*
Freightworld	www.freightworld.com/exp_geo.html
How to Redesign Your Website to Play to Your Audience, from *CIO Magazine*	www.cio.com/archive/111503/play.html
Package Tracking Links, from Copresco	www.copresco.com/pkgtrack.htm
TeleTransport Shipping Tracking	www.teletransport.it/newweb/eng/pagine/servizi-ship.asp
track-trace	www.track-trace.com

Chapter 14

Kaching! Kaching! Gettin' Paid

*I*f you're operating a regular store, taking in money from customers is a pretty easy matter. Cash, checks, credit cards, debit cards — you name it, and some well-established process is in place to handle it. From night-deposit drops to armored car pickups, the bricks-and-mortar merchant is already well covered when it comes to getting paid.

You won't find any cash registers online, though, so you need to look at other options. The major approach is to take credit cards. You can, however, arrange to be paid in other ways, like accepting checks by phone or using digital money. However, none of the other ways can really compete with the power of plastic.

Checking Out Online Payment Methods

Credit cards are king. If you do nothing but take MasterCard and VISA, you're pretty thoroughly covered. Nearly everyone who can afford a computer has one or both of them. Toss in American Express for the high-end customer and the business client, and you're all set. But some alternatives are out there, and you may want to add some or all of them to your setup.

PayPal

When it comes to online payments, one very impressive option is PayPal, now part of the eBay empire. PayPal takes a slightly different approach to online payments, and it's worth a good look. With PayPal, you can accept credit card payments without having a merchant account, and your customers can pay you directly from their bank accounts.

What do you have to do? Not much. Just sign up for an account at www.paypal.com. (See Figure 14-1.) What does it cost? Nothing, unless you actually make some sales. In that case, you pay $0.30 per transaction and anywhere from 2.2 to 2.9 percent of the selling price on top of that. Rates can be higher for international sales.

PayPal offers a complete payment system for you to use at no extra cost. You can integrate its free Web tools into your site's pages easily. Throw in a thorough payment-reporting system, which PayPal does, and you couldn't ask for a better setup for a startup business — or even an established one.

Google Checkout

Google Checkout is an exciting new opportunity for the online entrepreneur. Part of Google's ever-expanding variety of services, it may be the easiest way yet to set up the most important part of your store: the part where you actually get paid.

Figure 14-1:
PayPal provides easy shopping and payment facilities.

It's not very different from using PayPal; you simply place a Google Checkout button on your site. When your buyers click it, they're taken to an order form like the one in Figure 14-2. Except for the specific information from your store (item, price, and so on), it's the same form for all Google Checkout customers. This familiarity helps to create a high degree of comfort in your buyers.

Considering the vast user base that Google brings to the fray, this is a sales tool you can't do without, especially considering the price — it's free until 2008.

To sign up for the program, point your browser to:

```
https://checkout.google.com/sell
```

Once there, sign in via your Google account. If you don't have one, see Chapter 6 for the details on how to get it.

Cash alternatives

E-cash. Digital wallets. Sounds cool. Nice, easy-to-understand metaphor. You use digitally signed certificates online just like you'd use cash in the non-Net world. But it really hasn't worked out. There's no standard yet, although something called *ECML* — the Electronic Commerce Modeling Language — seems to be the first fitful attempt at one.

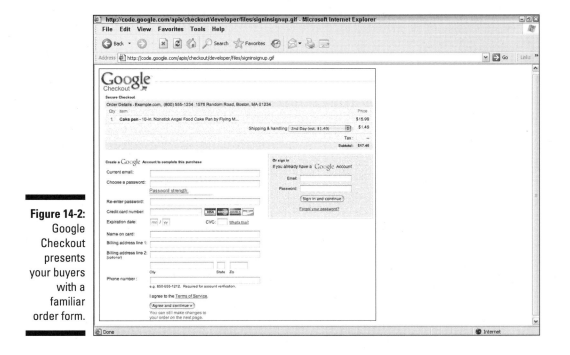

Figure 14-2: Google Checkout presents your buyers with a familiar order form.

The most telling thing, though, is that no one's telling. What I mean is that when you ask the folks who are trying to market e-cash exactly how many customers they have, exactly how many merchants are using their systems, and exactly how profitable this all is, they clam up real fast. This is not a good sign. When people are winning, they generally like to trumpet it to the world. But e-cash has nothing to show so far but hype and broken promises.

Phone checks currently offer a more accepted alternative. Here's the scenario — you print checks with other people's account numbers on them, take them to your bank and deposit them, and then watch the money roll in. It's not some kind of criminal operation, either. It's a perfectly legitimate business practice — as long as you have permission from your customers to do it.

The way it works is that your customers give you authorization to create a *draft* on their accounts. A draft is a check. You ask your customers to give you the information off their checks — bank name, check number, those little bank and account numbers across the bottom, and so on — and then you enter that information into a check-writing program. Next, you toss some special *safety paper* into your printer — that's the kind of paper checks are printed on — print those checks, and you've gotten paid just as if you had received a check in the mail.

Figure 14-3 shows a sample screen for creating a draft with Draft Creator from www.advancemeants.com/draft. See Table 14-4, at the end of this chapter, for more sources.

This is one of those systems that you really should have in place. It has only two drawbacks. One is that few people are familiar with this system, but that situation is changing rapidly. The other is not a problem for you, but some of your more savvy customers may object that they're paying the full amount up front (whereas with a credit card, they can repay the purchase price over time in small amounts).

There's one thing you just can't beat about this payment approach: All you pay for is the software and the paper (which you can get at any good office supply company). You have no monthly fee, no minimum charges, no discount rate, no nothin' that you've gotta put up with when you deal with credit card companies.

Phones, faxes, and snail mail

You should always give your customers some way to purchase from you offline. Even if you've got a fully secure system, plenty of people are still uncomfortable with entering their financial information online. If you can have someone answering the phone (at least during normal business hours), put that phone number on the order form. If you have a fax, put your fax number on there, too. And don't forget to add a physical address. That way, anyone who wants to order, but fears online security gaps, can still do so in the old, traditional ways.

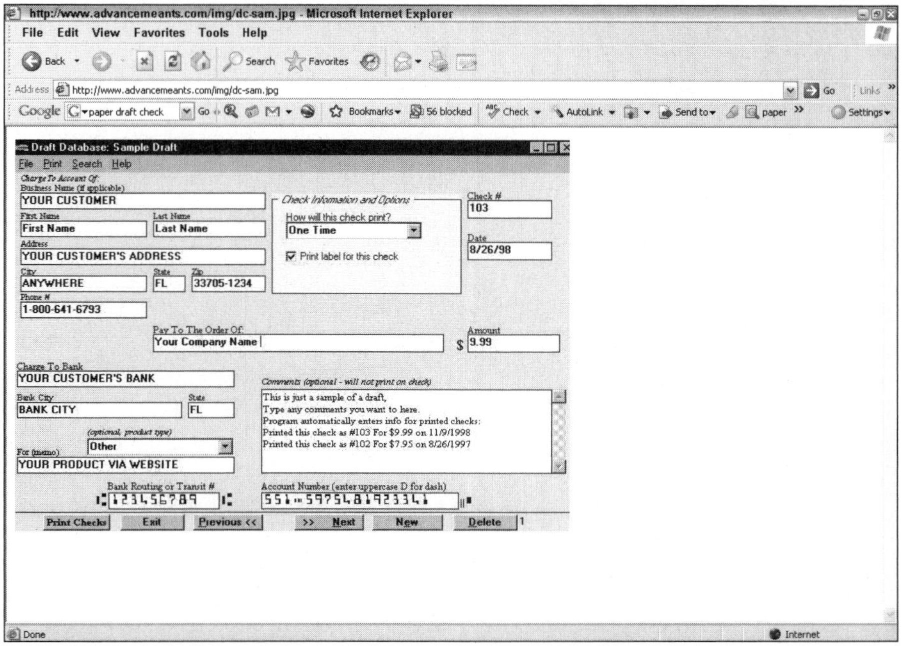

Figure 14-3:
You can use
a paper
draft in
place of a
normal
check.

If you work from your home and don't want to give out your home address, you can easily get an office address by renting a private mailbox for about a buck a day at most package-shipping companies (not the big ones like UPS that drive trucks around, but the small storefront operations, like Pak Mail or Mail Boxes Etc., which wrap and send packages for you). Many of them will even forward your mail to anywhere in the world. Table 14-1 gives the URLs of several private mailbox companies.

Table 14-1	Mailbox Rental Sources
Mailbox Company	*Web Address*
Box4me.com	www.box4me.com
Mail Boxes Etc.	www.mbe.com
Pak Mail	www.pakmail.com
Postal Connections	www.postalconnections.com
PostalAnnex+	www.postalannex.com

Getting a Merchant Account

You know that old line of Groucho Marx's? The one that went something like, "I wouldn't want to join any club that would have someone like me as a member." Well, if you're just getting started and don't have any kind of business or financial track record, you may have to settle for a credit card merchant account — giving you the ability to accept credit cards — that doesn't necessarily give you the best deal.

Even if you're really good at what you do and you're going into all this with your eyes wide open, the odds are pretty good that a financial analyst will classify you right alongside the starry-eyed dreamers who don't have a chance — unless you have a solid business plan, a proven staff, and some serious money behind your operation. That doesn't necessarily mean that you can't get a merchant account; after all, some credit card companies will give merchant accounts to businesses that they consider high-risk clients, just as there are loan companies that give a loan to someone with poor credit. But it probably means that you'll end up paying more for the privilege than a well-established firm would. Maybe lots more.

So what do you need to do to get established? And what are the pitfalls you have to guard against?

Choosing which acquirers to sign up with

If you think that you have a good relationship with your local bank, going into e-commerce might make you think again. Bankers are notoriously conservative. This is a good trait, of course, in people whom you need to trust with your money. But that conservative streak isn't so nice when you find out that the conservatism means that they don't get the whole e-commerce idea.

Even if your bank isn't Internet friendly, you still have tons of other places you can turn to. However, you can't get accepted directly by MasterCard or VISA. You have to go through some kind of intermediary, called a *merchant account acquirer,* along the way. Acquirers just take applications and pass them on to the banks that set up the merchant accounts and do the actual transaction processing. To find out whom you can talk to about getting set up as an Internet merchant, check out these official Web sites:

- **MasterCard:** Check out `http://www.mastercard.com/cgi-bin/acqdir/merchantReg.cgi`. Type the information about your company into the form there (see Figure 14-4), and MasterCard will take care of the rest. If you'd rather go outside the company, you can try `www.infomerchant.net/merchantaccounts/mastercard_acquirers.html` for an outside view.

- ✔ **VISA:** You can find a list of recommended companies at `http://usa.visa.com/merchants/new_acceptance/acquirer_list.html`.

- ✔ **American Express:** American Express is refreshingly simple — you apply directly to American Express. Drop in to `https://home.americanexpress.com/homepage/merchant_ne.shtml` and go at it. If you prefer to keep everything under one roof, you can usually also sign up with American Express through the same merchant account provider you use for MasterCard and VISA. Or check out both approaches and see which method gives you the best deal.

The American Express Web site is one fine example of design. It's both functional and attractive. Anyone can learn a lot about Web design and structure from studying it.

In addition to the official Web sites, there are so many acquirers online that it'll make your head spin. Go to any good search engine and type the phrase *accept credit cards.* You should get millions of results. Even allowing for duplicate listings and bad links, that's a lot to dig through. I've pared the list down a bit for you, though. Check out Table 14-4 for some of the major acquirers.

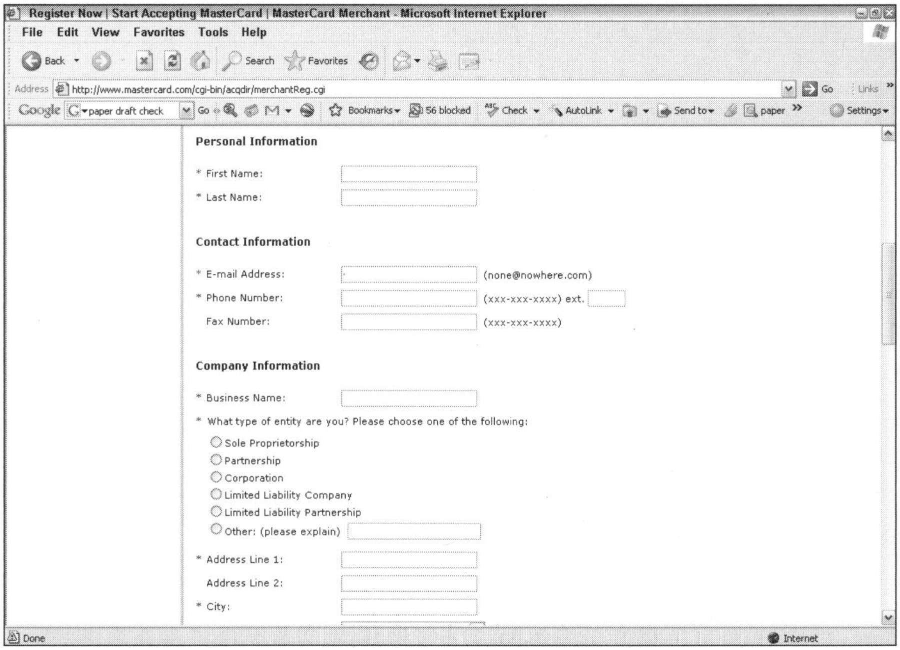

Figure 14-4:
Starting things with MasterCard.

Deciding which cards to take

So which card should you take? Or which cards? Well, the obvious answer is this: all of them. But the obvious answer isn't always the best. MasterCard and VISA for sure. They're the real biggies that almost everyone has. Beyond that, each card that you sign up for usually adds to your expenses. Most credit card firms charge you for the ability to accept the cards, even if you never process a single transaction with them. American Express doesn't. Well, actually, American Express has two plans. With the first one, you don't pay American Express any monthly fee, but you do pay the company a percentage of the take. The second plan is just the opposite — American Express doesn't get a cut, but you pay a flat fee every month. The choice is up to you.

If you're dealing with the general public, American Express is mostly useful for high-end purchases. If you're dealing with the business market, though, it's another story. Zillions of businesses have corporate American Express cards, and you can lose a significant amount of money if you can't take orders with these corporate cards, even for low-priced items. When it comes to the smaller cards, like Discover and Diner's Club, you should probably take them only if you're a really big company that does millions of dollars in sales. It's just not worth it for a typical small business to accept Discover or Diner's Club. Fortunately, most customers who have those cards will also have VISA, MasterCard, or American Express.

Signing up

After you decide which acquirers you want to sign up with, contact them and ask for an application. From that point, the exact details vary somewhat from one company to the next — make sure that you ask each company about the process before you get involved so that you'll have everything ready ahead of time — but the basic procedure goes something like this:

- ✔ **Fill out application forms.** Tons of sheets of them. And those forms are always too long to photocopy the whole sheet at once, so you'll have to keep turning them around and shooting them again to make a copy of the whole thing. You'll also need a magnifying glass to read some parts of the forms. These people take fine print seriously.

  Most merchant account providers now have an online application form. You fill it out and submit it online; then the provider mails a printed copy to you for your signature.

  When you're getting ready to fill out the forms, don't neglect to have the information handy about where the credit card company should send the money you make — your bank name, business account number, and ABA routing code. (Ask your bank.)

Some merchant account providers require you to open an account in a bank of their choosing. Run, don't walk, away from this kind of arrangement. It's a lot easier to handle your money if it's in your own bank.

✔ **Provide copies of your business documentation.** This may include a business license, corporate papers, or a partnership agreement, licenses to perform various services, or even copies of tax returns. Remember that merchant accounts are issued to companies, not individuals. Even if you're running a one-person shop, you have to do whatever your locality requires to be a legal business.

✔ **Estimate how many credit card orders you will process each month and how much money those orders will involve.** This is rough with a start-up business, but it's important because the merchant account provider will set a limit on how much you can submit for processing. If you end up making more than you thought, you have to ask the provider's permission to submit more orders than you signed up for. Most people deliberately overestimate the number of orders and the amount of money they expect, just to avoid this problem, but that can mean you end up paying more than you're required.

✔ **Have an on-site inspection.** That's right. Even though your business may not have a physical location and may exist only in cyberspace, you may have to put up with someone coming out to your house to look at it. These folks may even take a picture of your computer as your "place of business" for the record. This is nothing but a bit of red tape left over from the days before e-commerce.

Watching out for fees

At the top of the list of things to watch out for are fees. Merchants pay for the privilege of taking credit card orders, and the credit card companies have all sorts of little ways of sticking it to you. Here's a sampling:

✔ **Application fee:** This is pure gravy for the bank or — more likely — the sales agents, for whom it may be the main source of income. Double-check whether the application fee will be refunded if you don't get account approval and take the answer with a grain of salt. Get it in writing. Better yet, stay away from companies that charge one. Plenty of companies out there don't charge you just for looking at your application.

✔ **Setup fee for starting the account:** Again, lots of companies will set you up for nothing. Try to avoid the ones that charge you for the simple act of becoming a customer.

✔ **Monthly statement fee:** This is a charge that the credit card companies levy on you because they have to keep track of how much money they're making from you. You'd think that they'd be glad to do this for nothing, but that's not the case.

✔ **Percentage of each sale:** This is called the *discount rate*.

✔ **Transaction fee:** Yes, you're already paying a percentage. But the company still wants a few more cents.

✔ **Minimum monthly charge:** If you don't make enough sales for the credit card company's cut to meet a certain minimum amount, you have to pay the minimum amount anyway. Hey, the company isn't going to lose money just because you might. American Express has a refreshing difference — it doesn't have a monthly minimum.

✔ **Equipment charges:** If you're strictly online, you don't need any kind of equipment. Don't get suckered into buying a point-of-sale system or anything else you're not going to use.

Leaving off equipment, because it's unnecessary and wildly variable in cost, Table 14-2 shows the lowest costs typically associated with these fees. Lots of places claim to offer lower costs, but those firms must be running charities because these are the minimums that MasterCard and VISA charge Internet companies. (They do offer lower rates for more "stable" traditional bricks-and-mortar firms, however.)

Table 14-2	Low Internet Company Fees	
Fee	*Amount*	*When Paid*
Application	$0	One-time
Setup	$0	One-time
Statement	$9	Monthly
Discount rate	2.30%	Per transaction
Transaction	$0.30	Per transaction
Monthly minimum*	$20	Monthly

* If company's income from your transactions doesn't reach this amount

How do you pay all this and still make a profit? The same way every other merchant does: You raise your prices and pass the increase on to the consumer. However, a number of factors can make it hard to figure out exactly how much it costs you to accept credit cards. Sales that include the *CVV number* (the three-digit code on the signature strip on the back of the credit card) usually qualify for lower rates than sales that don't include it, for example. And, if you're in a specialty business (about 30 types of businesses fit this category, including adult entertainment, credit repair, jewelry, and airlines), the rate you pay will be about double the standard rate for other types of businesses.

Some companies, of course, actually care about your business and have nice, helpful people working for them. The best way to find out whom you're dealing with — before you sign up for a merchant account with any company — is to talk to some of its current customers. You can ask the company for references, but its employees will likely steer you only to people they know will say nice things about the company. Think about the references on your résumé. You don't include the boss who thought you were a turkey or the coworker who always tried to take the credit for your work, do you? The credit card companies don't want to send you to the people who are mad at them either.

Well, it's kind of hard to track down the clients of a company without asking someone at the company, so why not do it the other way around? Every Web site that takes credit cards has to be doing business with an acquirer. And almost all sites have an e-mail link to the Webmaster. Just surf the Web and keep leaving messages. "Who do you use? How do you like them? Have you had any problems with them?" (That kind of thing.) Pretty soon, you'll start to build up a consensus about which companies are currently the best to do business with.

Protecting against credit card fraud

The worst problem is credit card fraud. So what happens if you get a bad order? The answer's simple — you don't get paid. It's called a *chargeback* — the folks who handle your account issue a debit instead of a credit, and the amount of the bad charge is deducted from your business bank account. The same thing happens if a customer complains to the credit card company, saying that you didn't fulfill your duties (like if the customer never received the order, or the product didn't work). And if you get too many chargebacks, you can lose your merchant account. Worse, you can get charged big-time fees. That's right — more fees. Not only do you lose the money from the sale, but also if more than 1 percent of your sales in one month comes back as chargebacks, the credit card companies jack up your discount rate, which means that your profit on future sales shrinks.

Even if you successfully dispute the chargeback, you still have to pay a processing fee to cover the credit card company's expenses in falsely accusing you. Then comes the ultimate "insult to injury" stunt: If you keep getting lots of chargebacks, the company charges you to review your account. And that review can run into many thousands of dollars — MasterCard chargeback fees can even go up to $100,000 in a single month for repeat offenders. Not many Internet companies can afford that kind of expense.

The problem here is that Internet companies — like mail order or telephone order ones — have no way of ever seeing the credit card or the person who uses it. Normal fraud prevention wisdom (like watching to see if the credit card comes out of a wallet or a pocket) can't work. Nor, except in rare cases where people mail in Web pages they printed out, can Internet companies get a signature on an order form. All the company can do is accept a credit card number. There's no way to prove who provided that number. That's the nature of the Net. No doubt, this will be resolved in some manner some day, but for now, that's the way it is. Credit card companies have a phrase for this: *high risk*. That's right: MasterCard and VISA consider every company on the Internet to be a high risk. Well . . . not every company. If you're successful enough to make zillions of dollars, they pretend that you're not in the same boat as everyone else on the Net, even though nothing but the amount of profit is any different. Short of that, though, they've got the entire e-commerce world in their sights.

Make sure that the software you're using to process credit cards has an antifraud feature called *address verification*. Because the credit card issuer knows where it sends the bill, the address on the order can be checked against the credit card issuer's records. If the address isn't the same, you may not want to fulfill that order. Some companies, such as florists and fruit shippers, pretty well have to handle such orders because many of their products get ordered by one person to be sent to another person at another address. If you decide to take a risk like that, at least have two address areas on your form. One should be for the address to ship to, and the other one should be for the purchaser's home address if it's different from the address the item's being shipped to. It's not perfect protection, but it's a step in the right direction. And always make sure to require a signature for delivery. That way, you can prove the item reached the right address — assuming you ship a physical product, anyway.

Building on a Business Platform

If building your whole business from scratch while designing a Web site to boot seems like a big task, you might want to consider using an existing business platform to build on. There are malls online just as there are in suburbia, and they provide you with a ready stream of traffic — the same reason stores cluster in malls in the real world. Many online malls also provide merchant account services (such as Yahoo! Merchant Solutions from Yahoo! Stores, as shown in Figure 14-5). And most of the virtual and dedicated server providers (see Chapter 16) have some sort of shopping-cart software available as well. If you're looking for an all-in-one solution to your e-commerce needs, you should check out some of the sites in Table 14-3.

Table 14-3	Online Malls and Shopping Carts
Mall	*Web Address*
Americart Shopping Cart Service	`www.americart.com`
Clockwatchers	`www.clockwatchers.com/shopping.html`
Code9 Software	`www.code9software.com`
Coreave	`www.coreave.com`
Electronic Merchant Systems	`www.emscorporate.com/ecomm.htm`
StoreFront	`www.storefront.net`
Verio	`http://hosting.verio.com/index.php/ecommerce.html`
Yahoo! Merchant Services	`http://smallbusiness.yahoo.com/merchant`

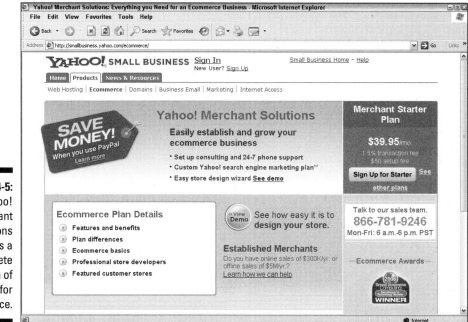

Figure 14-5:
Yahoo!
Merchant
Solutions
presents a
complete
selection of
options for
e-commerce.

Many of the malls offer complete e-commerce solutions — Web sites, merchant services, integrated shopping carts, and so on — and have some pretty sophisticated antifraud capabilities. In fact, they may be better options for many small companies than going the traditional route.

Converting Currencies

Whatever you're up to with e-commerce, your audience is global. Even if that's not your intent, you're going to have potential customers who aren't necessarily familiar with the current value of the U.S. dollar. Is there a solution? Oh, yeah. A really good one.

The Universal Currency Converter (UCC) from XE.com is a must-have for any commercial site that expects to handle international business. Like most free services, it has a banner ad built into it, but you can negotiate with XE.com to remove it for a fee. The converter lets anyone convert any amount in any currency to the equivalent amount in any other currency.

The basic module has only the major world currencies in it. Don't sweat it, though; if you need to include others, it doesn't cost you anything. This limitation is only for practical reasons. After all, nearly every transaction takes place in one of the top currencies, and the more options you add, the slower things get. Really, how often do you need to figure out how many Seborga luiginos are equal to 800 Uzbekistan soms?

Adding the converter to your Web page

To add the converter to your Web page, follow these steps:

1. **Go to www.xe.net/ucc/customize.php.**

2. **Read through the terms of use.**

3. **Fill out the required form with your URL and contact information.**

   Notice that the URL must be the address of the Web page on which you will actually put the converter, not just the general URL of your domain.

4. **Click the Go! button.**

   You need to register each page you use the converter on.

5. **On the resulting page, click the Fast Track Instructions button.**

   Now, you're back on the earlier page, right below the form you filled out. Yes, it's a roundabout way to get there, but the registration process is legally required if you want to use the converter.

From here, you have two options. Both of them work fine, so it's just a matter of how you like to do things.

6. **Use one of the following methods to get the code for the converter:**

   • Download the compressed file for either Windows or Mac. You then need to unzip it and load the resulting HTML page into an editor before you can use the code.

   • Click the Click Here to See the Raw HTML link and just copy the code off your browser screen.

If you download the file, you see that the enclosed Web page, `samp-ucc.htm`, has none of the usual elements you're used to — HTML, HEAD, and BODY. Yet it will still load into any browser and will work just fine. That's because, as useful as those elements are for envisioning the structure of your Web page, they're not technically required under the HTML standard. I'm not recommending that you leave them out of your pages, and I'm sure that XE.com did it just because the purpose of that page is only to hold the code for you to copy and paste. But it's a decent bit of tech trivia you can amaze and amuse your friends with.

7. **Whichever way you get your hands on the code, paste it into your Web page and save the file.**

8. **Upload the page to your Web server and try it out.**

   Figure 14-6 shows the converter on a Web page.

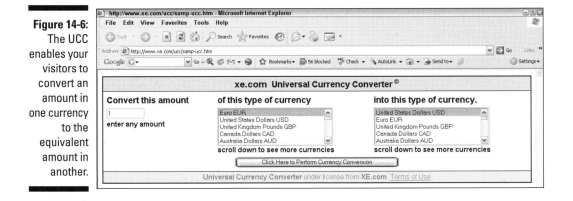

Figure 14-6:
The UCC enables your visitors to convert an amount in one currency to the equivalent amount in another.

Customizing the converter

Now, this is one fine service as is. But you can customize it, too. XE.com will change practically anything about the currency converter for a fee, but the company has also built plenty of options into it that you can use on your own.

Changing the default currencies

If you know the country from which most of your foreign customers come, you may want to set the converter so that it's ready to convert from your customers' currency to yours right away. Say, for example, that you're in the United States and you know that almost every one of your overseas customers is from the United Kingdom. You'd probably do well to set the conversion to default values of dollars to pounds in that case. This won't prevent anyone from another country from using the converter in the normal way. All it does is set which currencies are selected at the start, so visitors can still choose other currencies if they want.

This is what you need to do to set the default currencies in the converter:

1. **Go into the HTML source code and find the SELECT elements.**

   The one whose `name` attribute has a value of `From` is — you guessed it — the currency to convert from. The one whose `name` attribute has a value of `To` is the currency to convert to.

   One of the `OPTION` elements in each has the `selected` attribute. In the original version, the default From currency is the euro, and the default To currency is the U.S. dollar.

2. **To change the default, just delete the word `selected` from the OPTION elements for the current currency and add it to the ones you want to use.**

   Simple, ain't it?

Setting the default amount

Now, what if you have only one product, or what if all your products are the same price? For example, suppose you have a price of USD $49.95 that most people will want to convert to some other currency. Having already set the From currency to U.S. dollars, you can now set the default amount to 49.95. This default makes it really easy on your customers — all they have to do is pick their native currency, and they're off and running. To set the default amount, look for the following code line near the beginning of the form:

```
<INPUT type="text" name="Amount" value="1" SIZE=10><BR>
```

Just change the value of the `value` attribute. To set it to 49.95, change the code to this:

```
<INPUT type="text" name="Amount" value="49.95"
       SIZE=10><BR>
```

Users can still change the default value to anything they want by simply typing over it, just like they can select different currencies by selecting something other than the default selections.

If you want to change the order of the currency choices from alphabetical to some other method — such as placing the most likely currencies on the top of the list — all you have to do is to cut and paste the OPTION elements that reflect the currency values in the listings. Remove them from their current positions and paste them into their new positions. That's all there is to it.

If, for some reason, you don't want to give your users any choice in these things, UCC accommodates your wishes through the use of hidden variables. To do this, you add some INPUT type="hidden" elements right after the <FORM> tag and just before the <TABLE> tag.

To set the From currency so that it can't be changed, use the following code:

```
<INPUT type="hidden" name="From" value="xyz">
```

Replace the placeholder *xyz* with the three-digit code for the currency — such as USD for U.S. dollars or GBP for United Kingdom (or Great Britain) pounds.

To set the To currency, you do the same thing, but the line reads as follows:

```
<INPUT type="hidden" name="To" value="xyz">
```

To set the value so that it can't be altered (which prevents people from using your version of the UCC for test purposes unrelated to your site), add the following line of code:

```
<INPUT type="hidden" name="Amount" value="xyz">
```

Replace the placeholder *xyz* with the amount to be converted (for example, 49.95).

Adding and deleting currencies

If you want to add more currencies, check out the Full Universal Currency Converter at www.xe.net/ucc/full.shtml and copy and paste the appropriate currency to your version. Just add a new OPTION element under the To and/or From SELECT element for each new currency.

If you want to delete currencies from the listings, you need to delete the entire line for that currency, beginning with the <OPTION> tag and ending with the </OPTION> tag.

Customizing the results page

If you want to customize the default results page that appears after a currency conversion calculation, as shown in Figure 14-7, you need to go a bit deeper. Customization requires creating not only an element or an attribute, but also a *header* and a *footer*. The header contains HTML that is displayed before the calculation results, and the code in the footer goes in after them.

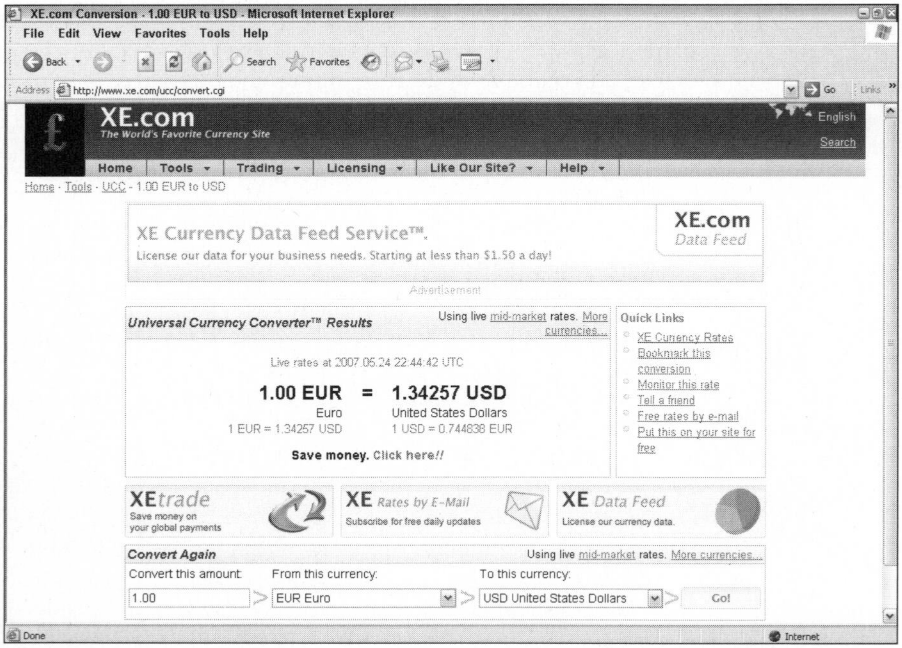

Figure 14-7:
The UCC
results
page.

To set up the header and footer, think about your HTML code ahead of time, as well as consider the variations that the UCC demands of you. The header has to go right after the line with the <FORM> tag and has to include the [HTML], [HEAD], [/HEAD], and [BODY] tags. Notice anything weird about these? Yeah, the brackets aren't the regular angle braces; they're regular brackets. This way, a Web browser that reads this code won't get confused by encountering two identical tags such as <HTML> in the same page. You put these odd-looking quasi-HTML elements in as values of a hidden INPUT element, and the UCC software reinterprets the squared brackets just as though they were angle braces when it comes time to create the results page.

So if you wanted to put in the following regular HTML code as your header . . .

```
<HTML>
<HEAD>
<TITLE>
This is a currency converter.
</TITLE>
</HEAD>
<BODY>
```

. . . you'd add it to the line in the currency converter code, like this:

```
<INPUT type="hidden" name="Header"
        value="[HTML][HEAD][TITLE]This is a currency
        converter.[/TITLE][/HEAD][BODY]">
```

Then comes the regular output of the converter. After that comes the footer. If you wanted to add the following HTML code to it . . .

```
<B>Thanks for using the converter!</B>
</BODY>
</HTML>
```

. . . you'd do it like this:

```
<INPUT type="hidden" name="Footer" value="[B]Thanks for
        using the converter![/B][/BODY]">
```

The Shopper's Currency Converter (www.xe.net/ecc/shoppers) provides the same functionality as the UCC, and versions are available that work in both Internet Explorer and Netscape Navigator.

Online Sources for Merchant Services

Table 14-4 lists some places on the World Wide Web where you can find more information on the topics covered in this chapter.

Table 14-4	Online Resources for Merchant Services
Web Site Name	**Web Address**
AIS Media	www.aismerchantservices.com
AMS Merchant Account Services	www.merchant-accounts.com
Best Payment Solutions	www.bestpaymentsolutions.com
ClickBank	www.clickbank.com
Discover Financial Services	www.discovernetwork.com/merchant/home/data/index.html
ePayment Solutions	www.epaymentsolutions.com

(continued)

Table 14-4 *(continued)*

Web Site Name	Web Address
EZ Merchant Accounts	www.ezmerchantaccounts.com
Instant Check	www.easydesksoftware.com/check.htm
Merchant Systems	www.merchant-systems.com
MerchantAccount.com	www.merchantaccount.com
Network Solutions Merchant Accounts	http://merchantaccounts.networksolutions.com
Paymentech	www.paymentech.com
Skipjack Financial Services	www.skipjack.com
Total Merchant Services	www.totalmerchantservices.com

Chapter 15

Examining Affiliate Programs

. . . .

. . . .

*W*hatever you call them — affiliates, associates, independent agents — businesses that operate on the World Wide Web have turned in a big way to letting other people do their advertising for them. Why should you care? Because you can make money at it. They don't just want you to plug their stuff; they're willing to cut you in on a piece of the action.

Zillions of companies are jumping on the affiliate bandwagon, where you sell another company's products and services for a slice of the pie. Companies from one end of the Web to the other are lining up to ask you to make your Web site their billboard. And the good news is that they don't want any of your money.

Table 15-1 lists a few major companies with affiliate programs.

Table 15-1	Major Companies with Affiliate Programs
Company	*Web Address*
Amazon.com	`https://associates.amazon.com/exec/panama/associates/apply`
PetSmart	`www.petsmart.com/global/affiliate/ap_affiliate_program.jsp`
Stamps.com	`www.stamps.com/affiliates`
Staples Office Supplies	`www.staples.com/sbd/content/about/affiliate`

Yeah, Sure It's Free

No, really, it's true. Joining an affiliate program doesn't cost you a bloody thing. The folks who offer the affiliate programs would be crazy to ask you for money. If you sign up as an affiliate, you already work for nothing, so what more could they ask? Any company that asks you to put up money to become an affiliate is probably running some kind of scam. It doesn't cost companies anything for you to sign up for their programs, and there's always the possibility that your Web site may actually make them some money.

Affiliate programs are just like most sales organizations. Salespeople don't get paid unless they generate money for the company. If a salesperson sells a product, he or she gets a percentage of the profit. Lots of people swear by that approach. After all, you may never starve on a regular paycheck, but you rarely feast either. If you're on commission, the sky's the limit. If you make enough sales, you can certainly manage a feast or two. Salaried employees who do a great job make no more money than the ones who do a lousy job. The salespeople who do a great job have something solid to show for their efforts.

Not all affiliates are paid a percentage of the profit, however. Sometimes, they get a flat fee instead. Either way, you get your slice of the pie every time it's cut. Okay, your slice goes into the fridge, so to speak. You don't get it right away. Don't panic; this is just one of those accounting things, as annoying as it is. Remember how I said that it doesn't cost a merchant anything to have you become an affiliate? Well, it's ironic, but it does cost merchants something when you actually drive business their way. It costs merchants money to run an accounting system to keep track of how much they owe you and to cut checks and mail them to you. If you manage to generate only five bucks in commissions, it's not worth their accountants' time to pay you. Sad, but true.

But don't panic — you do get paid. It's only a matter of earning a certain minimum amount. How much is that? It depends on the merchant. After you reach the minimum amount, the check is cut on a specific schedule. Many programs don't pay monthly, but quarterly. Make sure that you read the fine print before you sign up as an affiliate. Table 15-2 shows the payment schedule and minimum income necessary to trigger a payment from some representative affiliate programs.

Table 15-2	Payment Triggers	
Company	*Schedule*	*Amount Required*
Amazon.com	Quarterly	$100 ($10 for gift certificate or direct deposit)
Focalex.com	Monthly	$25

Company	Schedule	Amount Required
SearchTraffic.com	Monthly	$25
SnackExchange.com	Quarterly	$25
WebSponsors.com	Monthly	$15

If you don't earn the minimum amount by the time a check would be cut, the amount you earned carries over into the next pay period. In other words, if you need to make $50 to get a check sent out and you make only $30 by the deadline, you need to make only $20 more to meet the minimum for the next deadline. You may never get paid at all if you don't ever meet the minimum requirement.

So what's the best program to sign up with? Well, obviously, it's one that pays lots of money, doesn't have a high minimum amount before it issues a check, and issues checks more often than other programs. But you need to consider several other factors, too. First, you've got to find a program.

Can I Join?

Yes, of course, you can join an affiliate program. A company would be crazy to say that you can't join. After all, it's possible that you might send some business its way, and it doesn't cost the company anything to sign you up. Actually, about the only way not to get approved for an affiliate program is to run a Web site that the company finds objectionable — like a XXX adult site or one that tells how to rob banks with a homemade nuclear weapon.

Finding partners

So who's running affiliate programs? Where do you go to sign up? The short answer is that just about everyone's doing some kind of affiliate program these days. If you just use your Web browser's page-search function, you can hunt for the word *affiliate* on the sites that you visit in the normal course of your surfing, and you're guaranteed to trip over tons of programs. Many of the outfits that I list in other chapters of this book offer them, too.

You can also go to particular Web sites to find out the lowdown on affiliate programs. Table 15-3 lists some of the best sites for finding up-to-date news on the latest and greatest of these programs. (Figure 15-1 shows one of them.)

Table 15-3	Top Affiliate Information Sites
Company	*Web Address*
AffiliateMatch.com	www.affiliatematch.com
AssociatePrograms.com	www.associateprograms.com
ClickQuick.com	www.clickquick.com
LinkShare	www.linkshare.com
Refer-it.com	www.refer-it.com
WhichAffiliate	www.whichaffiliate.com

It's not a bad idea to cruise the search engines on a regular basis and hunt down any new programs that have come up since you last looked. In addition to keywords limiting things to your site's subject area, try some of these search terms: *affiliate program, associate program,* and *bounty program.* Don't forget the *program* part, or you'll spend the rest of your natural life trying to dig out from under all the results.

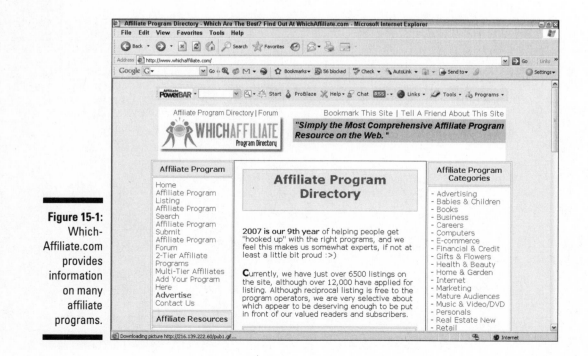

Figure 15-1:
Which-
Affiliate.com
provides
information
on many
affiliate
programs.

Working with a network

Not long after the idea of affiliate programs arose, people came up with the idea of affiliate-program networks. Program networks aren't just Web sites that offer you a large choice of programs to sign up for. They actually take care of nearly everything for you. All you do is go to a network's Web site, sign up, and state what kind of companies you want to sign up with. The network advises you and sets you up with some good ones. It's kind of like an e-commerce dating service.

LinkShare (www.linkshare.com) is an affiliate network that brings several programs together under one roof. You can find Commission Junction, a service similar to LinkShare's, at www.cj.com. Check out both Web sites to see what they can offer you.

Here's how to sign up as a Commission Junction affiliate:

1. **Go to https://signup.cj.com/member/publisherSignUp.do.**

   The Commission Junction Publisher Application page appears, as shown in Figure 15-2.

2. **Choose** your language and **which country you're in.**

3. **Select the currency in which you want your figures calculated.**

4. **Click the Next button.**

5. **Read the legal agreement in the box at the top of the page. When you reach the bottom of the agreement, click the Accept button. (See Figure 15-3.)**

   The check box beneath the agreement is automatically selected.

6. **Select the next two check boxes as well, affirming that you have read the privacy policy (you can click a link if you want to read it) and that you are of legal age.**

7. **Under the Site Information heading, fill out the appropriate information for your site (Web Site Name, Description, Category, and so on).**

8. **Under the Contact Information and Company information heading, enter the pertinent data.**

9. **Under Payment Information, select either Check or Direct Deposit. (The latter is available only in the U.S., U.K., and Canada.)**

   If you select Direct Deposit, more options appear, asking you for your bank information.

   This is a secure Web page.

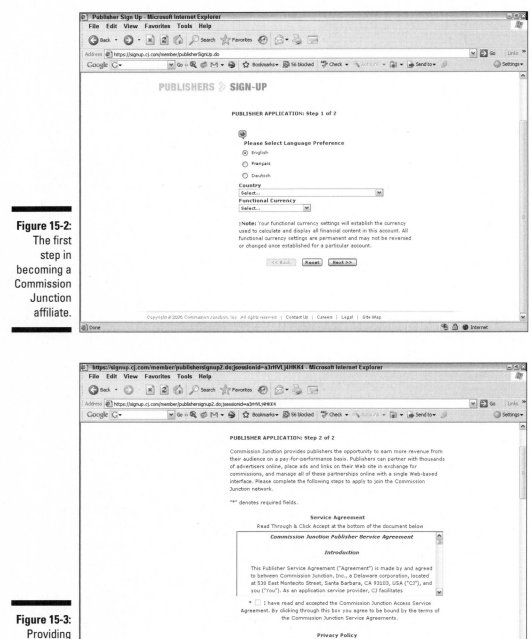

Figure 15-2:
The first
step in
becoming a
Commission
Junction
affiliate.

Figure 15-3:
Providing
the detailed
information.

10. **In the text box at the bottom of the page, enter the printed characters next to that text box.**

    This is simply a method for proving that you are an actual human being who is manually entering this information. That keeps automated programs from using the forms.

11. **Click the Accept Terms button at the bottom of the page.**

    You receive an e-mail with your account number, password, and so on.

From now on, just go to www.cj.com, enter your e-mail address (it has to be the same one you signed up with) and your password, click the Go button, and you're in. From here, you can explore all that Commission Junction has to offer, from new affiliate advertising possibilities to managing your account with it.

Profiting from Your Program

Most affiliate programs depend on the vast number of people they can get to advertise products or services for them. But you have no guarantee that you'll actually make any money — let alone any significant money — if you sign up with them. The odds, after all, are all with the affiliate programs. (See the section "Running Your Own Affiliate Program," later in this chapter.) But you can do some things to increase your chances that you'll actually find a check or two in your mailbox. And, if you really do it right, that check will be more than a joke.

Taking time to find the right programs

It's easy to get caught up in a heady rush and sign up with every affiliate program you can find right away. After all, you could JOIN RIGHT NOW and be up and running in JUST A FEW MINUTES! If you're wise, though, you'll take it slow and easy. Trust me, you're not missing the key to instant riches by not acting immediately. Billions of dollars are not going to suddenly flow into your mailbox the day after you get started.

If you're going to make a profit — and you can — a big part of the reason will be that you carefully studied the programs that are out there and made the right choice for you.

Use this checklist to get some basic answers about an affiliate program before you commit your time and energy to it:

- ✔ Go to the Web site that offers the program and read the affiliate FAQ (Frequently Asked Questions) and legal agreement. If it doesn't have a FAQ or it doesn't have clear answers to obvious questions, you should be a trifle suspicious of its intentions. All the legal agreements are more or less obscure to nonlawyers, however, so that's no true indicator of the program's purpose.

- ✔ Find out exactly what the program pays for. Does it pay for someone to just click a link on your site? Or does it pay only if that person places an order?

- ✔ How much does the program pay and how often does it issue checks?

- ✔ What's the minimum amount that you can earn and still get paid?

- ✔ How good is the program's support? Does it provide you with anything besides an advertising banner?

- ✔ Can you monitor, in real time, how much the program owes you?

- ✔ Does the program list others who are currently signed up for it? If so, go to those Web sites and e-mail the Webmasters to ask them how satisfied they are with the program.

- ✔ How long has the program been in operation? Are there any complaints filed against it with the Better Business Bureau (www.bbb.org), Direct Marketing Association (www.the-dma.org), or any regulatory agencies?

Choosing programs that fit with your audience

First, you need a Web site that appeals to the kind of people who would buy the product or service. It does you no good to sign up with a gardening supply house's affiliate program if you run a Web site that details the naval conflicts of the Napoleonic Wars.

If you do run a gardening site, go to www.bloomingbulb.com and click the Affiliate Program link at the bottom of the main page to get to the page shown in Figure 15-4. For Napoleon, well, I'm still looking. Maybe try one of the book chains.

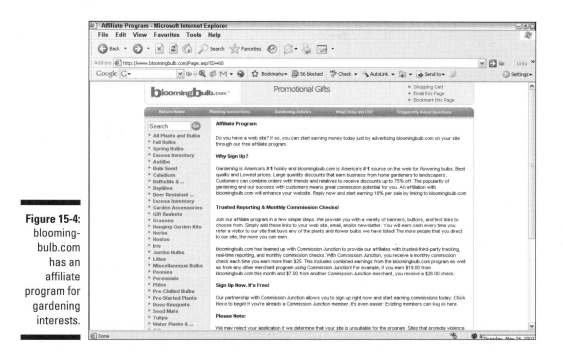

Figure 15-4:
blooming-
bulb.com
has an
affiliate
program for
gardening
interests.

Doing it the hard way

You can sign up with any programs you want — very few affiliate programs really care who their agents are — but what's the point if you're not likely to be profitable? Being an affiliate is just like running a business, and as with any other business, it's best to be involved in something that you already love and know very well.

What if you find an affiliate program that you like but you're not already running a site that fits in with its products? The short answer: Create a new site. With the incredibly low cost of starting an online site, running anywhere from totally free up to a few hundred bucks a year, you'd be crazy to walk away from a program that excites you.

If you really like the program, it's a matter of doing some research. If the subject matter turns you off, run — don't walk — away. Regardless of the potential rewards, you can't turn your visitors on if the topic doesn't excite you. If it does catch your heart and get you genuinely interested, though, you have a real chance to make something that people want to visit.

Taking it easy with Google AdSense

If you don't like the idea of doing your own research to place ads on your Web site, Google AdSense (`www.google.com/adsense`) is a welcome relief. The Google AdSense program has two sides to it: AdSense for Content and AdSense for Search. Both of them provide your users with content that is relevant to them while providing you with some welcome funding.

Google AdSense for Content works like other affiliate programs by placing banner ads on your Web page. As you can see in Figure 15-5, you can choose from lots of different styles, so you can work the ads easily into just about any kind of site design. There's even a provision for streaming video ads that's going into action soon.

Google AdSense for Search works just like the ads on the main Google search page, except that the search originates on your own Web site. (See Chapter 6 for how to add Google Site Search to your site.) As shown in Figure 15-6, paid advertisements appear to the side and above the regular search results. If one of your users clicks a paid link — not one of the regular ones — you earn a commission.

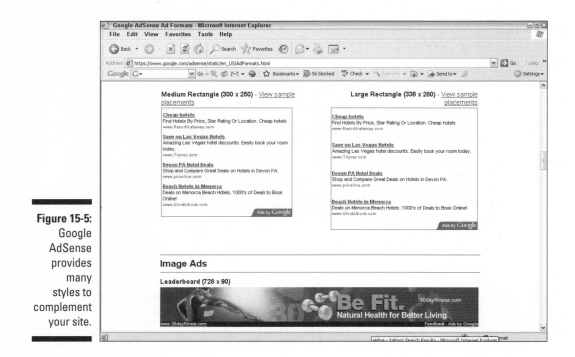

Figure 15-5:
Google AdSense provides many styles to complement your site.

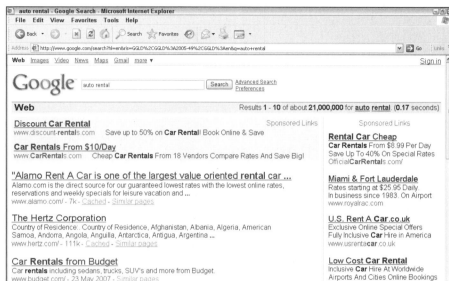

Figure 15-6:
Sponsored ads appear in response to a keyword search on Google.

Adding value to your site to keep visitors coming back

Even if your site's visitors are likely to be interested in the topic you're signed up for, you need to be especially vigilant about giving them full value for their visits. After all, even if you haven't planned primarily for an e-commerce site, you must remember that, after you join an affiliate program, you're running an online business.

You have to keep the visitors happy and keep them coming back for more. To do that, you have to give them a site that's worth their time. If all you do is set up a page with a bunch of links to programs that pay you if someone clicks their links or even buys their products, you've lost your focus. The focus of any Web site must be on the people who visit it. If you forget that or fail to take that approach for any reason, you're setting yourself up for total failure — in or out of the e-commerce world.

You have to offer something that no one else in the world can — your own unique viewpoint and outlook on the topic or your own personal contacts. If you sell books, do a book-review site, not just a book-listing site. (Don't forget to add this book!) If you sell baby products, try to get something in print from your local pediatrician — someone whom you know but who isn't already on other Web sites. If you sell gardening supplies, get out in the yard and get your hands dirty so that you can tell it like it is.

People will visit your site more than once, but only if you give them a reason to.

Focusing on your site

Tons of affiliate programs offer *two-tier* payment plans, which means that if you get someone else to sign up for the same program, you get a percentage of that person's income in addition to your own. Of course, that amount is smaller than what you make by direct purchases from your own site, but it still sounds like a pretty good deal. And it probably is, but a hazard is involved. You can get so caught up in trying to sign up other people that you forget what affiliates are for: getting your visitors to buy the products or services you're advertising for the program. If you overlook that fact, you start to see your own profits heading for the basement. When it comes to two-tier programs, take anything over your own direct involvement as gravy, because you have to rely on repeat customers, just like any business does. And you probably aren't going to get anybody to sign up as an affiliate twice.

Running Your Own Affiliate Program

It must have occurred to you by now that this affiliates bit is a pretty good thing to use if you set up your business online. I couldn't agree more. In fact, if anything, it's better for the business owner than it is for the affiliates. The following sections tell you what you need to know to run your own affiliate program.

Doing the math

Just look at the numbers. Say, for example, that you're selling a product for $20 that costs you $10, so you make $10 per sale. You pay your affiliates a 10 percent commission on each sale. If you have 1,000 affiliates selling your product, and each one generates a single sale in a month, you're getting an extra $20,000 income per month, and it costs you only $2,000 to generate it.

Take off the $10,000 for your costs and the $2,000 for the affiliates, and that's $8,000 per month profit — or $96,000 per year of free money. For a lot of small e-businesses, that's enough to justify their existence. The individual affiliate, though, gets just $2 per month.

Of course, a savvy affiliate makes more than that, but it does show that the affiliate system is heavily weighted in favor of the merchant.

Using software to host affiliates

Some software is designed to enable you to host your own affiliate program. (See Figure 15-7.) Table 15-4 shows some of the products that you can get. As with reciprocal linking, you have to hunt down the people you're going to be connecting with. On top of that, you have to manage everything. Rather than handling all the tedious details yourself, though, you may want to consider letting someone else do all the work.

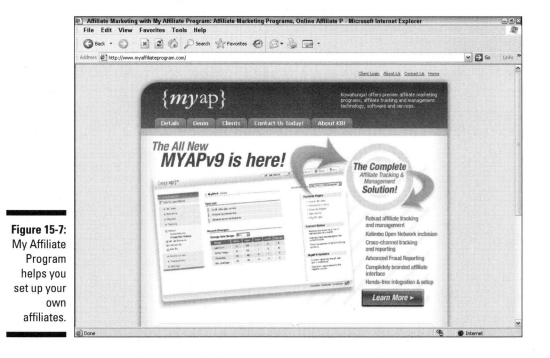

Figure 15-7: My Affiliate Program helps you set up your own affiliates.

Table 15-4	Affiliate Program Software
Web Site Name	*Web Address*
Interneka Affiliate	www.interneka.com
My Affiliate Program	www.myaffiliateprogram.com
ProTrack	www.affiliatesoftware.net
Ultimate Affiliate	www.groundbreak.com/ua_index.html

The Affiliate Tracking Network (www.affiliatetracking.com) occupies a kind of gray area here — it sells the software for you to do it yourself but also offers to do it for you. Both LinkShare and Commission Junction are mentioned as sources of income for affiliates in the section "Working with a network," earlier in this chapter, but they're also a prime source of affiliates. They've got both sides of this street well covered. Refer-it.com (www.refer-it.com) maintains a list of other firms that can help you set up a program. Limber up your fingers and go to www.refer-it.com/search.asp to check it out.

Online Sources for Affiliate Programs

Table 15-5 lists some places on the World Wide Web where you can find more information on the topics that are covered in this chapter.

Table 15-5	Online Resources for Affiliate Programs
Web Site Name	*Web Address*
AffiliateGuide.com	www.affiliateguide.com
AffiliatesDirectory.com	www.affiliatesdirectory.com
AffiliateShop	www.affiliateshop.com
Associate Search	www.associatesearch.com
ATL Affiliate Programs	www.atlnetwork.com
Cyberbounty	www.cyberbounty.com
DirectLeads	http://directleads.com
ValueClick	www.valueclick.com

Part VI
Publishing and Publicizing Your Site

The 5th Wave   By Rich Tennant

"Try putting a person in the photo with the product you're trying to sell. We generated a lot of interest in our eBay Listing once Leo started modeling my hats and scarves."

In this part . . .

This part discusses getting your site online and letting people know you're there. Chapter 16 gives you everything you need to know about different Web-hosting options. Chapter 17 covers getting your Web site listed in the search engines and establishing reciprocal links with other sites. Chapter 18 shows you how to keep your site in tip-top shape. Chapter 19 shows you how to keep in touch with your visitors after they've left, without falling into the spam trap and getting input from the folks who come to your site through surveys and forms.

Chapter 16

Letting the World In: Choosing a Host and Domain Name

- -

In This Chapter

▶ Choosing a host

▶ Finding free Web site providers

▶ Picking and registering domain names

- -

*I*f you don't already have a Web site or if you're unhappy with your current Web space provider, you have several options. You can run your own Web server, of course. With a DSL connection and Linux, it's even possible to put together a creditable setup in your own home. But that's a lot of work — ask network administrators just how much leisure time they have. And many broadband providers have policies forbidding you from doing it, anyway.

If you want to focus on developing and maintaining your site, your best bet is to leave the day-to-day grunge work of keeping the server up and running to someone else.

Practically every Web hosting provider offers all sorts of extended services in addition to plain Web space. These often include some form of e-commerce hosting, ranging from simply supplying the software to setting up a complete turnkey solution for you.

Going Live: Choosing a Host

You have three basic options when it comes to Web hosting:

- ISPs
- Virtual servers
- Dedicated servers

ISPs

The same people who provide you with Internet access can also be your Web space provider. Almost certainly, you have at least some room for Web pages as part of your basic service. If you're not interested in a very extensive site or in one that has tons of glitzy features, the basic setup the ISP gives you will probably suffice. Even if you don't have any kind of CGI access (see Chapter 8), you can probably still use remotely hosted services, like the ones described in this book, to enhance your site.

Many domain name registrars (described in "Finding a registrar," later in this chapter) also provide a limited amount of Web site space as a part of their services.

Virtual servers

Virtual servers are nothing more than directories on a hard drive. If that hard drive is on an existing Web server that supports virtual server capabilities, however, the Webmaster can make each one of those directories seem as though it is a fully functional Web server.

Other than being a really clever example of how you can use computer technology, does this have a practical application for you? It depends on your budget and your site's traffic expectations. It's certainly one of the cheapest ways to get your site up and running. You could pay for a couple of months' worth of a typical virtual server by skipping one good dinner at a decent restaurant. Some virtual servers are so cheap that you could pay for them just by skipping dessert.

On the other hand, you're sharing one physical server with lots of other virtual servers. Any physical server's performance degrades as it gets busier, with more and more people connecting to it and placing demands on it. But if you're on a virtual server, that scenario has a slightly different meaning. People visiting a Web site on one of the other virtual servers that's hosted on the same physical server as yours are putting a drain on your resources, too, because those resources are shared. Basically, if someone else's site gets too busy, yours can look like a turtle in molasses. And vice versa.

Dedicated servers

Nearly every company that handles virtual servers also leases dedicated ones. A *dedicated server* is a step up from a virtual server: Although it costs a bit more, it's your very own physical computer holding your Web site, with nobody else on it.

REMEMBER

Both virtual and dedicated servers offer more than just Web hosting. For example, they also handle e-mail. The focus here is only on the Web hosting aspect because this book is about Web sites.

Dedicated servers used to cost a small fortune, but a combination of generally lower computer prices and competitive pressures has dropped the expense of leasing one. At a bottom price of around $300 per month, dedicated servers are still a bit pricey for a private individual, but for any serious commercial operation, they're a great bargain. After all, that's only $3,600 a year, although hiring a single network administrator to work at your company can easily set you back 20 times that or even more.

Why compare those two costs? Aren't they apples and oranges? No, not at all. When you lease a dedicated server, the people you're leasing it from take care of keeping it up and running, which is what a network administrator does. Dedicated servers, like virtual servers, are located at the facility of a Web space provider, such as Verio (www.verio.com — see Figure 16-1), and you don't have to worry about regularly backing up your data, restoring after a crash, upgrading things like Linux kernels, or any of the million things that keep technical staffs hopping.

Finding your match

You can always run through the standard search engines and site guides looking for information on Web hosts. Some search engines, however, such as HostIndex (www.hostindex.com), are specifically designed to help you track down the right host for you (see Figure 16-2). The Web sites in Table 16-1 will help you do some comparison shopping.

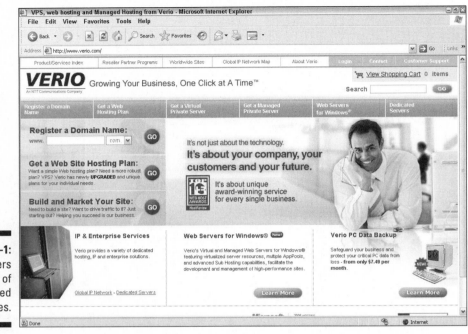

Figure 16-1:
Verio offers a variety of specialized services.

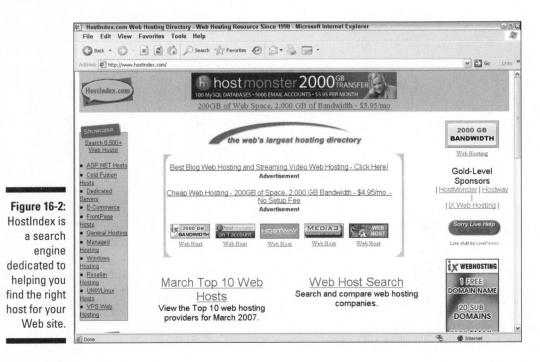

Figure 16-2:
HostIndex is a search engine dedicated to helping you find the right host for your Web site.

Table 16-1	Web Hosting Indexes
Web Site Name	*Web Address*
budgetweb.com	`www.budgetweb.com/budgetweb/index.html`
CNET Reviews	`http://reviews.cnet.com/Host_power_search/7011-6540_7-0.html`
Findahost.com	`www.findahost.com`
HostReview.com	`www.hostreview.com/power_search.html`
WebHostingTalk.com	`www.webhostingtalk.com`

Keeping It Cheap: Free Web Site Providers

More than 23 zillion Web space providers have an unbeatable price, which you probably guessed already from the title of this section. If you set up a personal or limited-interest site (such as a condo association newsletter), free Web space providers may be the way to go. You can get lots more space than your local ISP provides. It's not unusual to get 50 or more megabytes (MB) of Web storage space without having to pay a dime for it.

If you plan on running any sort of professional site, though, the free Web space providers aren't really the ticket for you. You need your own domain name — `.com`, `.org`, or whatever — in order to be taken seriously. (See the section "Getting Your Own Domain Name," later in this chapter.) Also, free Web hosts make their money by slapping ads onto your site, and you can't usually put up your own in competition with them.

Having to post a free Web host's ad on your site means you may not be able to use any add-ins such as opinion polls and chat rooms that feature their own banner ads either.

Table 16-2 lists some free Web hosts.

Table 16-2	Free Web Hosts
Web Site Name	*Web Address*
50Megs.com	`www.50megs.com`
Angelfire	`www.angelfire.lycos.com`

(continued)

Table 16-2 *(continued)*

Web Site Name	Web Address
Crosswinds	www.crosswinds.net
Dreamwater	www.dreamwater.com
TopCities	www.topcities.com
Tripod	www.tripod.lycos.com

Getting Your Own Domain Name

Domain names, like dummies.com, are the addresses of sites on the World Wide Web. Picking and registering your own domain name are two of the most critical phases in your site planning, and I show you how to do both in this section. When you tell your Web browser to go to www.dummies.com, it's obvious where you're going to end up — at the *For Dummies* Web site. Your computer doesn't know that, though. It can't actually go to a named site; instead, it asks a *domain name server* (DNS) to translate that name into a more computer-friendly set of numbers known as an *IP address*. It's like getting into a cab and telling the driver to go to the Acme Building. He asks you where it is, and you tell him it's at 1123 Main Street.

Domain extensions — the final letters at the end of an Internet address — are known as the *top-level domain,* or TLD. They're called "top level" because you read Internet addresses from right to left, and the part after the last dot is the highest step in a hierarchy that eventually leads down from the Internet as a whole, step by dotted step, to the particular computer you're going to. Here are the current domain extensions:

- .aero   Air transportation companies
- .biz   Business firms
- .cat   Catalan language sites
- .com   Commercial operations
- .coop   Cooperatives
- .edu   Educational institutions
- .gov   U.S. government and agencies
- .info   All uses
- .jobs   Human resources
- .mil   U.S. military

  ✔ .mobi   Mobile services

  ✔ .museum   Museums

  ✔ .name   Private individuals' sites

  ✔ .net   Internet service providers (ISPs)

  ✔ .org   Nonprofit organizations

  ✔ .pro   Professions

  ✔ .tel   For contact data

  ✔ .travel   For the travel industry

One problem with all these newer domains is that the general public identifies old standards with reliability, and some folks may tend to see the lesser-known alternatives as misprints or typographical errors. "Dot what? Don't you mean 'dot com?'" The term *dotcom* has, in fact, come into colloquial usage as meaning an Internet-based company.

The funny thing about all these TLDs is that there's no requirement in many cases for people to use any of them in the manner in which they were intended. Plenty of nonprofit organizations have .com addresses, and quite a few .nets have nothing at all to do with ISPs. Go figure. Some of the new TLDs, like .museum, have stringent requirements; if you're not a museum, you can't get a .museum address.

The domain extensions that I mention in the preceding bulleted lists are called *generic TLDs,* but another kind of TLD exists as well — the *country-level TLD.* These TLDs specify the country in which the Web site is based. That's not necessarily where the Web server that holds the site is located, thanks to the global nature of the Internet. Registering the same name in many countries can be useful if you're an international organization with multiple languages to support. That way, you can have a Spanish-language page at mysite.es, a Japanese-language page at mysite.jp, and so on.

If you're into alphabet soup, you can toss around such terms as *gTLD* and *CLTLD* for the generic and country-level extensions or even *iTLD* for international ones. Why there's a small *g* and *i* but an uppercase *CL* before the TLD parts is one of the Internet's great mysteries.

Picking a name

In the early days, it was easy to create a domain name because there weren't many of them in use yet. Today, though, if you want to pick a three- or four-letter abbreviation or a single word for your domain name, you're very likely to be out of luck. Everything short is already taken. The solution? Forget the acronyms and short names. Use phrases instead. The basic idea is to go for anything long enough that it's unlikely to have been used yet, but short enough to remember.

To find out whether a name is available, you use a WhoIs utility. One of the most familiar ones on the Web is the Network Solutions page at `www.networksolutions.com/cgi-bin/whois/whois`. You might also try the nice set of tools at `www.whois.net` (see Figure 16-3) or use a stand-alone tool like WhoIs ULTRA, which you can get your hands on at `www.analogx.com/contents/download/network/whois.htm`.

Take your time and poke around the AnalogX site. You can get some other wonderful utilities there, too.

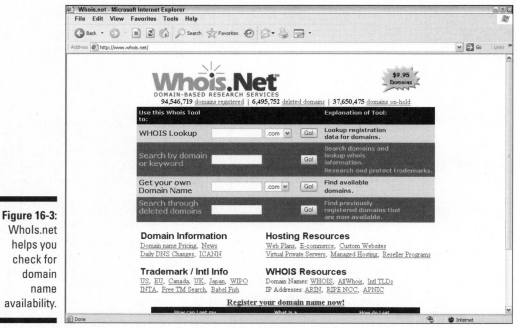

Figure 16-3:
WhoIs.net
helps you
check for
domain
name
availability.

What do you do if you come up with a great domain name, but it's already taken — and you've just gotta have it? Well, it depends. If you're a company that already has a trademark, the domain name may well already "belong" to you as a matter of course, even if you haven't registered it yet. Well, at any rate, it probably can't legally be used by anyone else. If you've been doing business as, say, Joe's Acme Fabuloso Garbanzo Beans and Unicyle Maintenance Company, and that name's your registered trademark, anyone running a site named `www.JoesAcmeFabulosoGarbanzoBeansAndUnicycle-MaintenanceCompany.com` is probably easy game for your lawyers.

You can often buy a domain name from the person or organization that's currently using it. It can't hurt to ask, anyway.

Another factor you need to consider when picking a domain name, besides the fact that some organization that's actually using the name has already registered it, is that some companies exist to do nothing but think up good names and register them. These companies, sometimes called "domain squatters," seem to have no intention of ever running real Web sites that use those names, but only . . . — well, it's hard to think of it as anything but holding the names hostage. The only purpose they have is to own the name and sell it to you. And if you think you'll get it away from them for pocket change, think again. It'll cost hundreds of dollars at least — and the upper end? Limitless for a good name.

Finding a registrar

After you pick a name, you need to register it so that nobody else can use it. This task is usually handled for you by your Web space provider, who's used to the job, probably has a bulk account with a major registrar, and fills out zillions of these applications every year.

The best-known registrar of domain names in America is Network Solutions (www.networksolutions.com). It registers your domain name for $35 a year if you sign up for one year or as little as $9.99 for a hundred-year commitment.

It used to be that you had to pay for the first two years at once, but in early 2000 this changed so that you can pay for only one year if you prefer. Many sites that offer assistance in registering your domain name still say that you need to cough up two years' money.

For a long time, Network Solutions was the only registrar on the block, but this is no longer the case. Today, many other registrars compete with it. The prices vary quite a bit, so it's a good idea to shop around. The popular GoDaddy.com, for instance, has prices in the pocket change range.

The organization that accredits domain name registrars is the Internet Corporation for Assigned Names and Numbers (ICANN). It maintains lists of the outfits that are authorized to register your domain name. To register a domain name by using one of the generic TLDs, go to www.icann.org/registrars/accredited-list.html and pick one of the registrars in your region.

To register one of the country-level TLDs, go to www.iana.org/cctld/cctld-whois.htm and click the name of the country; you find the URL of the country-level registrar at the bottom of the resulting page.

If you decide you don't like your current registrar, you can change. Any of the others will happily take your business away from its competitors.

Online Sources for Web Hosting and Domain Registration

Table 16-3 lists some places on the World Wide Web where you can find more information on the topics that are covered in this chapter.

Table 16-3	Online Resources for Web Hosting and Domain Registration
Web Site Name	*Web Address*
Better-Whois.com	www.betterwhois.com
checkdomain.com	www.checkdomain.com
Freedomlist	www.freedomlist.com
FreeWebspace.net	www.freewebspace.net
IANA (Internet Assigned Numbers Authority)	www.iana.org/domain-names.htm
ICANN	www.icann.org
Netcraft	www.netcraft.com
ServerWatch	http://serverwatch.internet.com/webservers.html

Chapter 17

Publicizing Your Site

In This Chapter

▶ Choosing keywords wisely

▶ Getting listed with search engines

▶ Checking your search engine ranking

▶ Trading links

▶ Using banner ads

Search sites (also called *search engines*) are a critical part of the World Wide Web. Without them, it's nearly impossible for most people to find what they're looking for. Therefore, if you're serious about your Web site (and I assume that you are because you're reading this book), it's important to know as much about search sites as possible (such as by hands-on, real-life experiences). And you can't do much better than trying out the search sites yourself. You can find out which ones give helpful responses to your queries and which ones return nonsense. For even more info, check out *Search Engine Optimization For Dummies,* by Peter Kent (Wiley Publishing), which goes into very fine detail about what readers can do to get their sites listed in the search engines.

Table 17-1 lists the major search sites.

Table 17-1	Major Search Sites
Search Site	*Web Address*
AlltheWeb	`www.alltheweb.com`
AltaVista	`www.altavista.com`
Ask.com	`www.ask.com`
Excite	`www.excite.com`
Google	`www.google.com`
Lycos	`www.lycos.com`

(continued)

Table 17-1 *(continued)*	
Search Site	**Web Address**
WebCrawler	www.webcrawler.com
Yahoo!	www.yahoo.com

If you're tired of slow search response times, try AlltheWeb. It gives you answers so fast that your head spins.

To make sure that people know your Web site exists, you should have it listed in lots of search engines. How many you should list it in is a matter of opinion. There's certainly no harm in going for broke and listing your site with every search engine, but about a zillion of them are out there — and most of them aren't very well known. In my opinion, after you're listed with all the ones in Table 17-1, any more effort runs into the law of diminishing returns. Yes, you will generate more visits by listing your site at even more search sites, but you don't get anywhere near as many visits from obscure search sites as you do from the more popular ones.

Speaking of popularity, the number one search engine is the oddly named but fantastically functional Google (www.google.com). Not that it needs the push, but I highly recommend it. If your site isn't listed on Google, you'll miss out on a lot of potential visitors.

There are many reasons for Google's success, but the main one is simply that it gives better results than many of its competitors. This is in large part due to its sophisticated page-analysis software, and you would do well to keep in mind what it looks for when you design your site's pages. Here are some tips on how to do that:

- ✔ Make sure that the important terms describing your site (the ones you think people will use as search terms when they're hunting for information on Google) appear in both your page title and in the first paragraph of your Web page.

- ✔ Use the same words at least a few times elsewhere on the page, but don't go hog wild — if you overdo it, you'll lower your ranking.

- ✔ Break up your page's text by using heading elements (H1, H2, and so on) that contain key phrases. Google pays more attention to these than to normal text.

- ✔ If, for some reason, your page design can't utilize heading elements, use the B (bold text) element to emphasize your keywords. (The STRONG element does the same thing.)

- ✔ Exchange links with other Webmasters, especially with those who already have a high Google ranking.

Using search sites isn't the only way of getting the word out, though. You can also work out reciprocal link arrangements with other Web sites, either on a personal level or through the agency of a banner-link exchange. (See the section "Investigating Reciprocal Linking," later in this chapter.)

Working Keywords into Your Pages

Search sites have different ways of gathering information on the content of Web sites:

✔ Some search sites are put together by human effort. People visit Web sites that have been submitted to the search site and then manually categorize those sites.

✔ Other search sites are fully automated. Programs called *robots* or *spiders* surf the Web, cataloging their findings and adding Web pages to the search site's database. Robots and spiders don't just note the URL of a page, though. They also index all the words on the page (except for words like *a, an, the, for,* and so on).

When someone runs a search, the search terms are compared with the indexed words. Links to whatever sites match the search terms are then shown to the person doing the searching.

In addition to the words in the text of your page (and sometimes in the alt text fields of images and other elements as well), search engines also index meta keywords.

The following sections give you the lowdown on incorporating keywords into your site.

Adding meta tags

META is one of the most versatile elements in HTML because it's one of the most poorly defined ones. Some would just say it doesn't have many limits. Its name and content attributes enable you to put many types of information into your HTML documents.

META always goes within the HEAD element, and it has no end tag.

You can have all the META elements you want, but only two of its uses matter to a search engine: as a page description and as a list of keywords. Neither one is essential. In fact, despite the frenzy about META keywords, your page description and TITLE element are actually more useful for search engines. (Google, the most successful search engine, doesn't even look at META keywords.)

Page description

When someone performs a search that returns a hit to your site, the response usually shows your page title and a blurb of text from the beginning of your page. This response underscores the importance of a good title. If the first sentence of your page doesn't describe all its contents, that may not be the best possible enticement for someone to visit it. If your page has a META description, however, the search engine will use that description to — you guessed it — describe your page.

Imagine that you have a page titled "The Love Letters of Grover Cleveland." Well, that title might not mean much to a lot of folks, and if the first sentence is something like a tame quotation from one of those letters, you're not doing too well. But a good description like this can fix that:

```
<META name="description" content="The secret life of the
        24th President">
```

List of keywords

You add keywords in much the same way that you add a description:

```
<META name="keywords" content="Grover Cleveland, 24th
        President, Buffalo, New York, Mugwumps">
```

Mugwumps? Trust me — it's a Grover Cleveland thing.

The META keywords aren't that important because the content of the page itself should already have the important terms in it. And some search engines don't even look at META keywords. Where keywords are useful is in a special situation that you can't easily accommodate in the visible page content without looking silly: You need to intentionally misspell words.

It's a fact: Lots of people have trouble spelling or typing or both. Therefore, you should also add common spelling errors to your list of keywords. For example, if you list *flying saucers* and someone's looking for *flying sossers,* that person won't be able to find your site. Well, you may not want that person to, but I'm not going to get into that. You should also cover yourself for any legitimate spelling variants. For example, if you sell tires and don't want to miss out on the British market, you should also list *tyres* among your keywords.

When it comes to choosing keywords, don't neglect synonyms. One person may look for *car parts* while another searches for *automotive accessories.*

Incorporating keywords in the content

The actual content of your Web pages is much more important than META keywords. In fact, it's critical, both to your search engine ranking and to visitor retention. When you write the copy for your pages, make sure that you throw in as many terms as possible that accurately describe your topic. As far as the search engines are concerned, the more often you can reasonably include relevant keywords, the better. After all, search engines rank your Web site by how well the contents of your pages match up with the search term that someone enters.

When it comes to the human visitors to your pages, as opposed to the robotic ones, you need to write in a way that entertains your audience. As a professional writer, I always try to avoid using the same phrase too often. When I need to refer to the same thing or action over and over again, I strive to find new ways to say it. I practically live for synonyms and pronouns.

It can be a difficult balancing act to satisfy your human visitors while at the same time cater to the search engines' needs. You don't want to bore your readers by endlessly repeating the same terms, but you do want to nail down the ranking you deserve. Here are some general steps on how to do this:

1. **To start with, make up a list of terms that you think people might use if they search for your page.**

2. **Go ahead and write your content without paying any attention to your list.**

   Writing your content first is important because if you stare at your list of terms while you're working, you may stifle your creativity.

3. **After you've finished writing your page, look over the list and mark down how many times you've used each of the terms on the page.**

4. **Go over your page and see where you can work in the words that you *didn't* use. Then for words that you *did* use, look for places you might use them again without screwing up the flow of the writing.**

After you've done these things, toss the list in the trash and reread your page. If it's still good, go with it. If it doesn't read well, you may have to sacrifice some of the terms to make the text more reader-friendly.

Avoiding keyword trickery

Lots of the get-rich-quick sites advise you to raise your ratings with the search engines by stacking the deck. Typically, this involves using the same phrase over and over again in your meta tags, like this:

```
<META name="keywords" content="computer books, computer
        books, computer books, computer books, computer
        books, computer books, computer books">
```

Avoiding traps

The traps, in this case, are some of the perfectly normal Web site design approaches. If you use frames or image maps, you're asking for trouble with the search engines. Why? Because many of the search engines don't navigate frames properly, and none of them can read the text in an image map. The same problem crops up when people use images containing text as a part of the image itself — your human visitors can read it, but a search engine's robot won't even know it exists.

Does that mean that you can't do things like putting text-filled images in a table for layout purposes? No, and you don't have to give up on frames or image maps, either. But you do have to provide a plain old text-link-alternative approach to these fancier methods. Lots of Web designers do so anyway to accommodate old or off-brand Web browsers.

If you're using frames, make sure to include NOFRAMES content with all the same links the folks who go through the framed version get. If you're using image maps or image links, toss in a text link somewhere on the page that leads to another page that has text-link versions of all the links from the images.

Another common trick is to put content like that into the text of the page itself. Often, Webmasters hide this bogus text from their human readers by setting its color to the same as the page's background color or by making the text so small that it's barely visible — or both.

This common trick is not the same thing as legitimately using the same terms and phrases several times in different places within the real context of your Web page. If you run a site that deals with airports, for example, the word *runway* may show up hundreds of times on one page, and anyone searching for that term will rightly find your page.

So why not use the trick method? Well, for starters, it doesn't work. Playing these kinds of games with keywords is a fast way to get dropped from the major search engines altogether. The people who run search engines aren't stupid, and they're fully aware of this type of stunt. They don't care for sites that try to stack the deck, because they're in the business of providing good results, and these kinds of tricks skew the results. You don't want to make enemies of the search engine folks; it's much better to keep on their good side.

Even if you do manage to find a workable trick that artificially boosts your ranking, you're not doing yourself any favors. What if you end up number one on every search, but your actual content isn't what you said it was (it's all just a clever use of keywords)? Do you think that the people who drop into your site will be coming back? After they find out that you're not delivering what you promised, they'll be off to other destinations before you can blink, and they won't pay any attention to your listing after that, even if it does turn up on top in their next search.

Some of the Web sites that come up on the first page of search results turn out to be dead links. If those sites had paid more attention to site design fundamentals than to search engine rankings, they might still be around.

Analyzing keywords that other sites are using

Taking a look at what other people are doing with keywords can be instructive. You can find out just what people are searching for plenty of ways; if some of those terms fit in with what you're doing, you may want to work them in. Here are some ways to analyze keywords:

- **The Lycos 50:** The Lycos 50 (`http://50.lycos.com`), shown in Figure 17-1, shows the results of the most popular user searches on Lycos, which are tallied at the end of every week. This listing is particularly informative because it shows the rank for each term in the previous week as well, and it also shows how many weeks each term has been in the top 50.

- **Keyword Live:** One of the best programs you can lay your hands on is Keyword Live, shown in Figure 17-2. It runs a check on several search engines to see what keywords people are typing in and shows you the top 100 keywords for each search engine in real time. That's right — not yesterday's news, not what was hot last week, but right now. You can download it for free from `www.analogx.com/contents/download/network/keyword.htm`. Try it. You'll like it.

- **Keyword Extractor:** After you get Keyword Live, check out Keyword Extractor, another useful freebie by the same author. You can find it at `www.analogx.com/contents/download/network/keyex.htm`. Keyword Extractor lets you analyze Web pages just like search engines do. It indexes all the words on the page and assigns weights to them depending on their frequency of use and position on the page. One of the best ways to use this program is to perform a search at one of the major search sites, follow the links to the top-ranked pages, and run Keyword Extractor on each of those pages. Study the results to see how those pages earned their ranks.

Don't just toss in popular search terms in an attempt to generate bogus hits. Adding *sex* and *MP3* to a site that's about walrus migration patterns won't bring you the kind of visitors you're looking for.

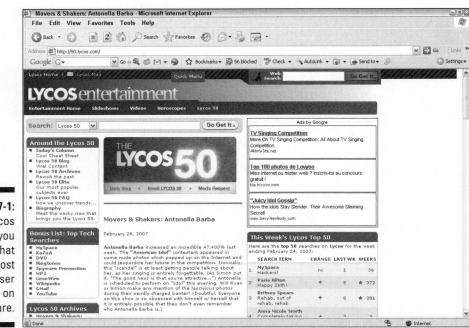

Figure 17-1:
The Lycos 50 lets you see what the most popular user searches on Lycos are.

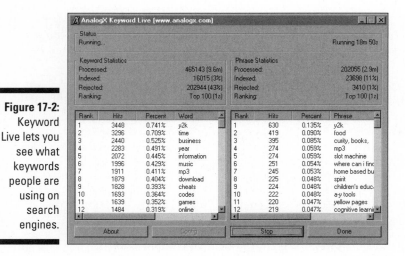

Figure 17-2:
Keyword Live lets you see what keywords people are using on search engines.

Keyword advertising

Analysis of your site's keywords is also important in the multifaceted world of *keyword advertising*. That phrase means a lot of things to a lot of people. I discuss one aspect of it in Chapter 15 — the use of Google AdSense to place targeted ads on Web sites and in search results. The flip side of this process is Google AdWords (`http://adwords.google.com`), which is where the advertisements come from.

The nice thing about Google AdSense is that it pays you to use it. With programs such as Google AdWords or Yahoo! Search Marketing (`http://searchmarketing.yahoo.com`), however, you'll be getting a bill rather than a check. If you've always thought of Google, Yahoo!, and such Web staples as free, think again — this is where they make their money. Just like TV or radio, it's the advertisers who pay for it all. They do this by buying space on a search engine's results page. (See Figure 17-3.) Which results page, though, and where? That depends upon the keyword the user entered and several other factors. All other things being equal, the advertiser who pays the most gets the top slot. The ad might also be limited to display in certain geographical regions.

If you're still with me, don't worry — the bill can fit within almost any type of budget. Perhaps the most important limitation you can specify is the most money you're willing to spend in a month. Although you can officially get started with pocket change (Google AdWords has a mere $5 registration fee at this writing), it's important to manage your advertising budget carefully. Fortunately, prompt feedback is a normal feature of these advertising programs. If you'd like to start advertising with Google AdWords, be sure to check out *AdWords For Dummies,* by Howie Jacobson (Wiley Publishing).

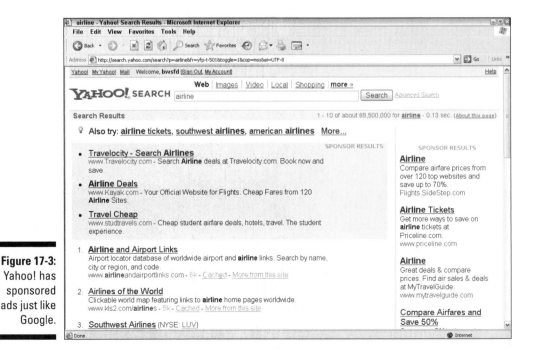

Figure 17-3: Yahoo! has sponsored ads just like Google.

Submitting to the Search Sites

You can just sit around and wait for a spider or robot to trip over your site. Sooner or later, that'll probably happen all by itself — the search engines are always hungry for more sites to add. But being proactive and making certain that your site is listed is a lot smarter. You can submit your site on your own, or you can use services that do it for you.

Doing it yourself

Why bother doing it yourself when you can pay someone else to do it for you? Well, there's the obvious advantage of saving money. If you're on a shoe-string budget, that can matter. If not, you're likely going to say something like, "It's more cost effective for me to pay someone to get my site submitted to search engines than for me to take time away from actually running the business." Well, there's something to be said for that reasoning, too.

But there's nothing like making sure that the job gets done right. And it's a wise Webmaster who gets thoroughly familiar with the many variations on how the search engines want Web page URLs to be submitted. I strongly recommend that you try submitting to at least a few of them yourself. Table 17-2 gives the URLs of the submission pages for several major search sites.

Table 17-2	Search Site Submission Pages
Submission Page	*Web Address*
AlltheWeb	`www.alltheweb.com/help/webmaster/submit_site`
AltaVista	`http://addurl.altavista.com/addurl/new`
Ask.com	`http://ask.ineedhits.com/sitesubmit.asp`
Google	`www.google.com/addurl.html`
Yahoo! (commercial sites)	`http://add.yahoo.com/fast/add?+Business`
Yahoo! (noncommercial sites)	`http://add.yahoo.com/fast/add`

Some search engines charge for adding your site to their listings, and more may do so. Yahoo! offers unpaid listings only for noncommercial sites. Make sure that you find out if it's free before you submit.

Most search engines accept submissions in pretty much the same way, and the process is pretty simple. With Google, for example, you simply go to `www.google.com/addurl.html` (see Figure 17-4), enter your URL, and click the Add URL button.

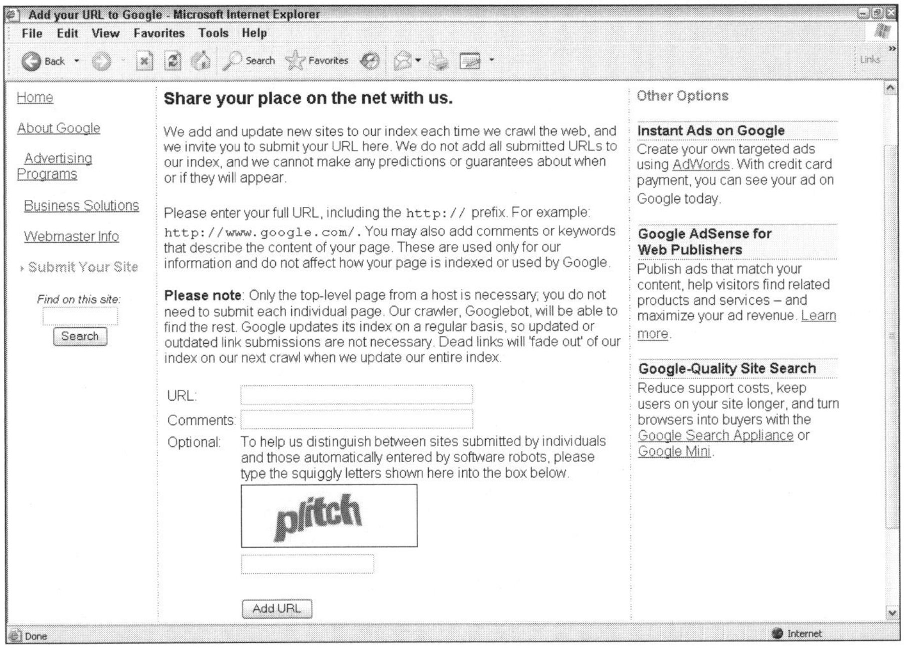

Figure 17-4: Google is the one search site you must list with.

With Yahoo!, you have to give a little bit more effort, but the process is still relatively easy. Here's how you do it:

1. **Go to `http://search.yahoo.com/dir` and browse until you find the category you want to be listed in.**

2. **Click the Suggest a Site link in the upper-right corner of the page. (See Figure 17-5.)**

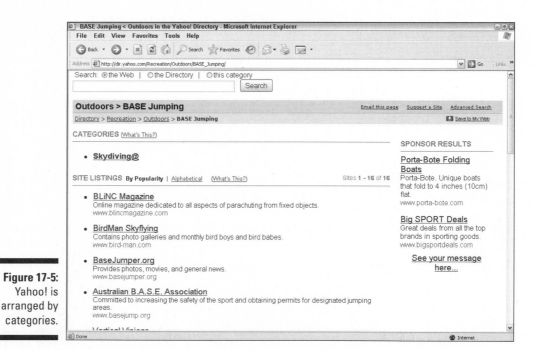

Figure 17-5:
Yahoo! is
arranged by
categories.

3. **On the resulting page, click the Standard Consideration button.**

The next thing that you'll see is a page that shows which category you've chosen.

4. **Scroll down and click the Continue button.**

5. **Enter your Yahoo! ID and password.**

This is the same as you use for Yahoo! Mail or Yahoo! Messenger. If you don't have one, just click the Sign Up link to get it. When you've finished that, move on to Step 6.

6. **Enter the requested information, such as title and URL of your site, on the page shown in Figure 17-6.**

7. **Click the Submit button.**

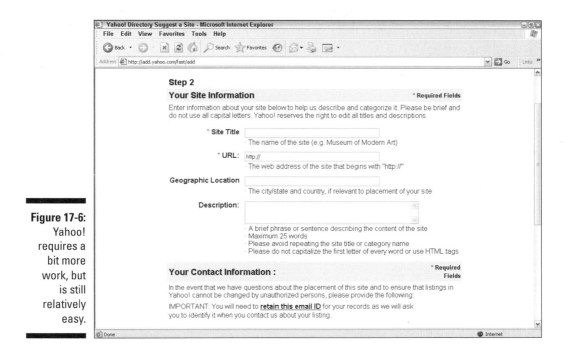

Figure 17-6:
Yahoo!
requires a
bit more
work, but
is still
relatively
easy.

Using submission services

You get what you pay for, you know? When it comes to Web site submission services, that saying really hits home. Very few of the free services submit your URL to anywhere near as many search sites as the paid ones do. However, the paid services submit your info to many more search engines, but you don't get much payback from listing in all the obscure ones.

Many Web site submission services fall into a gray area, offering limited free services but charging more for anything extra. The paid services may or may not be worthwhile, depending on how well they know their stuff. If you're going to part with your hard-earned bucks, you have the right to ask them a few questions first. Make sure that the people you're dealing with understand the differences among the search engines. If they can't tell you things like which ones accept HTML coding in their listings or how long a description is acceptable at a particular search site, you may not be getting much bang for your buck. You may be better off doing it yourself.

ProBoost (www.proboost.com), shown in Figure 17-7, is one classy example of folks who know what search engines are all about. With ProBoost, you don't just fill out a form. You can actually work with real, live people who are committed to your success. ProBoost has free telephone support and a chat room, too.

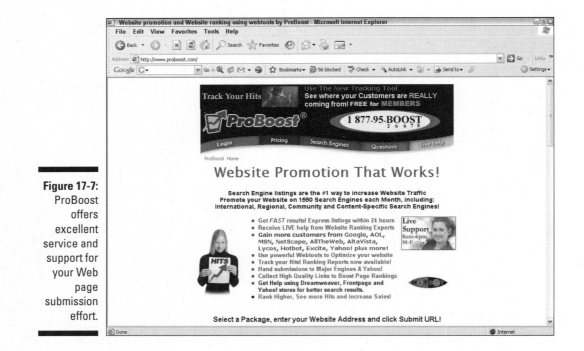

Figure 17-7: ProBoost offers excellent service and support for your Web page submission effort.

Keeping out of the search sites

Not everybody wants all their pages indexed and offered to the general public at a search site. There are two methods you can use to keep a search engine's robot from indexing your site. One may require the assistance of your network administrator or Internet service provider. The other you can do yourself.

Getting outside assistance

For a long time, the only way to lock a search engine out was to use a file called robots.txt. This file, located in the top-level domain directory (the same one your home page goes into), lists all banned search bots as well as directories that can't be searched. The reason you may need some professional help here is that unless you run your own dedicated server, you may not have access to the top-level domain directory. Putting `robots.txt` any-where else doesn't do you any good. If your Web site is housed on your ISP's server or on a virtual server, it's really in a subdirectory of a dedicated Web server. What you need to do in this case is to let the people who run your HTTP server know which directories you don't want searched. They'll take care of the rest, which consists of simply listing those directories in a text file.

The following example shows how to block all search bots from searching two sample directories:

```
User-agent: *
Disallow: /~mine/private/
Disallow: /~mine/personal/
```

Someone who wants to pry into your site can get a good start by looking at the contents of your `robots.txt` file. After all, it contains a list of all the directories and files you don't want the world to see. If you have anything confidential in those areas, `robots.txt` is a road map pointing straight to it.

Doing it yourself

If you want to grab control yourself, or if you just want to avoid using `robots.txt`, you can turn to that good old friend, the META tag. Remember that I said that tag is versatile. Well, this is another useful application for it. By assigning the `name` attribute a value of `robots` and adding one or more variables to the `content` attribute, you can specify your desires about the page it's in.

By default, a search robot will both index your page, adding the words in it to the search site's database, and follow all the links on the page. If you want to disallow both of these behaviors, add the following HTML code in the HEAD element of your file:

```
<META name="robots" content="noindex,nofollow">
```

You can accomplish the same thing by using a value of `none`:

```
<META name="robots" content="none">
```

Technically, you can do the opposite of this, allowing both options, by using a value of `all`, but there's no point to doing that. If you want both options working, just don't do anything.

To allow the indexing, but keep robots from following your links, you use this line of code:

```
<META name="robots" content="nofollow">
```

Remember that the robot's indexing and following of links are default behaviors, so you don't need to specify either one if you're allowing it. Thus, the preceding code doesn't mention indexing at all. You could, if you want to be pedantic about it, say the same thing like this:

```
<META name="robots" content="index,nofollow">
```

The situation would have to be unusual, but you may wish for a robot to follow the links in a particular directory without adding the pages in it to a search engine. To allow a robot to follow your links, but deny it from indexing, use this code:

```
<META name="robots" content="noindex">
```

Checking Your Search Site Position

You need to follow up on your submissions to make sure that you're listed (different search sites react on different timetables) as well as to find out where you land in the rankings when your keywords are used in a search.

Obviously, the fastest way to find out both of these things is to log on to the search engines you've submitted to and check things out. First, enter the name of your site and see if it comes up. If not, and it's been more time than the search engine is supposed to take, you may want to resubmit to it.

This is also a great way to find out which other Web sites have links to yours, because any page with your site's name on it will show up in the search results. (See the next section "Investigating Reciprocal Linking.")

If your site does come up, you'll want to enter the keywords from your site as search terms. This quickly shows you where you fall in the rankings. Assuming that some other sites show up on top of your own, it's worthwhile to take a look at their source code to see what keywords they use. Also, don't forget to look over their pages carefully. This is one of those rare instances where your competitors' techniques are literally an open book.

Investigating Reciprocal Linking

Reciprocal linking is the Web's equivalent of "You scratch my back, and I'll scratch yours." The way it works is this: You put in a link on your page to another Web site, and the other Web site returns the favor by putting in a link to yours. Even directly competing sites can benefit from linking to one another, just as two restaurants can happily exist side by side.

Finding sites to link to

So whom do you want to link with? Well, the simple answer is "anybody and everybody." The smart answer, though, is "the best and most popular sites in my category." What's best is a matter of opinion, but it's pretty easy to find the most popular ones, and you can use this technique to piggyback on their success.

What you need to do is to spend some time working the search engines. Here's the drill:

1. **Enter the keywords you think people would use to find your site.**

2. **Follow the links in the results to the other sites that are similar to your own.**

   All search engines will return some poor responses, so don't automatically assume that all the results would be good reciprocal link sources for your Web site. Use your own judgment.

3. **Look for an e-mail link to the site's owner.**

   Typically, you can find this type of link at the bottom of the page, but it may be anywhere.

4. **Click the e-mail link and send the site's Webmaster a message politely suggesting that you both link up.**

It may be helpful to put in a link to the other site first. That way, you can say something like, "I've linked to your site and would appreciate a return link from yours." This takes the discussion out of the realm of the hypothetical and puts the other site's Webmaster under an obligation to respond in kind. There are no guarantees, but most people do reciprocate.

Sometimes, you can't find any contact info on a Web site, no matter how hard you look. If that's the case and you really want to set up a reciprocal link with that site, you can run a search on the site's domain name by using a WhoIs service. WhoIs identifies the administrative, billing, and technical contacts for a domain. The best known one is at Network Solutions (www. networksolutions.com/whois/index.jsp). Or you can run a search from your own system with software such as WhoIs ULTRA from AnalogX (www. analogx.com/contents/download/network/whois.htm).

Another worthwhile program you may want to check out is Link Trader. You use Link Trader to create a database of all the people you've set up reciprocal links with, and it checks those sites to verify that the link back to you still exists. Keep the database up-to-date and run the program on a regular basis, and you can quickly spot any sites that drop your link. Then you can e-mail the Webmasters and ask them to put the link back in. You can download Link Trader Pro at www.homebizfactory.com/Link_Trader_Pro.html.

Many search engines (Google, for example) consider the number of other sites with links to yours when determining how high you rank. This means that of two sites, with everything else being equal, the one with more links leading to it from other sites shows up before the other one in search results. Reciprocal linking is a powerful tool that you can use to legitimately boost your own site's ratings.

Joining Web rings

Web rings are a kind of super reciprocal link arrangement. Instead of making a reciprocal link between two sites, you make it with an entire group of similar sites at a time. You can find Web rings on just about any topic you can think of, and many such rings are listed at `http:// dir.webring.com/rw` or `www.ringsurf.com`. (See Figure 17-8.) You can also start your own Web ring if you want.

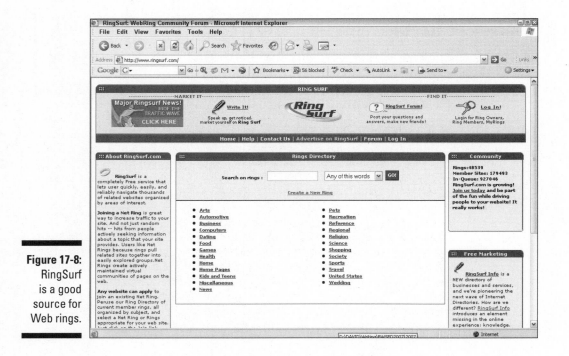

Figure 17-8: RingSurf is a good source for Web rings.

The weakness of Web rings is that they link in a ring. In other words, each one links to the previous one in the list and the next one in the list. If any site drops out of the ring, that messes up the whole thing, just as if you broke a link in a chain.

Joining a banner exchange

In a *banner exchange,* each member creates a banner ad and submits it to a central site. That site, the exchange itself, automates the process of displaying all the members' ads on all the other members' Web sites. A banner exchange sounds like a great idea, but in practice, few banner exchanges survive for very long. If you're considering joining one, make sure that you ask how long it's been in operation. Also make it a point to contact current members and see how satisfied they are with the exchange.

That said, joining a banner exchange is an easy task. You fill out a simple application form on the exchange's Web site; then you send the exchange your banner and place some HTML code on your site. That's all there is to it — the exchange handles everything else. Several reputable banner exchanges are listed in Table 17-3.

Online Sources for Getting the Word Out about Your Site

Table 17-3 lists some places on the World Wide Web where you can find more information on the topics covered in this chapter.

Table 17-3	Online Resources for Publicizing Your Site
Web Site Name	*Web Address*
Add Me.com	www.addme.com
Apex Pacific	www.edynamicsoft.com
Guerilla Marketing Online	www.gmarketing.com
HitExchange	www.hitx.net
LinkBuddies	www.linkbuddies.com
MetaSpy	www.metaspy.com
Search Engine Watch	www.searchenginewatch.com
WebCrawler Popular Searches	http://www.webcrawler.com/ info.wbcrwl/searchspy
Wordtracker	www.wordtracker.com

Chapter 18

Web Aerobics: Tuning Up Your Site

In This Chapter

▶ Validating your HTML

▶ Finding broken links

▶ Fine-tuning your site

*M*aking Web pages is pretty easy, but the one thing that many people overlook is that about a hundred zillion things can go wrong with them. Even if your Web pages work perfectly on your favorite Web browser, they may not work on all browsers. Even if all your links are functional, some of the sites they're aimed at will go down or out. Even if you have great graphics on your site, they may slow down your page load so much that nobody is willing to wait for them to download.

So this chapter takes a look at several tools that make your pages work. Here's a sampling of what these tools can do for you:

✔ **Examine your HTML code for errors:** These tools point out errors or possible problem areas.

✔ **Find broken links:** You can use programs that follow all your links for you and let you know which ones are working right and which are broken.

✔ **Check spelling:** Some handy tools make shoor yore spelling things rite.

Don't miss this tour — your visitors will appreciate what these tools can do for your site.

W3C HTML Validation Service

This one's the official site, the straight-from-the-horse's-mouth place. W3C is the short form of World Wide Web Consortium, and the folks there are the ones who put out the HTML standard. Now, anyone who's done much with Web pages already knows that some things that work on Internet Explorer don't work on Netscape Navigator, and vice versa. (And that's not even taking third-party Web browsers into consideration.) If you write your HTML to fit the official W3C standard, you'll miss out on some capabilities, such as setting page margins, but you'll also be guaranteed that your Web pages will work in every browser. Okay, some odd browsers out on the fringes may not support the W3C standard, but they're not much of a concern.

To do a quick check on whether your Web page meets the official standard, follow these steps:

1. **Go to http://validator.w3.org.**

   The W3C validation form appears, as shown in Figure 18-1.

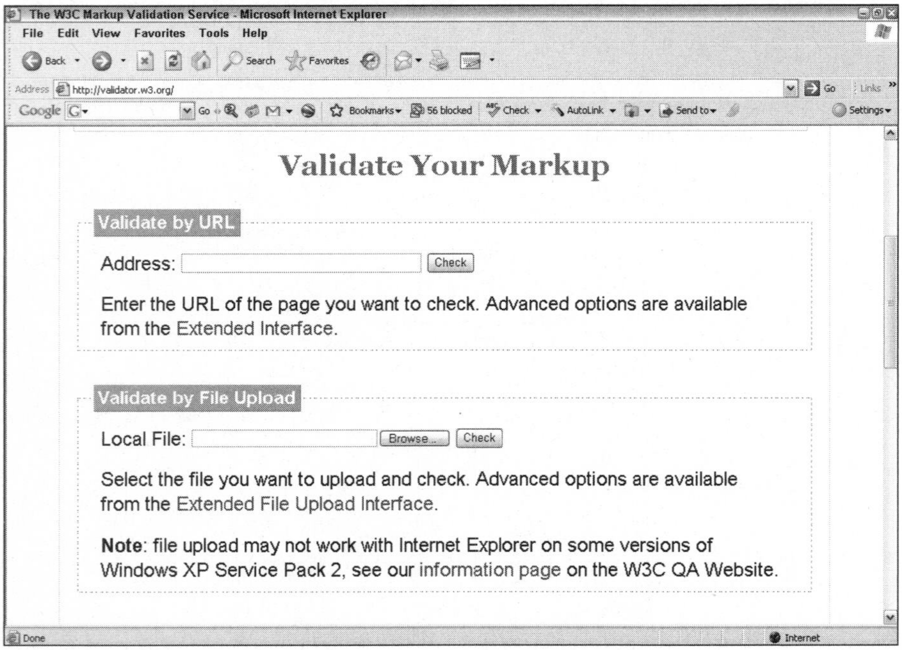

Figure 18-1:
The W3C validation form helps you check your pages for conformance to the HTML standard.

2. **If the Web page you want to check is on the World Wide Web, enter its URL in the Address text box under Validate by URL. If the Web page is**

on your hard drive, enter its location in the Local File text box under Validate by File Upload or, better yet, click the Browse button to navigate to the file.

Alternatively, you can scroll down and directly paste your HTML code into the text area under Validate by Direct Input. (See Figure 18-2.)

3. **Click the Check button for the type of input you're using.**

   The results of the test appear on a new page.

To run a test with more advanced options, follow these steps:

1. **If the Web page you want to check is on the World Wide Web, go to `http://validator.w3.org/detailed.html`; if it's on your hard drive, go to `http://validator.w3.org/file-upload.html`.**

2. **Enter the URL of the Web page in the Address text box. (See Figure 18-3.)**

   If you're testing a file on your local drive, the form at `http://validator.w3.org/file-upload.html` is slightly different from the one shown in Figure 18-3. A Browse button appears to the right of the File text box. Click that button to search your hard drive and select the file you want to test. From this point on, both approaches are identical.

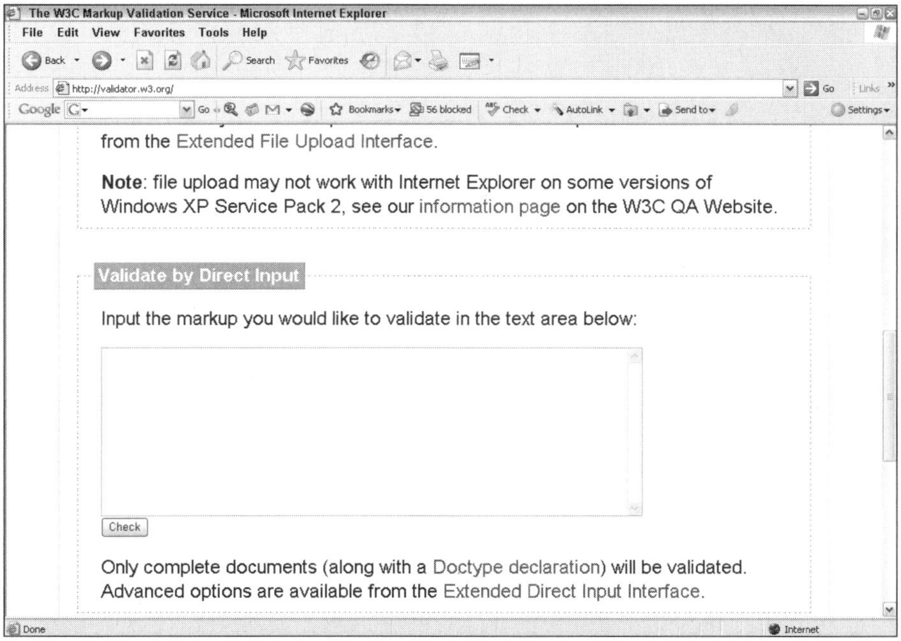

Figure 18-2:
The Validate by Direct Input option lets you paste code directly.

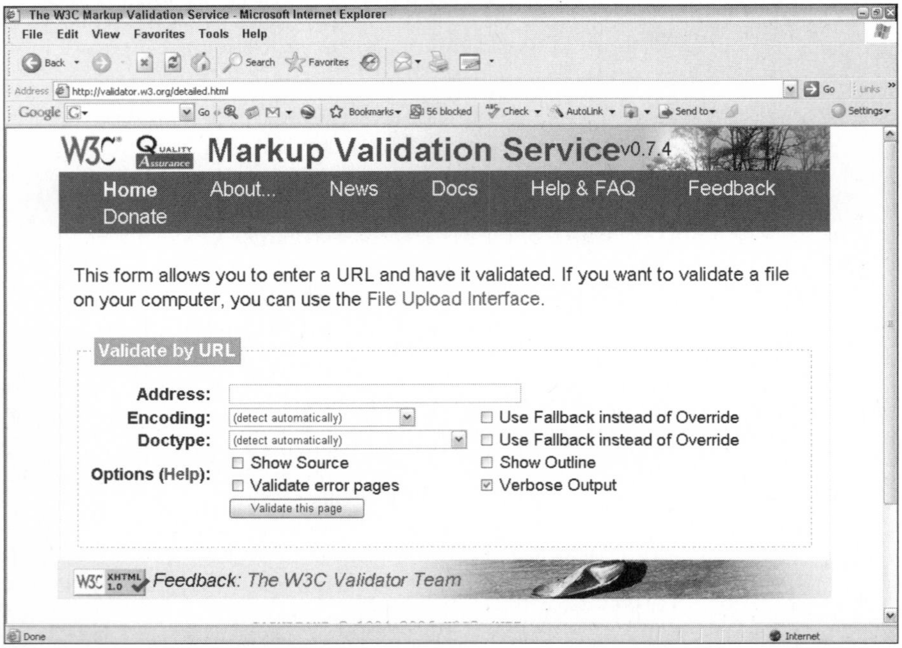

Figure 18-3:
The detailed version of the form gives you more options.

3. **If you want to specify the encoding scheme the page uses, select one from the Encoding drop-down list. Otherwise, leave it set to automatically detect the encoding.**

   When you select the Use Fallback instead of Override check box, the validator will use the specified encoding only if there is no encoding scheme specified in the code of your Web page.

4. **If you want to specify the version of HTML the page uses, select one from the Doctype drop-down list. Otherwise, leave it set to automatically detect the HTML version.**

5. **Select any combination of the following check boxes:**

   • *Show Source:* Select this check box if you want the HTML source code from the tested document to show up on the report. This is most useful if you want to sit down with a hard copy of the report, especially if you need to go over it with other members of a Web design team.

   • *Validate Error Pages:* Select this check box if you want to process pages that generate errors.

   • *Show Outline:* Select this check box if you want to have the hierarchy of heading elements (H1 through H6) shown on the report. If no heading elements are on the page, this option won't show any results.

   • *Verbose Output:* Leave this check box selected if you want the most detailed report.

6. **Click the Validate This Page button (or, for the file-upload version, the Validate This File button).**

The results of the test appear on a new page. They're pretty self-explanatory, but if you need more information, you can click the Explain link next to each error.

If your pages don't fit the official standard, it doesn't necessarily mean that your pages are bad. The most important thing is to find out whether your pages work properly in the Web browsers you expect your site visitors to be using.

The official standard is much stricter than the coding on a Web page has to be in order for the page to work. Both of the major Web browsers (Internet Explorer and Netscape Navigator) gleefully overlook all sorts of variations from the standard (or even outright errors) and still display the page as you intended. And in many instances, the people who wrote the standard just plain disagree with the majority of Web page authors on how things should be done.

Checking Those Links

Few things are more irritating than a bunch of broken links on a site. Visitors won't mind the occasional click that takes them to a Page Not Found error — after all, the Web is a fast-changing place. But when broken links show up over and over again, visitors will decide that your site isn't worth all the trouble you put them through.

So what can you do to minimize broken links? You can take all the care you want with your site's internal links, but the links that lead to other people's sites are out of your control. Sites go down, and pages and files change location, but the Webmasters in charge of those sites aren't likely to keep you notified. If you have lots of links, keeping track of all those updated links can be a full-time job.

The real solution is to click every single link in your entire site on a regular basis. Fortunately, you don't have to wear out your mousing finger doing this manually. This is the kind of thing that computers excel at. After all, one of their main purposes is to perform repetitive actions rapidly so that you don't have to. Here are a few programs that can do the work for you.

2bone.com's Link Checker

Link Checker by 2bone.com is a service that tests the links on any Web page, and it's totally free. Really, no strings attached. No advertising commitments, no registration — you don't even need to supply your e-mail address. How nice is that?

To check the links on a Web page, follow these steps:

1. **Go to www.2bone.com/links/linkchecker.shtml.**

   The Link Checker page appears, as shown in Figure 18-4.

2. **In the Step 1 text box, enter the URL of the page you want to check.**

   Note that you cannot check more than one page at a time.

3. **In the Step 2 area, select either the Express Lane option button or the I Can Wait Service option button.**

   The difference between the two is that the Express Lane option is limited to ten items per page, and the other takes a lot longer because it waits until it can display all the test results on one page (exactly how long depends on the number of links on the site).

4. **Click the Test My Links button.**

   While you wait for the test results, a pop-up window appears, which talks about the 2bone.com Web site. You need to click the Close link to get back to the Web page, which, depending upon how fast a service you selected, should be showing up any second now with the results of your links test.

Figure 18-4:
Link Checker by 2bone.com lets you know how many links on your Web page are broken.

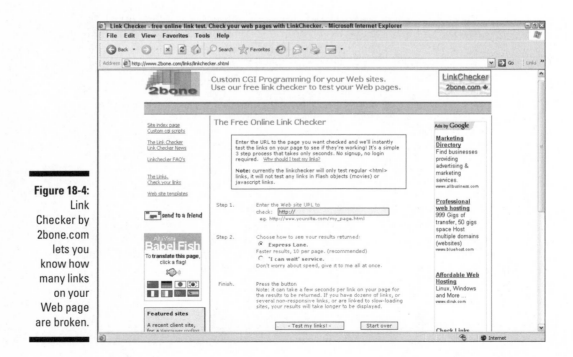

LinkAlarm

LinkAlarm (www.linkalarm.com) is a commercial operation that runs a good service at a reasonable price. One of the nicest features is that the LinkAlarm report separates internal and external links so that you can focus on your site's problems apart from the troubles that other Webmasters are having. The best news is that you can give it a try for a couple of weeks gratis. If free is wonderful, a free trial is the next best thing.

Here's how to get started:

1. **Go to www.linkalarm.com/trial.**

   The Register New Account page appears, as shown in Figure 18-5.

2. **Enter your first and last names and your e-mail address.**

3. **Enter the URL of the site you want to check.**

4. **Under How Did You Find Us, either select one of the options in the drop-down list or type another reason in the text box just below it.**

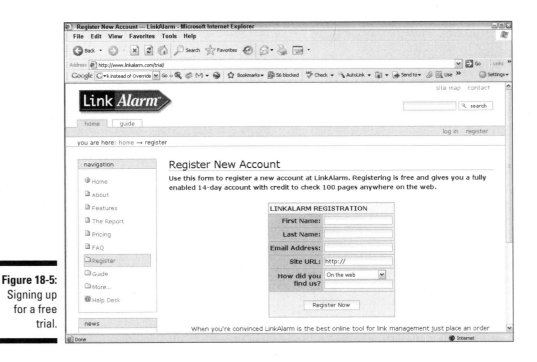

Figure 18-5:
Signing up for a free trial.

5. **Click the Register Now button.**

   Although you receive an e-mail message giving you the Web address you need to manage your free account, the service also automatically takes you there at this point. Figure 18-6 shows the resulting page.

6. **Make sure that the site URL is correct and then select one of the option buttons to choose the frequency of testing.**

7. **Select a category for your site from the Category drop-down list.**

8. **Click the Continue button.**

   This takes you to the Enter New Site page (see Figure 18-7) containing the URL and frequency you selected.

9. **Select the category again. (It doesn't carry over.)**

10. **Click the Enter This Site button.**

    The testing automatically begins. Note that the words *enter this site* mean that the information on this site is entered into your list of sites (which, at this point, contains only the one).

11. **When the testing is complete, you receive an e-mail message notification. Click the link in the message to view your broken links report.**

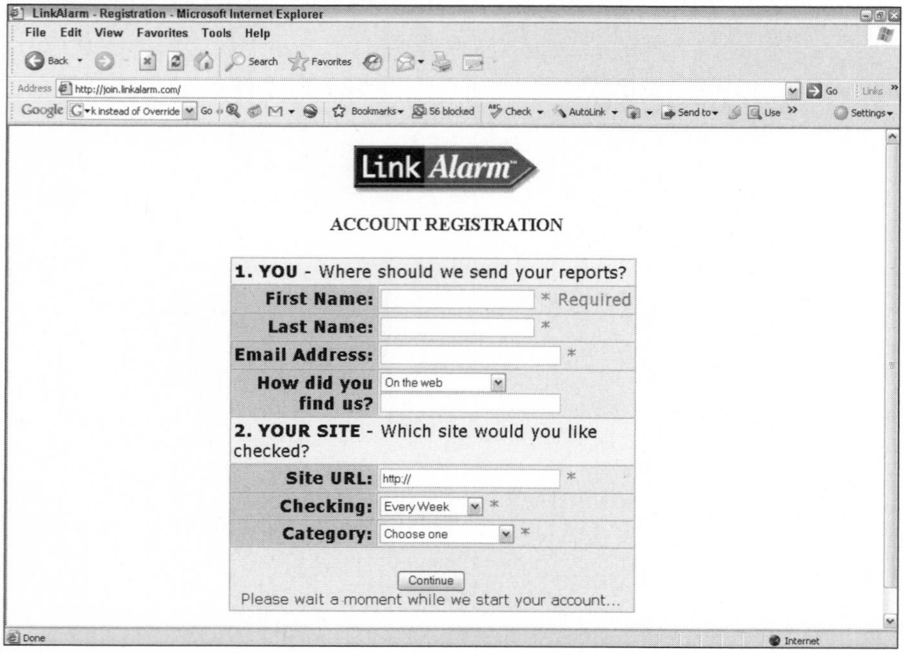

Figure 18-6:
Adding a new site.

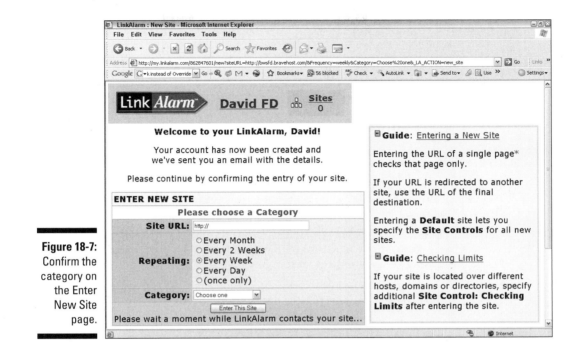

Figure 18-7: Confirm the category on the Enter New Site page.

Testing Your Site with NetMechanic

Although the tightly focused Web tool sites are very popular and extremely useful, you can find some really nice places on the World Wide Web that are like smorgasbords of Web tools. Sites like these are mostly fond of automotive metaphors — NetMechanic and the Web Site Garage, for instance. The Web Site Garage also includes GIF Lube. You get the idea. You won't find much of anything along the lines of The Site Garden or The Page Salon. Well, whatever these sites are called, go to them, bookmark them, and return to them often. You'll be glad to have them handy.

NetMechanic (www.netmechanic.com) does a whole bunch of things for you, all in one simple move. Or with a bit of effort, you can customize the process — using a custom dictionary for the spell-checker, for example. NetMechanic has both a free version and a paid one. The freebie is limited to a maximum of 5 pages with a maximum of 25 links per page, although the paid version handles up to 400 pages or 5,000 links on one site.

NetMechanic will run these five tests on the page or site you choose:

- ✔ Link Check
- ✔ HTML Check & Repair

✔ Browser Compatibility

✔ Load Time Check

✔ Spell Check

To run the site test with all the default settings, follow these steps:

1. **Go to www.netmechanic.com/products/HTML_Toolbox_ FreeSample.shtml.**

   NetMechanic's HTML Toolbox Free Sample page appears, as shown in Figure 18-8.

2. **Enter the URL of the page or site you want to check in the URL text box.**

3. **Select the option button for the number of pages you want to check. Your two options are 1 and 5 pages; if your total pages fall somewhere between those numbers, select 5.**

4. **Type your address in the Email text box; if you want to view the report on-screen, don't enter anything here.**

   If you selected the 5-page option, you have to enter an e-mail address.

5. **Click the Test Now button.**

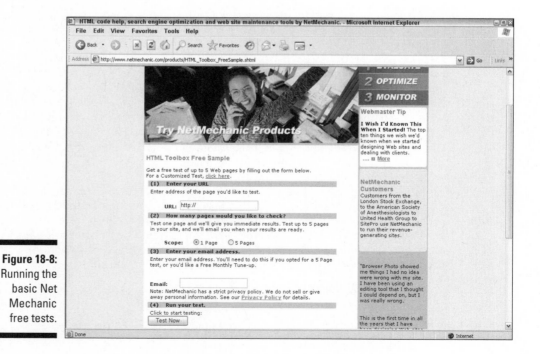

Figure 18-8: Running the basic Net Mechanic free tests.

NetMechanic runs its suite of tests on your site and generates a report on-screen or sends a report to your e-mail account, depending on which option you chose in Step 4 of the preceding steps. The on-screen version shows a progress bar while you're waiting. The more complex your site is, the longer the process takes to complete. If you want to abort the process, the progress screen has a Cancel button you can click.

To run a customized test, try this instead:

1. **Go to www.netmechanic.com/toolbox/power_user.htm.**

2. **Enter the URL of the page or site you want to check in the URL text box. (See Figure 18-9.)**

3. **Deselect the check boxes for any tests you don't want to run.**

4. **Select the option button for the number of pages you want to check. You can choose either 1 or 5 pages.**

   If your total pages fall somewhere between those numbers, select 5.

5. **Enter your address in the Email text box; if you want to view the report on-screen, don't enter anything here.**

   If you selected the 5-page option, you have to enter an e-mail address.

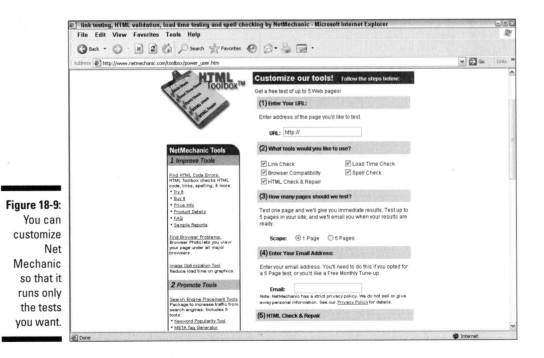

Figure 18-9:
You can customize Net Mechanic so that it runs only the tests you want.

6. **Under HTML Check & Repair, select the check box if you want to test for handicapped accessibility.**

   Under Browser Compatibility, NetMechanic lists the percentages of people who use different versions of the two major Web browsers when visiting its site.

7. **If you have different figures available from the site you're testing, enter those numbers for each of the listed Web browsers.**

8. **Under Spell Check, enter the URL of a custom dictionary (if you have one relating to the topic of the site you're testing) in the text box; if you don't want to spell check words in uppercase, leave the Ignore Words in Upper Case check box selected.**

9. **Click the Test Now button.**

NetMechanic runs the selected tests on your site and generates a report on-screen or sends a report to your e-mail account, depending on which option you selected in Step 5 in the preceding step list. The on-screen version shows a progress bar while you're waiting. The more complex your site is, the longer the process takes to complete. If you want to abort the process, the progress screen has a Cancel button you can click.

Check out the NetMechanic image file optimizer, GIFBot, at `www.netmechanic.com/GIFBot/optimize-graphic.htm`. It handles both GIF and JPEG file formats.

Online Sources for Fine-Tuning Your Site

Table 18-1 lists some places on the World Wide Web where you can find more resources like the ones covered in this chapter.

Table 18-1	Online Resources for Fine-Tuning Your Site
Web Site Name	**Web Address**
Dr. Watson	`http://watson.addy.com`
Google Analytics	`www.google.com/analytics/`
Link Valet	`www.htmlhelp.com/tools/valet`
LinkScan/QuickCheck	`www.elsop.com/quick`
OptiView Web Acceleration	`www.gifwizard.com`
Site Check	`www.siteowner.com/sitecheck.cfm`

Web Site Name	Web Address
W3C CSS Validation Service	`http://jigsaw.w3.org/cssvalidator`
W3C Link Checker	`http://validator.w3.org/checklink`
WDG HTML Validator	`www.htmlhelp.com/tools/validator`
WebXACT	`http://webxact.watchfire.com`
Xenu's Link Sleuth	`http://home.snafu.de/tilman/xenulink.html`

Chapter 19

Keeping in Touch with Visitors

· ·

· ·

*W*hen someone initially visits your site, you naturally want that person to keep coming back. One of the natural ways to do that is to keep in touch by letting visitors know what's new and reminding them that you're there. The problem is *spam* — no, not the canned meat — it's Internet slang for unsolicited commercial e-mail. If you haven't gotten plenty of it already, you probably don't have an e-mail address at all. Get-rich-quick schemes, health products that make you live forever, and all sorts of other garbage zoom back and forth across the Net, clogging mailboxes and raising hackles.

So how do you keep in touch without spamming? The answer is simple: You send e-mail messages only to those visitors who request them. That way, everybody's happy. You get to build up a following among your visitors, and they get to receive the information they ask for. This chapter presents tools that make it easy for your visitors to keep up with what's going on at your site while keeping you out of the doghouse with your Web space provider.

Using Autoresponders

Autoresponders are programs that automatically send e-mail messages to visitors who request them. The visitor makes the request either by sending an e-mail to your autoresponder address or by making the request through a form on your Web site.

What you can do with autoresponders

Okay, so what? Well, the way you use an autoresponder all depends on what your message says. Say, for example, that your e-mail message contains your current catalog or the sale of the week. Sound like something useful?

You can even set up several different documents that people can request. This technique is useful if the products or services you sell or talk about can be easily organized into categories. For example, a Web site that sells software might put together one gigantic catalog or set up several links, such as Click Here to Receive Our Productivity Catalog and Click Here to Get Information on Graphics Software.

So far, so good. What you have is a perfectly spam-free way for people to get detailed information on demand, and the autoresponder does all the work for you. All you do is write up the documents and upload them once. From then on, the autoresponder takes care of all the drudgery.

But another feature of autoresponders borders on spammishness. You can set them up so that they send not only one message but also several different messages over a period of time. The basic idea is that it often takes more than one contact to close a sale, which is true, as anyone in sales knows. The problem is that the person making the request for the first document isn't requesting a whole series of messages over several weeks or months. It's a gray area, and you should be well advised to carefully consider whether to use that feature.

Check with your Web space provider to see whether it has autoresponders available as part of your basic service. Or read on to find out about Get Response.com's autoresponder.

Using GetResponse.com

GetResponse.com (www.getresponse.com) has both free and paid autoresponders. The basic difference between them is that there's no advertising in the paid version. With both versions, you get multiple messaging, although there's a limit of five automated timed responses for the free version. GetResponse.com has covered the spam issue by adding removal information at the bottom of all autoresponses. Anyone who requests information and doesn't want to receive multiple messages can simply unsubscribe and he won't receive any of the follow-ups.

One of the nicest aspects of this autoresponder is the ability to format your autoresponse messages with HTML, so you aren't limited to plain text.

TIP

If you decide to go with the paid version of GetResponse, the company offers a 30-day money-back guarantee.

Signing up

To sign up with GetResponse.com, follow these steps:

1. **Go to www.getresponse.com/orderfree.html.**

2. **Enter the information requested in the form shown in Figure 19-1 and then click the Submit button at the bottom of the page.**

   The Web page that appears is filled with all the reasons why you should switch from a free to a paid service.

3. **If you want to switch to the paid service, click the Click for GetResponse Pro button. Otherwise, click the Click for GetResponse Free button.**

   You receive an e-mail message containing your password and a couple of useful links.

Figure 19-1:
The Get Response. com application page is where you enter your basic information.

Setting up your account

To set up your autoresponder message with GetResponse.com, follow these steps:

1. **Go to www.getresponse.com/login.html, enter your account name and password, and click the Log In button.**

   This takes you to the Easy Setup Wizard, shown in Figure 19-2.

2. **Enter the required information (company name, address, and so on).**

3. **Scroll down to the Signature section. (See Figure 19-3.)**

   The information you entered in Step 2 corresponds to simple codes — the address is [[address]], the country is [[country]], and so on. The default signature is shown in the Preview window. If this is not to your liking, simply click within the Signature text area and type your changes. You can use the leftward pointing arrow to insert the codes if you prefer.

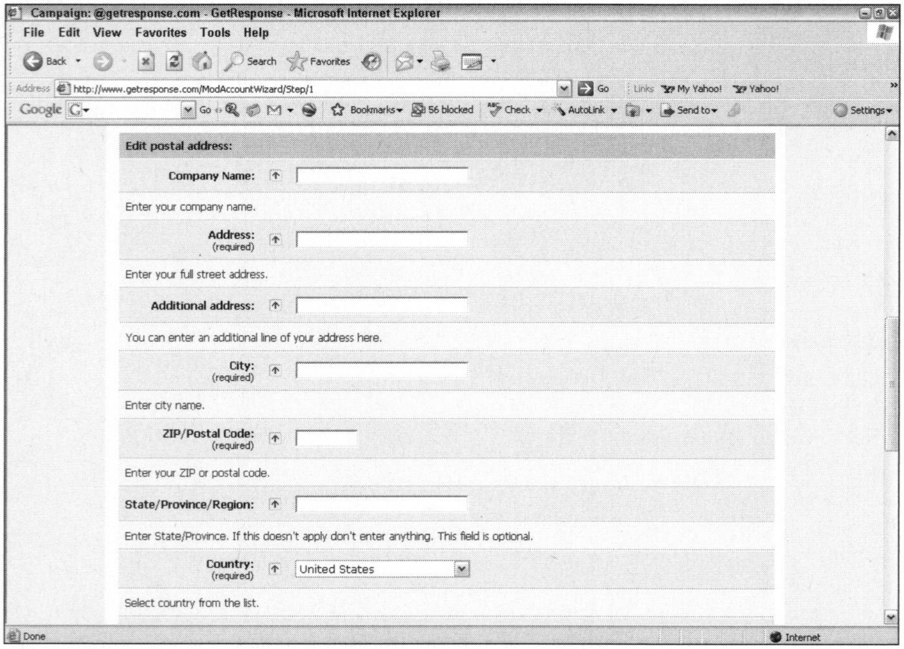

Figure 19-2:
Using the
Easy Setup
Wizard.

4. **Click the Next Step button.**

5. **In the resulting screen, shown in Figure 19-4, enter your personal information (name and e-mail address); then click the Next Step button.**

6. **On the next page, click the You Can Now Start Using Your Account! link.**

7. **Select Edit from the Campaign Actions drop-down list, shown in Figure 19-5.**

8. **Click the OK button.**

9. **Scroll down and click either of the two Create New Message links. (See Figure 19-6.)**

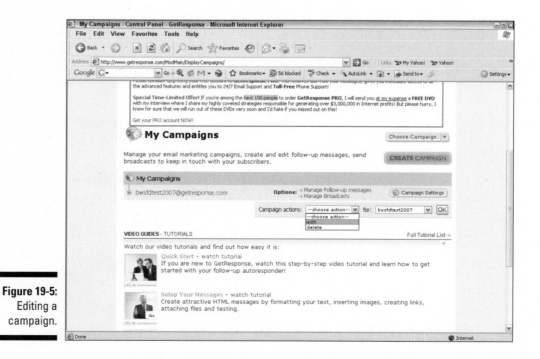

Figure 19-4:
Confirming
your
information.

Figure 19-5:
Editing a
campaign.

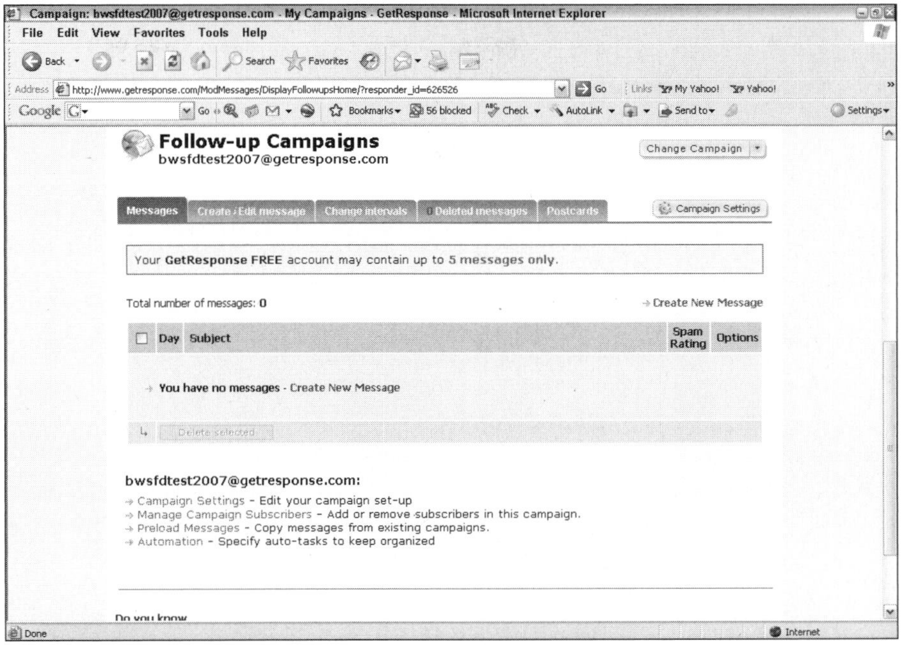

Figure 19-6:
Creating a
new
message.

10. **Type the subject of your message into the Subject text box.**

11. **Enter 0 in the Interval text box so that the message goes out as soon as it's requested.**

12. **Paste your response message into the Plain/text area.**

    Note that the free version has only plain text, but the paid version allows you to use HTML.

13. **In the Message options section, select the check boxes for the options you want.**

    The first two options, Track Click-Throughs of Your Links and Track Sales Generated by This Message, are for those who have signed up with GetResponse's affiliates program, which you can do at www. getresponse.com/affiliate_sign_up.html. (See Chapter 15 for more information on affiliate programs.)

    The third option, Validate HTML code, isn't valid for the free trial because you can't use HTML.

    The fourth and final option, Set Permission Reminder, automatically inserts a paragraph like the one in the upcoming section, "How an opt-in system works," which states that this message was requested by the recipient.

The Add/Remove Attachments link only functions for GetResponse Pro users.

14. **Click the Add Message button.**

15. **Repeat Steps 7 through 14 for any subsequent messages.**

The delay value for follow-up messages (Interval) sets the amount of time to wait from the date of the first request, not the amount of time between each message. So if you want to send a message every day, your first message should have a delay of 0, your second one should have a delay of 1, the third should have a delay of 2, and so on.

Opt-In Newsletters

Newsletters are short, privately produced publications that focus on a single topic. They've been around for hundreds of years, but rising postage costs drove many of them out of business. Now that e-mail is such a common part of life, newsletters are making a major comeback. In its purest form, a newsletter is dedicated to covering current situations, like a newspaper does, but it usually provides a deeper analytical approach. Other newsletters, on the other hand, have nothing to do with news and instead deal with business or professional interests. Because they're often written by one person or a small team of people, they tend to be informal and highly opinionated.

I once received a remarkably honest item that looked a great deal like a newsletter. Under the title, the masthead bore the motto "A Catalog Thinly Disguised as a Newsletter." That's probably the single most common use of newsletters. Even if they're not directly offering products for sale, they're still sales and marketing tools. Many consultants, for example, send out monthly newsletters packed with advice and insights. Yes, they're giving away a service for free this way, but they're also publicizing their expertise.

Many services let you send messages to their own targeted lists of e-mail addresses. Normally, this practice is considered spamming, but if the lists are generated from opt-ins, that's another matter entirely. Opt-in mailing lists are much less intrusive or prone to errors than normal mailing lists, because the safeguard makes it impossible for anybody to sign someone else up for one.

How an opt-in system works

With an opt-in system, a user can enter her e-mail addresses in a form. She then receives a message in her mailbox that asks her to confirm her subscription. If she doesn't reply to that message, her address doesn't go into the system.

The problem with using other people's lists is that because you didn't run the opt-in service yourself, you don't know for sure that all the names on the list are legitimate. And some of the companies that offer these "opportunities" also seem to be heavily into hype and get-rich-quick philosophies. You have to be very careful not to get caught up in spamming.

The Emailxtra.com service described in the next section doesn't adhere to get-rich-quick schemes and spamming. It helps you run your own opt-in system from your own site, while handling most of the workload for you. This setup gives you the best of both worlds.

Although you're using an opt-in system, it's still a good idea to begin your newsletter with something like this:

> "*For subscribers only.* You received this newsletter because you filled out the opt-in form for XYZ News at www.xyznewsoptin.com. We keep our subscriber information completely confidential. If you have any questions, e-mail us at subscriptions@xyznewsoptin.com."

Trying out Emailxtra.com

Emailxtra.com (found, as you might expect, at www.emailxtra.com) is a company that specializes in setting up e-zine newsletters for small- to medium-sized businesses. Its offerings range from self-service accounts where you do all the work to full-service ones where it handles everything.

To set up a free trial account with Emailxtra, follow these steps:

1. **Go to www.emailxtra.com/free_trial.htm.**
2. **Click the Click Here to Signup for Free link, shown in Figure 19-7.**

   The pop-up window, shown in Figure 19-8, appears.

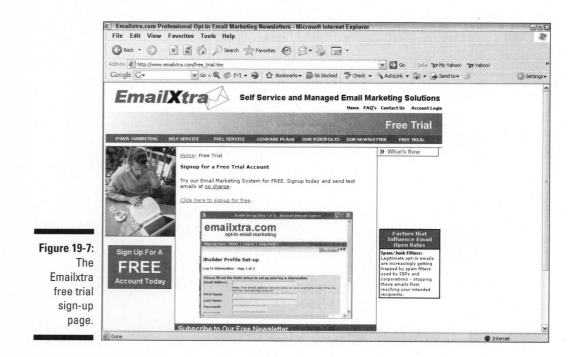

Figure 19-7:
The Emailxtra free trial sign-up page.

3. **In the pop-up window, enter the required information: your e-mail address, your first and last name, and a password (entered twice for confirmation purposes). Then click the Submit button in the lower-right corner of the window.**

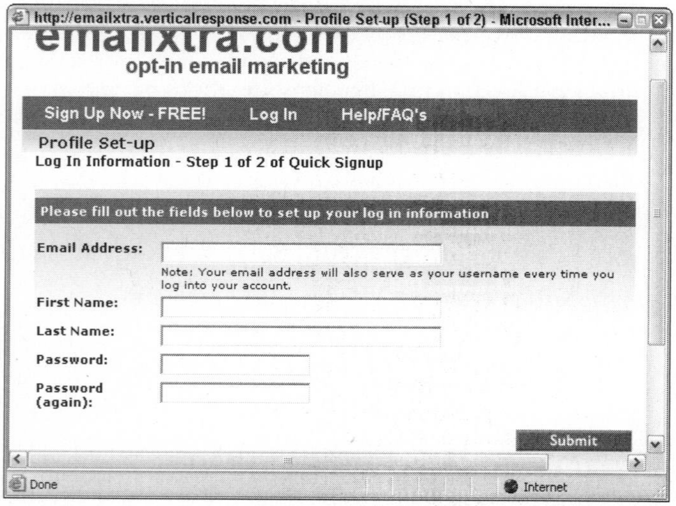

Figure 19-8:
Enter your login information.

The pop-up window, shown in Figure 19-9, appears.

4. **In the next pop-up window, enter the requested information about your company (such as its name and phone number). When you're finished, click the Submit button.**

   Emailxtra then sends you an e-mail message about your new account.

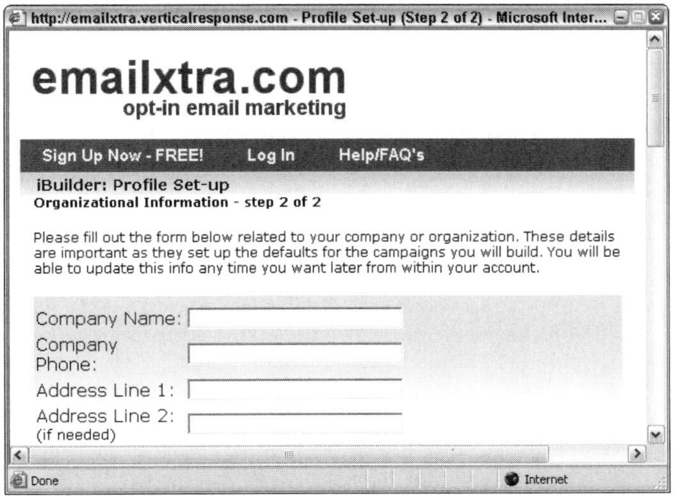

Figure 19-9:
Enter your organizational information.

http://emailxtra.verticalresponse.com - Profile Set-up (Step 2 of 2) - Microsoft Inter...

emailxtra.com
opt-in email marketing

Sign Up Now - FREE!	Log In	Help/FAQ's

iBuilder: Profile Set-up
Organizational Information - step 2 of 2

Please fill out the form below related to your company or organization. These details are important as they set up the defaults for the campaigns you will build. You will be able to update this info any time you want later from within your account.

Company Name:
Company Phone:
Address Line 1:
Address Line 2: (if needed)

Done   Internet

5. **When the resulting e-mail message arrives, open it and click the link.**

   Clicking this link verifies that your e-mail address is correct and opens a welcome page in your Web browser.

6. **Click the Click Here to Start E-Mail Marketing link.**

   This takes you to a login page where your e-mail address is already entered.

7. **Enter your password and click the Sign In button.**

In the future, you can just go to `https://emailxtra.verticalresponse.com/login.html` to log in.

Keeping Visitors Updated about Changes to Your Site

So you made some changes to your site. You worked hard on them from the conception to the follow-through, and you're thrilled with the results. Well, personal satisfaction is nice, but what about all those people who have already visited your site? Will they know about all the improvements that you've made?

Visitors will notice the changes if you use an update notification service such as ChangeNotes or ChangeDetection.com.

ChangeNotes

ChangeNotes (www.changenotes.com) keeps track of your site and automatically e-mails your visitors whenever there's a change. It performs this task by automatically downloading one copy of your page each day and comparing it with the copy it downloaded the day before. If the pages are the same, nothing happens. If the pages are different, the service sends an e-mail to everyone on your list of interested users.

ChangeNotes is an opt-in service, so you don't have to worry about a spam problem. You put a link on your Web pages, and your visitors get to choose whether to receive update notices.

No matter how many times a day your site changes, your users will never receive more than one notification in 24 hours. That notice contains all the changes noted during that time.

Adding ChangeNotes to your Web pages couldn't be much simpler. Just follow these few steps, and you'll be up and running in no time:

1. **In your favorite editor, open the Web page you want to add ChangeNotes to and (if necessary) select the option that displays the source code.**

2. **Go to www.changenotes.com/webmaster.php.**

3. **Scroll down to the text box that's near the middle of the page, shown in Figure 19-10.**

   This text box contains source code that you can copy and paste into your Web pages.

4. **The easiest way to handle copying the source code is to use an old and venerable series of key combinations. Just click anywhere within the text area and then press Ctrl+A.**

   This command selects all the text, visible or not, in the text area. The source code is highlighted to indicate that this has taken place.

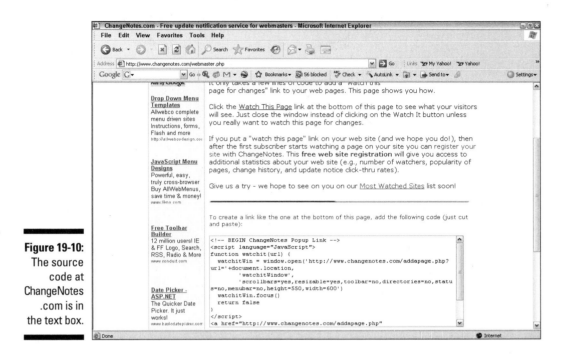

Figure 19-10:
The source
code at
ChangeNotes
.com is in
the text box.

5. **Press Ctrl+C to copy the source code.**

6. **Open your Web page–creation program and paste the copied source code into your Web page's code. Okay, for those of you who want all the key combos, you can use Ctrl+V to paste the code.**

7. **Save your Web page.**

8. **Upload the updated page to your Web server.**

That's all there is to it. You just add the link, and ChangeNotes does the work for you while you go on doing other things. Visitors who click that link see the window shown in Figure 19-11, which lets them sign up.

ChangeNotes keeps track of only the Web pages that have one of its links on them, so you must add the source code to each page on your site. One quick way to do this is to use a Web page–design program such as Dreamweaver to add the source code as a library item, which automatically puts it on all the pages in your site.

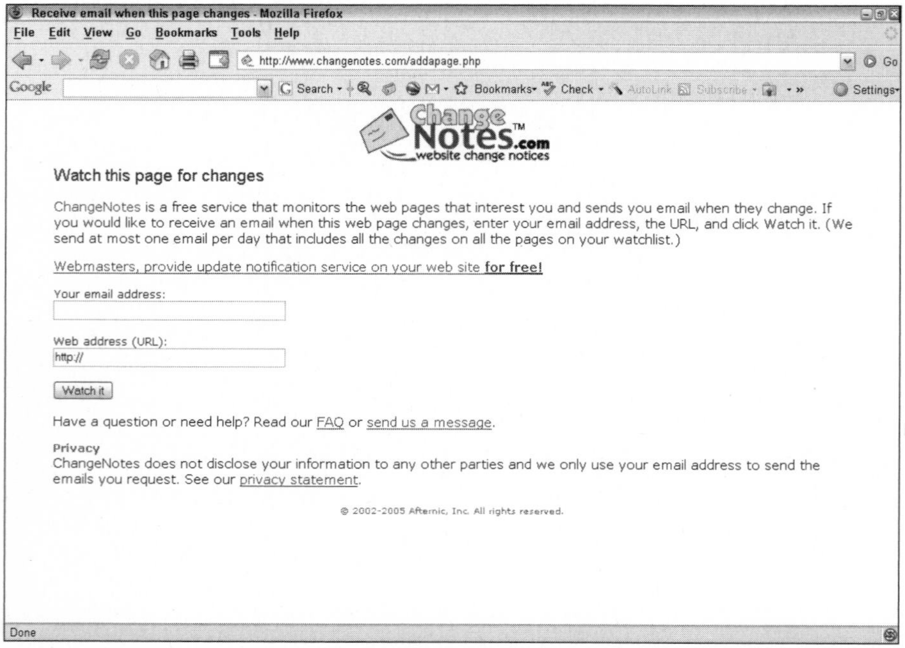

Figure 19-11:
Your visitors can fill out this form to keep updated about changes at your site.

In some situations — maybe many of them, depending on the design and layout of your site — you may not want users to get e-mail messages every time something changes in a particular area of a page. ChangeNotes has that base covered, too. You can set off a section of your page by using two custom tags:

```
<!-- BEGIN change-ignore -->
Your block to be ignored goes here.
<!-- END change-ignore -->
```

ChangesNotes ignores anything that lies between the tags when it checks your site. Those items can change without triggering any response from the service.

Don't worry about the strange tags. Any Web browser that finds them will simply ignore them, and they will have no impact on your visitors, who will still see everything that lies between the tags. The only thing that is affected by the tags is the ChangeNotes service itself.

ChangeDetection.com

ChangeDetection.com is another update-notification service for Web sites. This one, however, provides a bit of a nicer interface than ChangeNotes.com does, with a nice selection of panels you can add to your Web pages.

To sign up with ChangeDetection.com, follow these steps:

1. **Go to www.changedetection.com.**

2. **Enter your e-mail address in the form and click the Get It button.**

   You will quickly receive an e-mail message asking you to confirm that you're signing up. Click the link in the message to do so. ChangeDetection. com will now send you an e-mail message that includes the source code that you need in order to add the necessary signup panel to your Web pages.

3. **If you don't like the particular panel that you receive in the e-mail message, just check out the attachment to that message by opening it in a Web browser.**

   The attachment is an HTML file that includes the codes for a dozen different designs of signup panels, shown in Figure 19-12.

4. **Just copy the source code for the design you like best from that HTML file and paste it into your page's code.**

5. **Save your Web page.**

6. **Upload the changed page to your Web server.**

Figure 19-12:
ChangeDe tection.com gives you a variety of signup panel styles to choose from.

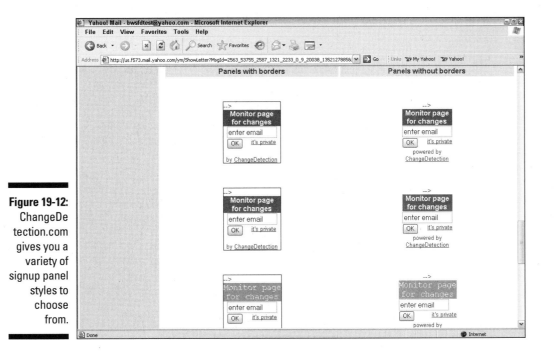

Trying Out Form and Poll Makers

Hardly a day passes without someone announcing the results of some kind of poll: "Thirty-two percent of city residents prefer smog." "The *For Dummies* nerd's approval rating climbed by 4 percent in the past week." "Quantum physics confuses nine people out of five." For whatever reason, people are fascinated by other people's feelings about different subjects. And people love to toss in their two bits' worth whenever they see a survey form. Here are a few common uses for Web site survey forms:

- ✓ **Feedback on product quality:** "How do you rate our new release?"

- ✓ **Opinions on social issues:** "Should we pay more attention to threatened species?"

- ✓ **Preferences between political candidates:** "Do you plan to vote Democrat, Republican, or Independent?"

- ✓ **Requests for new site features:** "Check the services you want us to add."

It's not just polls, though. The amount and variety of information gathered via forms on the Web are staggering. Visitor information, prospect inquiries, and product orders are only a few uses of forms. If the idea of using forms interests you, but you're not comfortable with CGI, or Common Gateway Interface (see Chapter 8), you may want to try out some of the form makers and processing services that are described in this section.

A tremendous amount of overlap exists between the folks who offer free forms and those who offer form-processing services. Many of the form makers also provide CGI services, although they usually limit them to servicing their own custom forms. A pure form-processing service, however, handles forms that you create on your own. This type of service gives you much more control and power over your Web site content.

Response-O-Matic

Response-O-Matic, which you predictably find at www.response-o-matic. com on the Web, is one of the best form-processing firms around, and it gives you tremendous flexibility. It handles any form that you want to throw at it. Well, okay, it does have a few restrictions. But they're minimal and reasonable. You can't, for example, transmit more than 50K of data with one form submission. That's plenty, however, with scads and bunches to spare.

The questions that you add to the form are up to you, but they require a bit of HTML knowledge. (If you're totally at sea when it comes to HTML, try Freedback.com instead, which is listed in Table 19-1 at the end of this chapter.)

To create a form by using Response-O-Matic's service, follow these steps:

1. **Go to www.response-o-matic.com and then click the Get Started button.**

2. **On the Sign Up page (see Figure 19-13), enter your name, e-mail address, and a password.**

3. **Click the Sign Up button.**

   You will get an e-mail message asking you to confirm your account creation. Click the link in it.

4. **The resulting Form Builder page, shown in Figure 19-14, has a rudimentary form that asks for only a name and e-mail address.**

   Don't fill in the information — it's just part of the form that you're building for someone else to fill in.

5. **If you don't want those two form elements, click the Delete link to the left of each of them.**

6. **To add other elements, click the Add a Question link.**

7. **In the Choose a Question Type box (see Figure 19-15), select the desired kind (check box, radio button, and so on).**

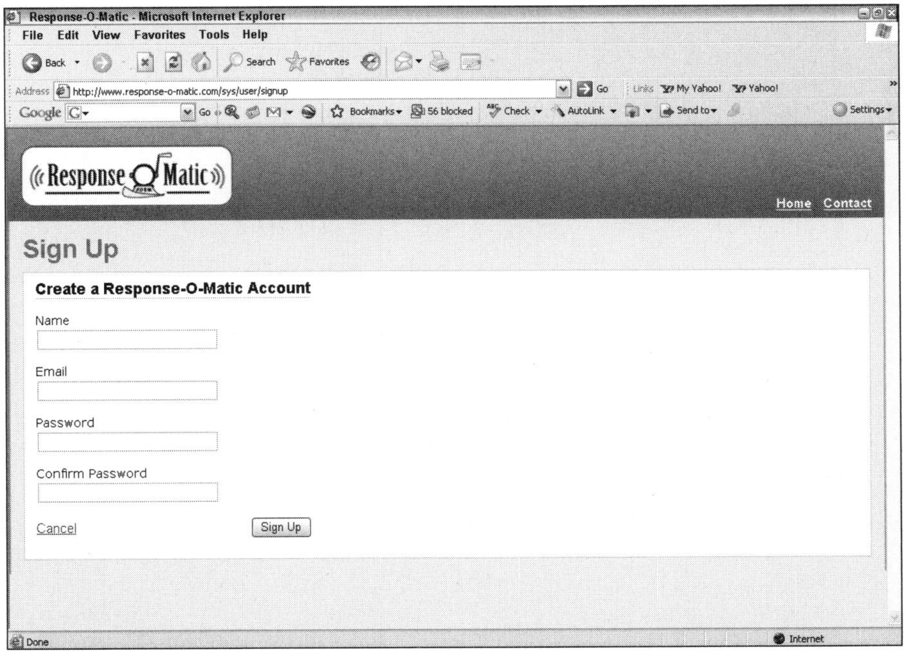

Figure 19-13:
Entering
your data.

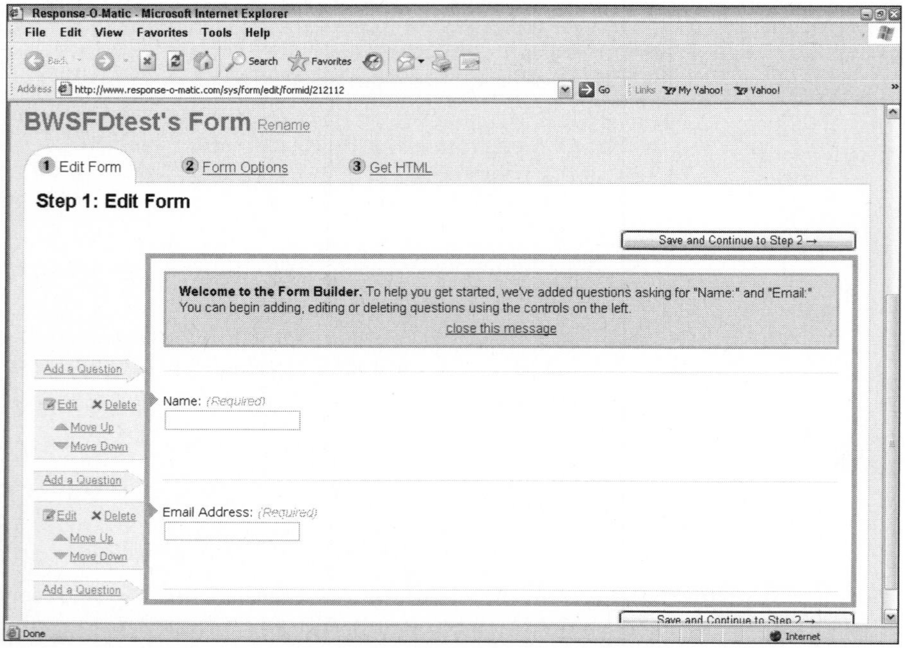

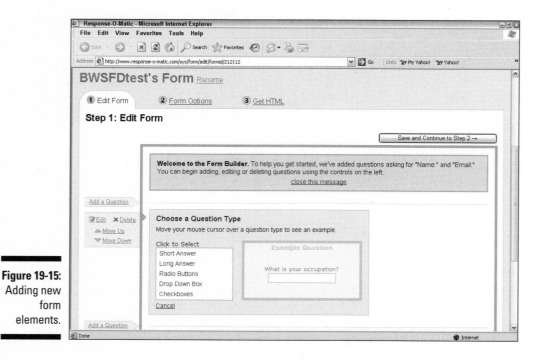

Figure 19-14:
Adding form
elements.

Figure 19-15:
Adding new
form
elements.

Figure 19-16 shows the results of selecting the Short Answer option.

8. **Enter the question you want to ask. If an answer is absolutely necessary, select the Required check box.**

9. **Click the Save button. Figure 19-17 shows the result.**

10. **When you're satisfied with your form, click the Save and Continue to Step 2 button.**

11. **On the Form Options page, shown in Figure 19-18, select whether to have your form users sent to your site or to the all-purpose Thank You page at Response-O-Matic.**

If you choose the Thank You page, you then see a box in which you can enter your Web site's address, which will be displayed on the Thank You page. You can also select an option to show the form results on that page.

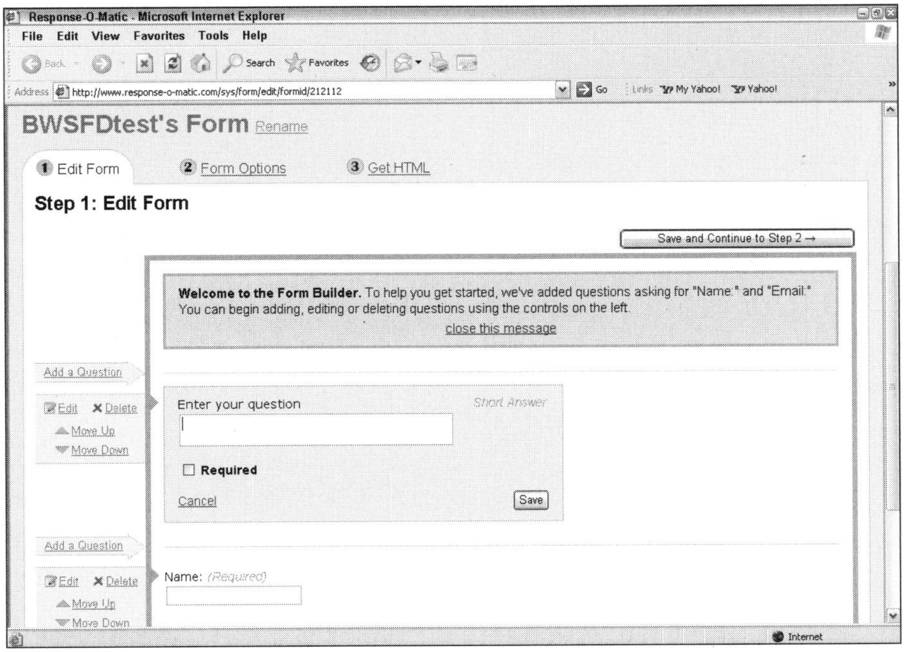

Figure 19-16: Selecting the Short Answer option.

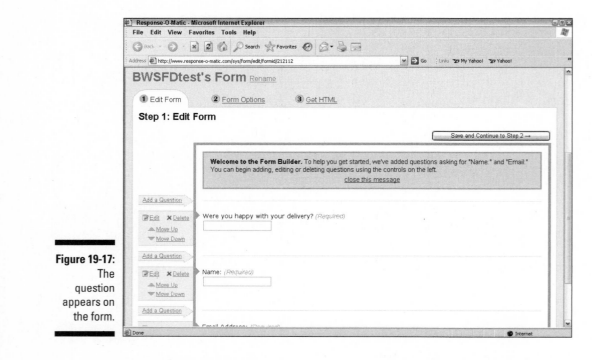

Figure 19-17:
The
question
appears on
the form.

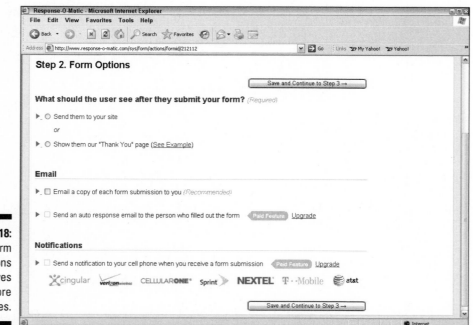

Figure 19-18:
The Form
Options
page gives
you more
choices.

12. **Under Email, it is advisable to select the check box to have the form submissions mailed to you.**

    You'll get to enter a subject for the form e-mails you'll receive.

13. **Click the Save and Continue to Step 3 button.**

14. **On the resulting Get HTML page (see Figure 19-19), copy the code and then paste it into your own Web page.**

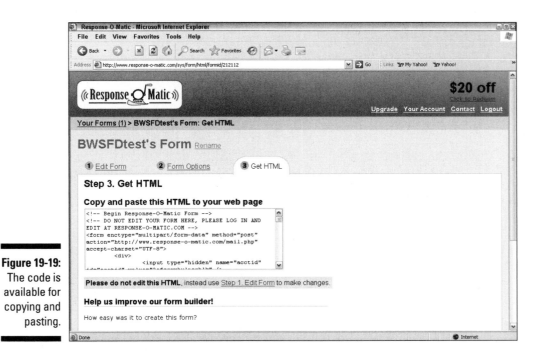

Figure 19-19:
The code is available for copying and pasting.

FormSite.com

FormSite.com (www.formsite.com) is another form maker that, in addition to creating a variety of general forms, has a specific survey form service. Like Response-O-Matic (described earlier in the chapter), the service is free if you accept its accompanying advertising — or you can pop for a few bucks to get rid of the advertising banners and pick up some extra features, such as secure forms.

To create a form with FormSite.com, follow these steps:

1. **Go to www.formsite.com.**

2. **Click the Sign Up Now button.**

3. **Type a username and a password in the appropriate text boxes on the User Profile form, shown in Figure 19-20.**

   You can optionally provide your e-mail address.

4. **Click the Submit button.**

5. **On the resultant New Form Web page, shown in Figure 19-21, type the name of your form in the — you guessed it — Form Name text box.**

6. **To use a predesigned template, select the option button next to the survey template that most closely resembles the one you want to create.**

7. **To start from scratch, select the From a Blank Form radio button; then click the Create button.**

8. **On the resulting page, click the Click to Continue link.**

9. **On the next page, click Add Before or Add After.**

   It doesn't matter which, since there isn't anything on the form yet; either one puts a new form element at the top of the blank form.

10. **The Standard Items page (see Figure 19-22) has a wide variety of sophisticated form elements you can add. Simply click the one you want and then select the desired options.**

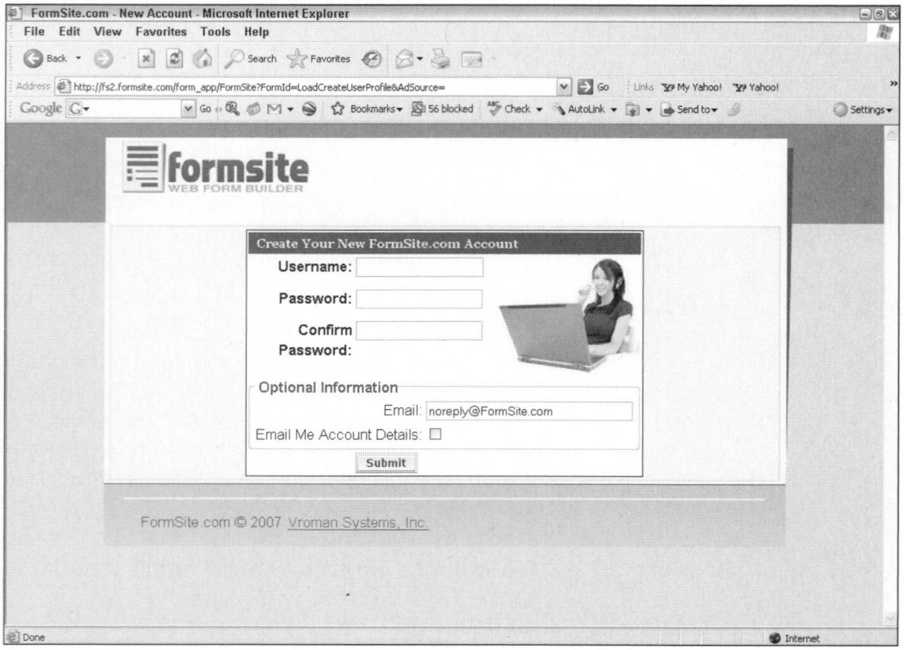

Figure 19-20: FormSite.com's User Profile page, your starting point for creating your survey.

Figure 19-21:
Creating a
new form.

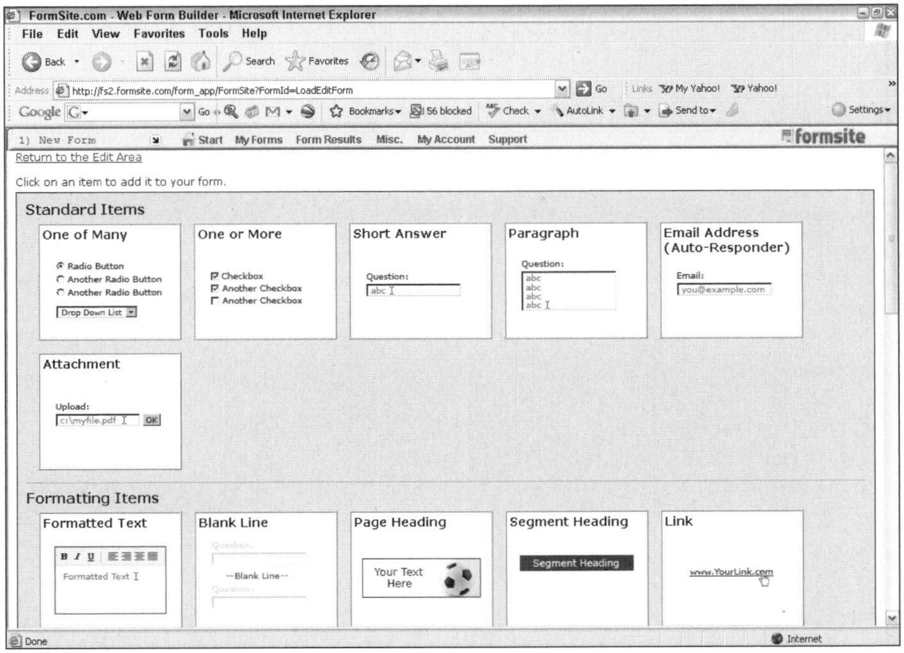

Figure 19-22:
Selecting a
new form
element.

Figure 19-23 shows the results of clicking the Image form element. To add an image to the form, click the Upload Image button. Among the available options, alternate text (shown in a Web browser if the image is unavailable) can be added, and you can make the image a clickable link by supplying a connecting URL.

11. **When you're satisfied with your choices, click the Submit button to add the element to your form.**

12. **Once the form is completed, click the Publish button.**

13. **On the resulting Web page, select the Embedded Form Link radio button.**

14. **Copy the HTML code and paste it into your own Web page.**

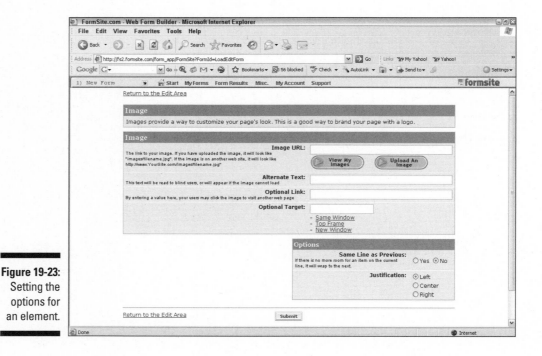

Figure 19-23:
Setting the options for an element.

Privacy and Security

First, if you submit your site's input to someone else for processing, you surrender control over that information. Make sure that you check out the form processor's privacy policy before you commit yourself. Look for a link that says something like Privacy Statement or Privacy Policy, click it, and carefully read the fine print that you find there. Print out a hard copy to keep in your files.

If the form processor doesn't post a clearly stated privacy policy on its site, you probably don't want to use its services. If the company doesn't promise in writing to keep your information and your users' information confidential and you still go with it, you may end up feeding everything from your site's forms right into a spammer's or telemarketer's data bank.

Another concern is that most form-processing services send the form contents to you by e-mail. Because the information in the form travels through the Internet's e-mail systems, anyone running a server through which it passes as it traverses the Internet can read the information. Now, your average network administrator has better things to do than read other people's passing e-mail, but you've got to keep in mind that this ain't exactly the most secure approach possible. A *sniffer program,* software that filters e-mail as it passes through a server, can grab sensitive information from those messages.

Obviously, using form-processing services isn't the ideal approach if you're getting information that would be useful to crooks — such as credit card numbers, for instance.

If you handle sensitive information, you need to make sure that any form processor that you use collects your data via a secure form and keeps the data on its server until you can pick it up yourself by logging on to a secure page at the processor's site, like with the professional-level version of FormSite.com (described in the preceding section).

Online Sources for Visitor Communications

Table 19-1 lists some places on the World Wide Web where you can find more resources like the ones that are covered in this chapter.

Table 19-1	Online Resources for Visitor Communications
Web Site Name	*Web Address*
Alxnet Poll	`www.alxnet.com/services/poll`
Autoresponders.org	`http://autoresponders.org`
AWeber Systems	`www.aweber.com`
EZpolls	`http://ezpolls.superstats.com`
Freedback.com	`www.freedback.com`
Freepolls.com	`www.freepolls.com`
SendFree	`www.sendfree.com`
SiteGadgets.com	`www.sitegadgets.com`
Sparklit	`www.sparklit.com`
Yesmail	`www.yesmail.com`

Part VII
The Part of Tens

The 5th Wave   By Rich Tennant

"Guess who found a Kiss merchandise site on
the Web while you were gone?"

In this part . . .

*W*ell, it just wouldn't be a *For Dummies* book without the Part of Tens. Chapter 20 shows you where to go when you need to find out the answers to everything from business and legal issues to grammar questions. Chapter 21 is a guide to some of the best things an e–commerce site can add. And Chapter 22 is a potpourri of ten more great add-ins.

Chapter 20

Ten Great Places to Get Advice

*W*e all need advice from time to time. Even if you're terribly independent, as nearly self-sufficient as can be, there are times when you
need to turn to others for assistance. Well, here are ten Web sites where you
can go if you feel the need to ask for help. Each site has its own special feeling and its own particular set of standards. But somewhere in this chapter,
you're gonna find a few places that you'll be so happy to know about that
you'll just burst from joy.

Bizy Moms

The Bizy Moms site (www.bizymoms.com) is shown in Figure 20-1.

Figure 20-1:
Bizy Moms
is a fabulous
resource for
the work-at-
home
crowd.

Despite its name, Bizy Moms appeals to both the mother and father who want to work from home while raising a family. The site hosts live chats on issues such as "The Internet, Money, and You" or "Business on a Shoestring." Bizy Moms is the best place to go if you want to know about free postage, Internet marketing, or just about anything else of interest to the home-working parent.

Toss in the advice on time management and paperwork control from those who've been there, and you're just beginning to explore this site.

Cozahost Newsletter

You can check out the Cozahost newsletter, shown in Figure 20-2, at `www.cozahost.com/news`.

The Cozahost newsletter is an e-commerce e-zine with a difference: It's actually worth reading. Granted, it doesn't have as many neat links as are packed into this book, but against competition like that, who stands a chance? (For the humor-impaired, that's a joke — consider yourself officially notified.)

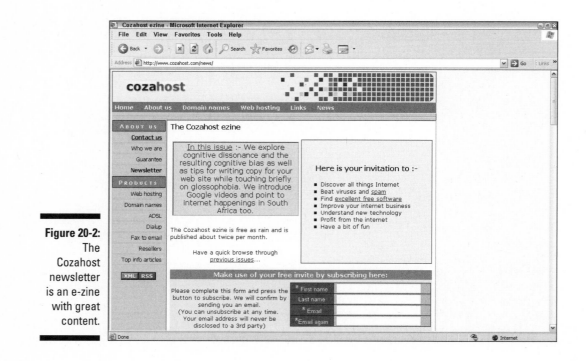

Figure 20-2: The Cozahost newsletter is an e-zine with great content.

Seriously, folks, the links in the Cozahost newsletter, although fewer than you find on some sites that have a lot less to offer, are premium. It's worth your time to follow them. If they're internal links, they lead to good articles on Web work; if they're external, they lead to decent tools that you should consider adding to your own repertoire.

geek/talk Forums for Webmasters

The Geek/Talk Forums site (www.geekvillage.com/forums) is shown in Figure 20-3.

Ah, fellow geeks! geek/talk (www.geekvillage.com/forums) is the place where you can let it all hang out. The geek/talk bulletin board (see Figure 20-3) is for those of us who just *love* technical stuff, who absolutely live for the last bit that we can squeeze out of HTML, who . . . well, you get the idea. Actually, you're welcome to pop in and ask the simplest questions in the world. Even if you don't know the first thing about HTML, this site is the place to ask your dumbest questions and expect a civil answer.

Figure 20-3:
The
geek/talk
Webmaster
forums.

This wonderland is a great place to visit. Here, you'll find folks who are interested in all the same things you are, from Web design to e-commerce. And you can find a different BBS (bulletin board service) for just about any topic you want to discuss.

grammarNOW!

Figure 20-4 shows the grammarNOW! site (`www.grammarnow.com`).

Do your participles dangle embarrassingly? Are your diphthongs out of style? If you ever stay awake wondering about these mighty questions, grammar NOW! is your kind of site. This site is one place where you can get free answers to those embarrassing questions with complete confidentiality. The folks who run this site e-mail you an answer without showing the world that you don't know what to do about the ablative absolute.

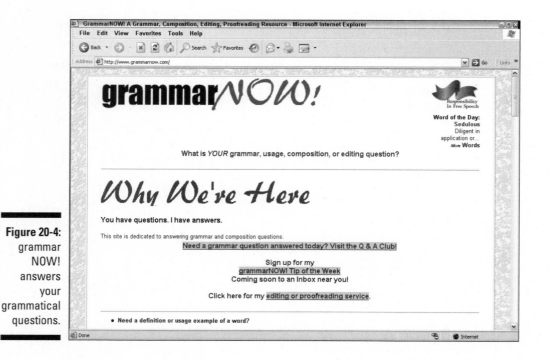

Figure 20-4: grammar NOW! answers your grammatical questions.

If you're really out on a limb, you'll be happy to know that not only can you get a quick answer for free, but you can actually hire the brains behind this site to go over your Web site with a fine-tooth comb and clear up any grammatical problems on it. And the site's list of grammar links is well worth exploring on its own.

Kasamba

The Kasamba site (`www.kasamba.com`) is shown in Figure 20-5.

Kasamba is a great place to get answers on a wide variety of topics, ranging from businesses to computers. It's also a great source of information on lots of things that Web people need to know. Interested in starting a home-based business? Want to know about tax liabilities? Or about e-commerce or Web design? Ask 'em.

Kasamba has the people who know all the answers, and they'll get back to you quickly with good, solid information.

Figure 20-5: Kasamba is the place to find the answer to just about any question.

LawGuru.com

Figure 20-6 shows the LawGuru.com site (`www.lawguru.com`).

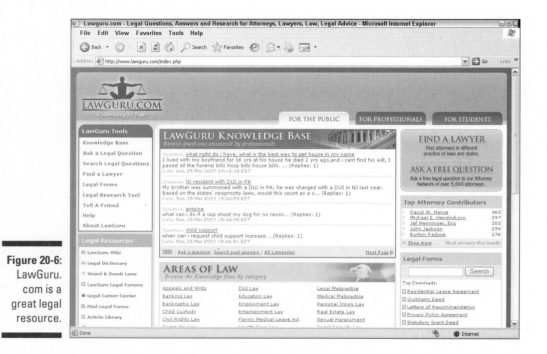

Figure 20-6:
LawGuru.
com is a
great legal
resource.

LawGuru.com is a nice source for legal research. At this site, you can check out everything from the latest U.S. Code revisions to that money you forgot you were owed.

This site has a huge database of legal questions and answers, and if you can't find what you're looking for in it, you can submit your own questions to the LawGuru folks. They've also got chat rooms for both attorneys and normal people and a no-nonsense FAQ (Frequently Asked Questions) on copyright.

Siteowners.com

The Siteowners.com site (`www.siteowners.com`) is shown in Figure 20-7.

Figure 20-7:
Siteowners.
com has
tips on
everything
about Web
develop-
ment.

Siteowners.com is just what it sounds like — a meeting place for people who run Web sites. If you're interested in Web design, this site is a pretty nice place to stop in and absorb things. The site even has its own Webmaster forums, including Web site critiques and discussions about topics like e-commerce and Web site programming techniques.

You can find articles on e-commerce, marketing, and Web design, just to name a few of the features of this premier site

The Small Business Advisor

The Small Business Advisor site (www.isquare.com) is shown in Figure 20-8.

The Small Business Advisor is one handy little resource for those of you who are thinking about opening up your own business. This site covers every-thing from taxes to insurance and has business news that actually makes sense to small business people (and tall ones, too). Its free e-mail newsletter is a prime source of savvy advice, useful information, and links that you'll want to click.

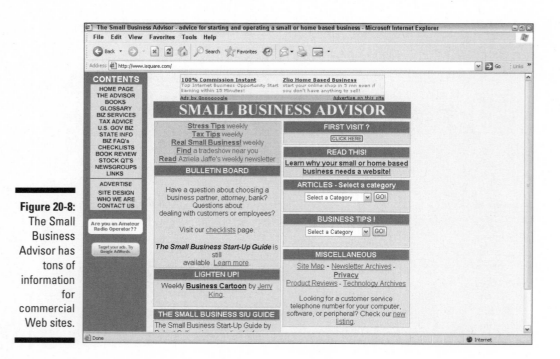

Figure 20-8:
The Small
Business
Advisor has
tons of
information
for
commercial
Web sites.

The site's various checklists alone are worth the visit — they cover everything from choosing a business partner or a bank to working with an attorney. Lists of business-oriented newsgroups, Internet-specific business commentary, and state-specific contact information are just a few of the tidbits that this site offers.

Web Developer's Journal

The Web Developer's Journal site (www.webdevelopersjournal.com) is shown in Figure 20-9.

What is there to say about a site that's just chock full of so many goodies? The Web Developer's Journal lives up to its name, providing tons of material on every aspect of life — at least as far as it affects the Web. Really. Everything from setting up forms to animation.

Figure 20-9:
Web
Developer's
Journal is a
great
source of
information.

Website Tips

The Website Tips site (www.websitetips.com) is shown in Figure 20-10.

If you're looking for one place to find information on everything from accessibility to XML, it's hard to beat Website Tips. You're talking several thousand listings here: hand-held wireless devices, JavaScript, e-commerce, legal considerations — all calculated to increase your Web design IQ.

Figure 20-10:
Website Tips
offers great
advice on
Internet
design and
over 2,000
worthwhile
links to
explore.

Chapter 21

Ten Fabulous Tools for E-Commerce

*Y*ou simply must try this blend of programs, add-ins, and services if you're into e-commerce. Even if you're not, some of the items in this chapter, such as HumanClick, MapQuest, or the Direct Marketing Association's Privacy Policy Generator, may come in handy. Some of these items are freebies, some cost serious money, and others offer a combination in which you can get a lesser version at no charge.

CafePress.com

The CafePress.com site (www.cafepress.com) is shown in Figure 21-1.

Figure 21-1: CafePress. com makes it easy to get into the art business.

Got some great ideas for T-shirts, coffee mugs, or mouse pads? If you don't want to spend lots of money for bulky and dangerous equipment, drop in to CafePress.com. It's not just another place that'll iron an image onto a mouse pad for a fee. It's a whole e-commerce setup that costs you nothing.

You can set up a store at the site with no investment except your image files. Just upload those files to CafePress.com, and it takes care of everything. Not only does it do the manufacturing and shipping for you, but you don't even have to get a credit card merchant account; it'll do your credit card order processing, too.

DMA Privacy Policy Generator

The DMA Privacy Policy Generator site (`www.the-dma.org/privacy/ creating.shtml`) is shown in Figure 21-2.

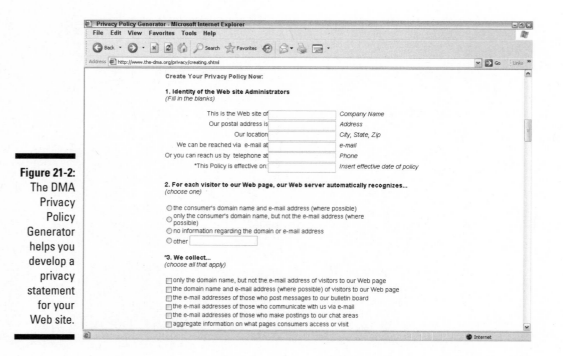

Figure 21-2:
The DMA Privacy Policy Generator helps you develop a privacy statement for your Web site.

The Direct Marketing Association (DMA) assists you in creating a privacy statement with its free DMA Privacy Policy Generator, a simple, easy-to-use online form. By filling out the form and selecting the check boxes that apply to your company's situation, you provide the basic material for your privacy statement. When you finish, you can have the completed statement e-mailed to you as plain text or as a ready-to-use Web page that you can drop into your site. To access the Privacy Policy form, go to `www.the-dma.org/privacy/creating.shtml`.

ECommerce Guide

Figure 21-3 shows the ECommerce Guide site (`http://ecommerce.internet.com`).

The ECommerce Guide is an e-zine that's a truly valuable resource for anyone involved in e-commerce. It's got reviews of online store software, the latest news for e-sales, and some really, really good columns. If you're not checking out this site, you're missing out on a lot of useful information.

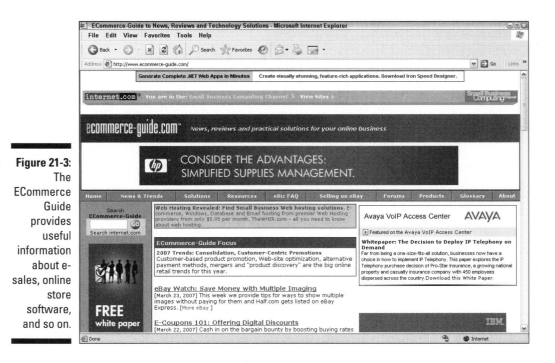

Figure 21-3:
The ECommerce Guide provides useful information about e-sales, online store software, and so on.

HumanClick

The HumanClick site (www.humanclick.com) is shown in Figure 21-4.

HumanClick is a fantastic way to add a human touch to your Web site. It's a service that enables you to respond instantly to your customers' needs. Imagine: You're looking at a page on someone's site, and you have some questions about the products you see. An icon there reads Click for a Real Person. You do so, and you go into a chat with someone who can answer your questions. Pretty nice, eh? Yep, this one's a must-have. Drop everything and go to this Web site. Click the Free Trial link and think about how nice having this feature on your site would be.

This service is definitely something you want on your Web site — and you don't even need to keep your people available 24 hours a day to use it. During the times that nobody's around to answer questions, you just tell the HumanClick client program on your computer that you're unavailable, and the icon on your site changes to read Leave a Message.

As if all that's not enough, the service places no burden on your customers because HumanClick is JavaScript that's embedded in your pages. It works with every major Web browser, and your visitors don't need to download anything to make it work.

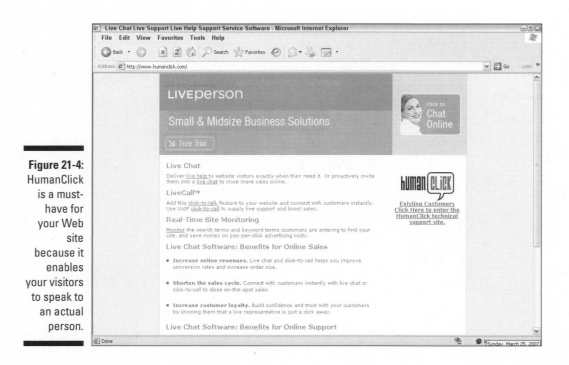

Figure 21-4: HumanClick is a must-have for your Web site because it enables your visitors to speak to an actual person.

MapQuest

The MapQuest site (www.mapquest.com) is shown in Figure 21-5.

MapQuest is a fabulous place to get maps. No kidding — maps. But not just plain old road maps. These beauties are customized maps that you can create for helping people find your location, for example, or showing them how to get from their hotel to a tourist attraction.

Although MapQuest charges for plenty of things on its site, it also offers a free service that you may want to take a look at: LinkFree. LinkFree links your site to the main MapQuest site so that your users can take advantage of its cartography services.

To access the MapQuest free services page, shown in Figure 21-5, go to www.mapquest.com/features/main.adp?page=lf_main.

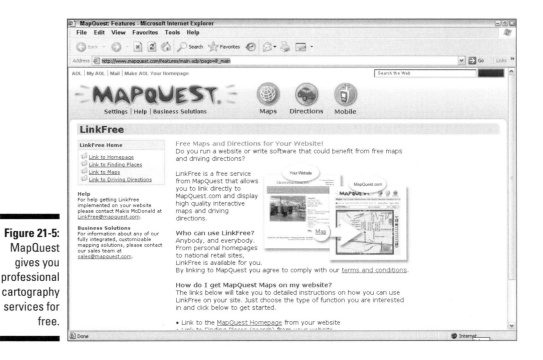

Figure 21-5: MapQuest gives you professional cartography services for free.

osCommerce

Figure 21-6 shows the osCommerce site (`www.oscommerce.com`).

osCommerce has a deal that's hard to refuse — you can download its osCommerce software for zero dollars with no limits, no time constraints, no nothing. It's open source software, which means that not only is it free, but you also get to play with the source code and change it to suit yourself. Ah, yes, that's the catch. If you're not a PHP programmer or don't have one on staff, you may get in a bit over your head with this software; if you are or do, however, you can download this software at `www.oscommerce.com`.

Still, even without custom modifications, using this package is a worthwhile way to get your store up and running. It handles everything from creating product pages to managing shipping and just about anything that you can imagine in between. It's easy to use, too. Figure 21-6 shows a demo catalog made with osCommerce.

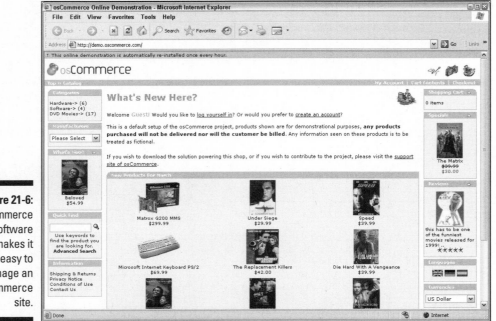

Figure 21-6: osCommerce software makes it easy to manage an e-commerce site.

S&H greenpoints

The S&H greenpoints site (www.greenpoints.com) is shown in Figure 21-7.

Ah, remember how you used to collect S&H Green Stamps? Okay, ask your parents about it. Or maybe your grandparents. At any rate, someone you know will remember. It used to be that you'd go to the grocery, fill your cart, and pay for your purchases. Then, along with your change, you'd get a certain number of stamps from the cashier, depending on how much money you'd just spent. You'd toss the stamps in the grocery bag along with your receipt and trot on home. You'd put the stamps in a kitchen drawer until you had so many that you couldn't open the drawer any more without stamps spilling out all over the floor.

When things reached that stage, you'd have to face the odious task of licking all the stamps and pasting them into the books that you also picked up at the grocery. When you had a whole bunch of books filled, you'd sit down with the S&H catalog and go on a shopping spree. Now the Internet is reviving this grand old piece of Americana. But this time around, you don't have to lick all those stamps! Now, it's S&H greenpoints, a new form of digital reward — kind of like the Web equivalent of frequent-flyer miles.

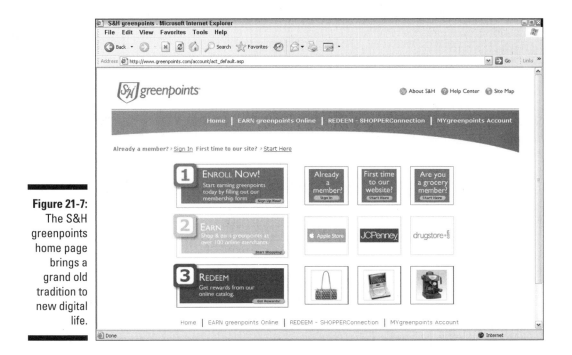

Figure 21-7:
The S&H greenpoints home page brings a grand old tradition to new digital life.

I have a major hunch that this arrangement is going to work out well for both online shoppers and e-merchants. If you're into any kind of e-commerce, look into this site at www.greenpoints.com.

SYSTRAN Translation Software

Figure 21-8 shows the SYSTRAN Translation Software site (www.systransoft.com).

One of the hottest sites on the Web is AltaVista's Babel Fish translation page. It works with SYSTRAN translation software, and you can go right to the source and set up your very own translation system. Anyone who's serious about e-commerce must deal with the fact that the World Wide Web is just that — a global setup. Your storefront is an international business, and although English is widely spoken, it's hardly the only language in the world.

With SYSTRAN translation software working on your site, visitors quickly translate your pages among more than half a dozen major Western languages: Dutch, English, French, German, Greek, Italian, Portuguese, and Spanish. And SYSTRAN doesn't stop there. The service also includes Chinese, Japanese, Korean, and Russian. So hurry up already and pop into SYSTRAN's Web site. The whole world is waiting. Run — don't walk — to www.systransoft.com.

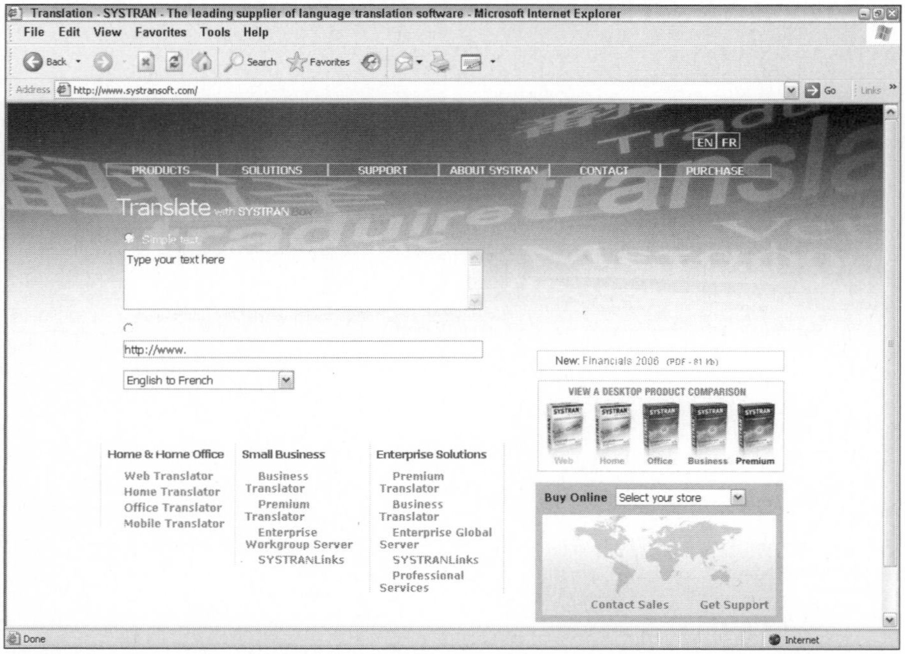

Figure 21-8:
SYSTRAN's home page, where you can sign up to add its translation service to your site.

TRUSTe

The TRUSTe site (www.truste.com) is shown in Figure 21-9.

This site is kind of an open question. What question is that? Well, whether paying hundreds or even thousands of dollars to an outside group to certify that your privacy policy means what it says is worth the price to your organization. To solidly quantify how much a trustmark such as the TRUSTe seal means in terms of extra sales is impossible, just as it is with things such as Chamber of Commerce or Better Business Bureau logos in a store window. Nonetheless, major outfits from MSN to eBay have jumped onto the TRUSTe bandwagon.

If you collect any kind of potentially embarrassing personal information, such as criminal records or health status, getting TRUSTe certification is probably worth the cost. Without it, people may be reluctant to provide honest answers to such questions. Still, unless you're in the employment or insurance business (or something similar), you're not likely to gather any kind of information other than names, addresses, phone numbers, credit card numbers, and so on.

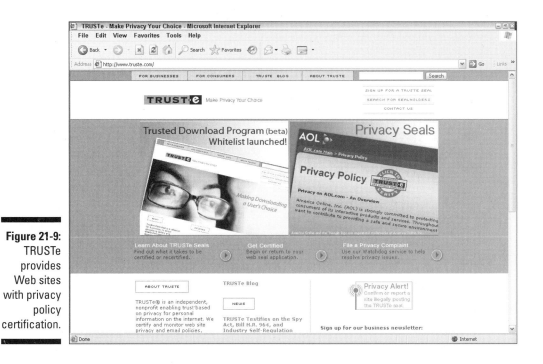

Figure 21-9:
TRUSTe provides Web sites with privacy policy certification.

Visit the TRUSTe site and read over all the materials there to decide for yourself whether its service is right for your situation. You also find valuable advice there on creating a privacy statement. You can access the site's home page at www.truste.com.

WorldPay

The WorldPay site (www.worldpay.com) is shown in Figure 21-10.

When it comes to finding a financial partner for an online business, you can't do much better than WorldPay. Unlike so many banks, the WorldPay folks "get it" — the Internet, that is. They truly understand that a Web business is a global business.

Figure 21-10: WorldPay is geared for e-commerce.

Let's face it — how many merchant account providers are comfortable dealing with payments via both American Express and Lastschriften? How many of them can help you comprehend payments in dollars and euros and yen? WorldPay also supports deferred payments, allowing you to let your customers spread their buying power over time.

On top of this, the WorldPay folks are happy to work with companies large and small, and they have a refreshingly simple application process for merchant accounts. So, what are you waiting for? Pop on over to www.worldpay.com.

Chapter 22

Ten More Great Add-Ins

*W*ell, you just know that every book has to have a final chapter. I'd like to keep on going forever, but I can't, so I'm using these last few pages to point you toward some more great Web site add-ins and services.

@watch

The @watch site (www.atwatch.com) is shown in Figure 22-1.

If you have deep pockets and need a detailed analysis of your Web server's downtimes and uptimes, you may want to take a look at @watch. Figure 22-1 shows an availability report from @watch.

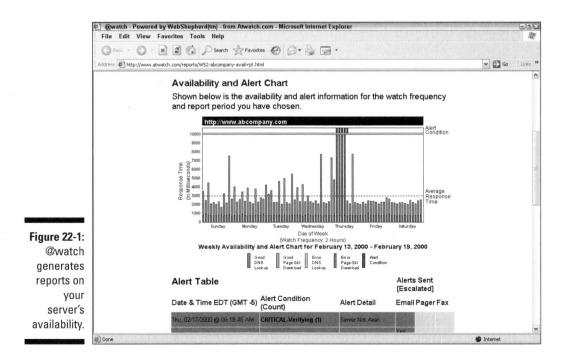

Figure 22-1: @watch generates reports on your server's availability.

@watch offers three program levels: @watch Advanced ($14.99 and up per month), @watch Pro ($29.99 and up per month), and @watch Enterprise ($39.99 and up per month). Prices decrease if you sign up for a year at a time, and you get volume discounts for multiple URLs.

Crossword Compiler

Figure 22-2 shows the Crossword Compiler site (www.crosswordcompiler.com).

If you want to add a crossword puzzle as a feature on your Web page, you need the right software — a program that understands what a Web designer wants, not just what someone with a pencil and paper does. Crossword Compiler is such a program. You'll be thrilled about how easy it is to use and the utility of its Java-enabled Web page connection. Prices range from $49 for a single-user license all the way up to $2,900 for a multiuser package with all the bells and whistles.

While you're at the site, check out the links at the bottom of the main page. They take you to goodies like multilanguage support.

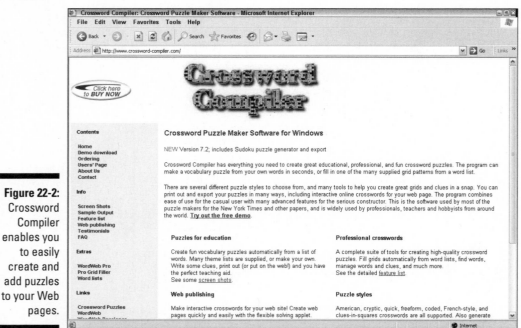

Figure 22-2: Crossword Compiler enables you to easily create and add puzzles to your Web pages.

Everyone.net

The Everyone.net site (www.everyone.net) is shown in Figure 22-3.

Figure 22-3:
Everyone.
net adds
regular mail
service to
your site.

You would like to offer your visitors an e-mail service, but you don't have much in the way of mailboxes available. You may have a handful that came along with your Web service, but they won't stretch very far. So, you turn to Everyone.net to save the day with their free service.

Just fill out a simple application and then eagerly count the hours until the e-mail message with all the details arrives. In it, you will discover the wondrous secrets of giving your users free 25MB mailboxes (not bad). Set your course for www.everyone.net/offer-free-email.html.

GeoPhrase

The GeoPhrase site (www.geobytes.com/GeoPhrase.htm) is shown in Figure 22-4.

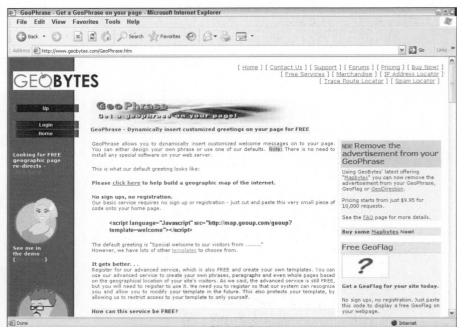

Figure 22-4:
GeoPhrase
lets you
personalize
things for a
global
audience.

It is *so* nice when you run across some people who really understand what the Internet is. And the first thing it is, is global. The visitor logging on to your home page right now could be sitting anywhere from Tulsa, Oklahoma, to Tokyo, Japan. It makes no difference to your Web server, but it probably makes a difference to the visitor.

That's where GeoPhrase comes in. It checks where your visitors come from and, depending on their location, offers a different greeting to them. And all you have to do is paste some HTML code into your Web page.

And that's just the beginning. You can customize the whole shebang, and GeoPhase will even help you do it. Oh, did I mention that all this is free? Fire up your Web browser and get on over to www.geobytes.com/GeoPhrase.htm.

Leonardo

Figure 22-5 shows the Leonardo site (www.leonardo.com).

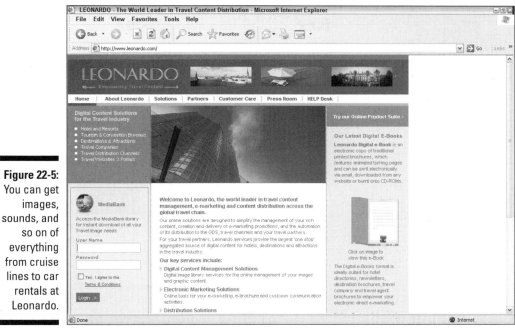

Figure 22-5:
You can get images, sounds, and so on of everything from cruise lines to car rentals at Leonardo.

Leonardo is a must for anyone in the travel industry. But even if your site isn't travel-oriented — if you just need some great content about tourist destinations around the world — you must see this place. It's like going on a shopping spree in a chocolate boutique.

One person's vacation spot is another person's banking center or technology mecca . . . or whatever.

These folks provide photos, recordings, video, and just about anything else you can imagine. Drop in, sign up, and take a look around at the stuff shown in Figure 22-5.

localendar

The localendar site (`www.localendar.com`) is shown in Figure 22-6.

This calendar is one of the best add-ons that you can have on your site — period. Aside from the fact that it's something you're likely to want to use yourself, localendar is an incredible facility to offer your Web site visitors. You don't even have to put up with hosting some banners on your calendar site — just the little localendar link icon.

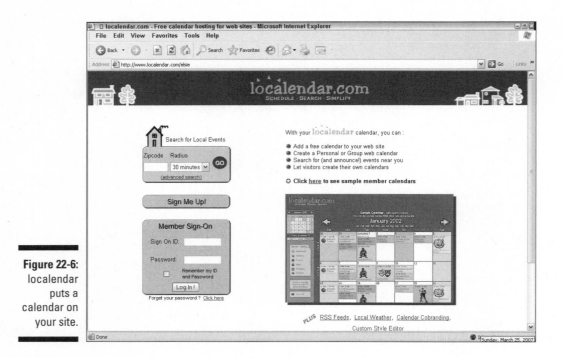

Figure 22-6:
localendar
puts a
calendar on
your site.

You can set up localendar in a variety of displays such as a daily, weekly, or monthly format, and you can set things up so that it blends in well with your site's layout. localendar is a freebie that you can pick up at www.localendar.com.

Merriam-Webster Online

Figure 22-7 shows the Merriam-Webster Online site (www.merriamwebster.com).

As you probably expect, Merriam-Webster offers dictionary and thesaurus services, and you just know from the nature of this book that you can latch onto those services for your own site, right? You can just go to the Merriam-Webster site and fill out a simple form. Then you choose from among a selection of search boxes and paste the code into your Web page. What could be simpler? Check it out at www.merriamwebster.com/searchbox/index.htm.

Figure 22-7:
You can choose which style of Merriam-Webster dictionary and thesaurus search box you want on your site.

SuperStats

The SuperStats site (`http://counter.superstats.com`) is shown in Figure 22-8.

If you want nothing more than a simple visual page counter or if you just gotta have the most detailed reports of page hits possible, what do you do? You head for the same place: SuperStats (`http://counter.superstat.com`). It's part of Network Solutions, a name that will be instantly familiar to you as the big-name domain registrar.

These folks know just about everything there is to know about Web sites, and they're a good thing to have on your side. They've got a variety of plans that cover the needs of Web sites both large and small.

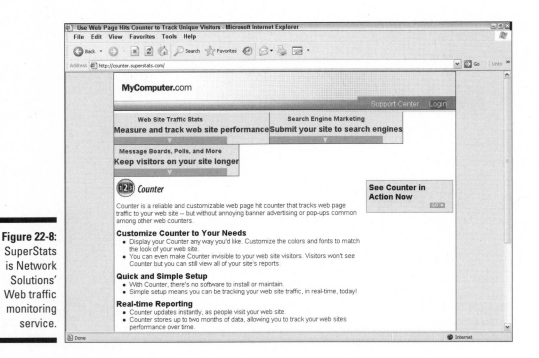

Figure 22-8: SuperStats is Network Solutions' Web traffic monitoring service.

Tell A Friend

The Tell A Friend site (`www.bravenet.com/webtools/announce/index.php`) is shown in Figure 22-9.

You see billions and billions, if not absolute zillions, of Web sites that display a Recommend This Site to a Friend link. You have good reason to include a link like this one on your site because a personal recommendation is a powerful sales tool. If people hear from someone they trust about a Web site that they ought to look at, they're much more inclined to check it out. With any other method, you have to ask people to rely on the word of strangers or maybe even just a search engine.

Even if you're not involved in e-commerce, you still want to attract quality visitors. And you still get more of the right people visiting your site if you help your current visitors tell their friends how much they like it. One of the easiest ways to do so is to use the free Tell A Friend service. Just go to `www.bravenet.com/webtools/announce/index.php`.

One of the benefits of the Tell A Friend service is that it offers prizes, which is an extra incentive for people to make a recommendation. One of the drawbacks is that the service is trying to get people to sign up for its newsletter, but even that has a silver lining. If people do sign up, Tell A Friend pays you as an affiliate. (See Chapter 15 for information about affiliate programs.)

Figure 22-9:
Tell A
Friend's
referral form
helps bring
new visitors
to your
Web site.

theFinancials.com

Figure 22-10 shows theFinacials.com site (`www.thefinancials.com/mfr_free.html`).

theFinancials.com is one of the most incredible sites for economic content that you can find anywhere. I kid you not, if you want to know something financial — or, more important, you want your site visitors to know it — drop everything and head to `www.thefinancials.com/mfr_free.html`.

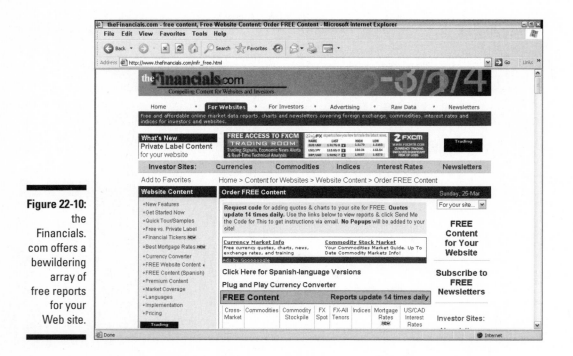

Figure 22-10:
the
Financials.
com offers a
bewildering
array of
free reports
for your
Web site.

You'll find Pacific Rim market reports, tickers, crude oil prices, mortgage rates . . . you name it. Just click the link for the report you want and then click the Send Me the Code for This link.

Part VIII
Appendixes

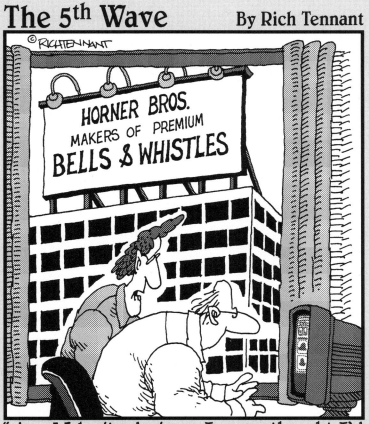

The 5th Wave   By Rich Tennant

HORNER BROS.
MAKERS OF PREMIUM
BELLS & WHISTLES

"As a Web site designer I never thought I'd say this, but I don't think your site has enough bells and whistles."

In this part . . .

All the new terms that have been invented to describe the Internet could drive even Daniel Webster nuts, so I put together a glossary of them for you. And I wouldn't want to leave you guessing about what's on the CD-ROM that's tucked into the back of this book, so I've tossed in an appendix about that, too.

Appendix A

Glossary

- -

aardvark: A type of anteater — its name means earth pig.

acceptable use policy: A policy that sets forth the type of user behavior that is accepted by the management of a Web site.

acquirer: See *merchant account.*

Acrobat: See *Portable Document Format (PDF).*

active link: See *link.*

Active Server Page (ASP): A Web page created with HTML and either VBScript or JScript (Microsoft's name for JavaScript) or both. Commands on Active Server Pages are processed via the ActiveX engine. See also *HTML, VBScript, JavaScript,* and *ActiveX.*

ActiveX: A system developed by Microsoft to enable a Web page utilizing ActiveX controls to interface with the Windows operating system.

Address Verification System (AVS): An antifraud feature for credit card transactions in which the address of the credit card holder is compared to the address on an order form. If the two addresses aren't the same, the probability of fraud is higher.

AJAX: Short for Asynchronous JavaScript and XML, a version of DHTML (Dynamic HTML).

anonymizer: A Web server that strips identifying information from a visitor's Web browser, thus preventing any Web page that the user visits from gathering data about the user. It does this by reissuing the user's request for a Web page instead of simply passing it along. The reissued request contains only the identifying information of the anonymizing server itself, not the identifying information about the user.

applet: Major programs are known as *applications.* Short programs, especially those written in the Java programming language for use on the Web, are called by the diminutive *applet.*

ARPANET: The original test bed for the Internet, a computer network developed by the Advanced Research Projects Agency.

ASCII (American Standard Code for Information Interchange): A common method for representing textual characters.

ASP: See *Active Server Page.*

attachment: A file that is sent along with an e-mail message. Most e-mail clients place an attachment into a separate directory from the one in which they store the e-mail messages. E-mail attachments are one of the primary means of spreading viruses.

authentication: Verifying the identity of a person or service, usually through digital IDs.

autoresponder: A program that automatically responds to an e-mail message by sending back a preprogrammed e-mail message of its own. Autoresponders are useful for providing price lists, back issues of newsletters, and so on.

AVS: See *Address Verification System.*

axis: In three-dimensional (3D) graphics, each of the three directions is indicated by an axis. The typical coordinate system uses an x-axis that runs horizontally, a y-axis that runs vertically, and a z-axis that runs, essentially, between the front and back of the monitor.

B2B: Business to business e-commerce, such as sales of photocopiers.

B2C: Business to consumer e-commerce — general products or services not related to business.

bandwidth: The total amount of data that a particular network connection can handle. The higher the bandwidth, the more data that can be sent in the same amount of time.

banner: An image link that appears on a Web page (generally at the top of the page) and contains advertising for a sponsor.

binary file: A program file. In transferring files through FTP, you must be careful to send program files as binary files rather than as text files because text files have a different format.

blog: A shortening of *web log.* A personal diary on the World Wide Web.

blogosphere: The sum of all the blogs in the world.

browser: See *Web browser.*

Cascading Style Sheet (CSS): A method of specifying the layout and appearance of a Web page that gives greater control than HTML at the cost of greater complexity.

cat: A creature that deigns to permit humans to inhabit the same planet.

CFML: See *ColdFusion Markup Language.*

CGI: See *Common Gateway Interface.*

chargeback: A debit issued against your merchant account by a credit card company because of a dispute over the validity of a transaction.

chat room: A place where people meet online and exchange messages in real time.

click-through: The action of a site visitor in clicking an advertising link to visit the advertiser's site.

client/server: A computer that provides resources to other computers over a network. The main computer provides a network service and is known as a *server.* Computers that use the services of a server are *clients.* You also use the term *server* to refer to the software that provides the service. The software that accesses the server is also known as the *client* or *client agent.*

ColdFusion Markup Language (CFML): A proprietary Adobe markup language that provides Web designers with the capability to easily create Web-based database query forms and the Web pages that present their responses. See also *markup language.*

colocation: Similar to leasing a dedicated server; the server is located at a site that provides technical services to you (such as network monitoring), but you own the server instead of leasing it. You may provide your own equipment or purchase it from the colocation firm.

Common Gateway Interface (CGI): A program that can take information gathered from users in a Web page form and pass that information to other programs for processing.

compile: The source code that you create with languages, such as Java or C, is run through a *compiler* that prepares a stand-alone, ready-to-run program.

configuration: The particular arrangement of practically anything having to do with computing. Configuration, for example, may refer to how many and what types of peripherals are connected to a computer. It may also refer to the settings in the preferences section of a program.

cookie: A text file that a Web site places on a visitor's computer. Cookies typically contain information such as an identification code, the date of last visit, visitor preferences, and so on.

copyright: The right to make copies. The creators of works such as books, paintings, songs, or computer programs own the copyrights to those works unless they transfer their rights to another person or company.

CSS: See *Cascading Style Sheet.*

dedicated server: A computer that is reserved for the use of a single person, company, or organization. See also *virtual server.*

default: Failure to pay bills. Seriously, defaults are the normal settings for software and hardware as they come from the manufacturers. In most cases, you can change the default settings to suit yourself.

demographics: Information that you gather from visitors to your site. Commonly, demographics include such things as the computer systems that visitors use, their income levels, and any other information that you require to understand your audience. Be careful about gathering data on age, race, sex, ethnicity, religious persuasion, and such because this may lead to discrimination charges. Make sure that, if you do ask for this type of information, you make clear that such disclosures are purely optional. And never, never, *never* make any of this information available to anyone else, except as a lump-sum total. You need to keep the individual input absolutely confidential.

Denmark: A country in northern Europe, of which about 75 percent is composed of farms.

DHTML: See *Dynamic HTML.*

digital ID: An encrypted identifier that you keep on file at a central repository known as a *Certificate Authority.* It certifies that you *are* who you say you are (just in case you're wondering).

Digital Subscriber Line (DSL): A popular method of high-speed Internet access that utilizes existing telephone lines. Normal telephone operation is also possible on the same line, so you can use phones and fax machines while the DSL connection is active. The DSL connection doesn't interfere with normal phone signals because it goes out at a different frequency.

discount rate: A percentage of each sale that you pay to the bank that processes credit card transactions.

DNS: See *Domain Name System.*

domain extension: See *top-level domain.*

Domain Name System (DNS): A system to translate the human-readable domain names, such as www.dummies.com, into the numerical IP addresses that computers understand (in this case, 38.170.216.18).

dot com (or dotcom): Colloquial expression meaning an Internet-based company.

download: Transferring a file to your computer from another computer. Also refers to the file that you download. See also *upload.*

draft: A check that you print to draw funds from another person's account after the person provides you with account information and authorization.

drop shipping: An arrangement by which you gather orders and submit them to another company; that company then sends its merchandise to your customer with your return address on it. You pay the company a wholesale rate and keep the difference as profit.

DSL: See *Digital Subscriber Line.*

Dynamic HTML(DHTML): The combination of HTML along with JavaScript and Cascading Style Sheets to create a Web page with dynamic elements. See also *JavaScript* and *Cascading Style Sheet.*

e-commerce: Business conducted on the World Wide Web or via intranets. Although some elements of e-commerce may contain traditional bricks-and-mortar aspects such as mailed order forms, it takes place primarily via the Internet or some similar network system.

e-mail: The sending and receiving of written messages via computer networks such as the Internet.

Emerald City: The home base of the Wizard of Oz.

emoticon: A symbol used to express the emotion of the writer, such as a *smiley* like :-) to indicate pleasure or harmless intent, or a wink like ;-) to show the writer's words are intended as a joke.

encryption: The encoding of data (such as e-mail messages or personal information entered into online order forms) so that it can't be read by anyone who does not have the key to the code.

end tag: See *tag.*

eXtensible HyperText Markup Language (XHTML): A version of HTML that follows the XML specification. See *HyperText Markup Language* and *eXtensible Markup Language.*

eXtensible Markup Language (XML): A markup language that allows users to create custom tags, in effect allowing them to create their own personalized markup language. See also *markup language, tag.*

eXtensible Style Language (XSL): A language for adding style sheets to XML documents. The relationship between XML and XSL is the same as between HTML and CSS. See also *eXtensible Markup Language, HyperText Markup Language,* and *Cascading Style Sheet.*

FAQ: A listing of Frequently Asked Questions and their answers.

Fargo: A city in North Dakota.

feed: The transmission of information from a server to either its clients or another server.

feed reader: A program for deciphering RSS feeds.

File Transfer Protocol (FTP): A method for transferring files from one computer to another across a network or the Internet.

flame: A message that contains insults or inflammatory material.

flame war: An extended exchange of messages containing flames. Flame wars disrupt the normal process of communication in mailing lists, newsgroups, message boards, and chat rooms.

font: A complete set of letters, numbers, punctuation, and special characters that all have a particular look and shape. For example, this is in the Arial font, whereas `this` is in the Courier New font.

frame/frameset: A method enabling you to display multiple Web pages on a single browser screen. Framesets set off different areas of the screen. Each area is known as a *frame,* and each frame contains its own Web page.

FTP: See *File Transfer Protocol.*

GIF: An image file that follows the standards of the Graphics Interchange Format. You commonly use GIFs for limited animation.

guillemot: A type of sea bird famous for waddling.

high risk: The category into which credit card companies place businesses that they believe are particularly prone to suffering from fraudulent transactions.

hit: A single access of a Web page.

home page: The main Web page from which all other pages in the site branch out. It is commonly called `index.html`, although this is not a requirement. In fact, any name will work, although if you use another name, visitors may see a listing of available files instead of instantly viewing your home page. The users then have to figure out which file among those listed is the home page.

Other common names include `index.htm` and `default.htm`. The difference between the `.htm` and `.html` extensions is practically nonexistent, by the way, going back to the days when the early DOS operating system recognized only three-letter extensions. All modern operating systems are capable of recognizing longer file type extensions, and few professionals limit themselves to the old DOS conventions anymore.

horizontal rule: A line across a Web page that you use to visually separate one section of a page from another. The HR element in HTML creates a horizontal rule.

HTML: See *HyperText Markup Language.*

HTML editor: Text editor with special features designed to assist you in creating Web pages.

HTTP: See *HyperText Transfer Protocol.*

hyperlink: See *link.*

hypertext: Text on a computer that includes links to other text, images, sound, and so on.

HyperText Markup Language (HTML): The native language of the World Wide Web, which you use to construct Web pages.

HyperText Transfer Protocol (HTTP): System for transferring files across the World Wide Web.

ICANN: See *Internet Corporation for Assigned Names and Numbers.*

image: General term for any picture or artwork on a Web page. Web images are usually stored in GIF, JPEG, or PNG formats.

image map: An image that contains multiple links. Users viewing an image map select different links by moving the mouse pointer to different parts of the image and clicking. You must carefully design the images that you use in image maps to provide visual clues to the links that they contain.

image repository: A Web site that contains a large amount of digital art, mostly simple icons. Image repositories typically gather these files without any attention to avoiding copyright and trademark violations.

InterBank: An organization that processes merchant credit card transactions for its member banks.

Internet: Short for *Internetwork*. The Internet consists of several different computer networks that all link together into a network of networks.

Internet access: The capability to connect to the Internet; usually an ISP provides this capability.

Internet Corporation for Assigned Names and Numbers (ICANN): The organization that accredits domain-name registrars.

Internet service provider (ISP): Company that provides Internet access, usually by dial-up connections, although many also offer high-speed dedicated connections.

interpret: Source code from languages such as JavaScript and Perl is read by another program (such as a Web browser or Web server). That program then interprets the instructions in the code and carries them out. See also *compile.*

intranet: A network consisting of several computer networks linked together. Unlike the Internet, an intranet is private and access to it is limited to its membership. Intranets are commonly used in B2B e-commerce situations.

IP address: The numerical equivalent of a domain name.

Isopoda: A type of crustacean with a small head.

ISP: See *Internet service provider.*

Java: A programming language that is often used to create applets for the Web. See also *applet.*

JavaScript: A simple but powerful programming language that programmers use to create scripts for Web pages. See also *script.*

JPEG: Also known as JPG. An image file that follows the standards of the Joint Photographic Experts Group. JPEG files are generally smaller than other file formats but maintain high-quality images nonetheless.

John of Lancaster: Admiral of the British fleet in 1422.

JPG: See *JPEG.*

keyword: A word or phrase that search engines use to locate Web pages containing matching terms.

link (hyperlink): A connection between a Web page and another Internet resource. Usually, a link contains the URL (Internet address) of another Web page, but it can also link to other resources, such as images. By convention, a link appears as blue underlined text that, after you activate it (usually by a mouse click), causes a Web browser to load the linked resource. You also often use images as links. An *active link* is one that you're currently clicking, and a *visited link* is one that you activated previously.

list owner: The person who manages a mailing list. Usually, the list owner is the person who conceives and launches the list. This person is also known as a *list manager* and may be the *moderator* of the list as well. See also ***moderator.***

list server: A program that processes the e-mail messages that comprise a mailing list. The list server usually also handles such routine administrative matters as subscribing and unsubscribing list members if they send it a message containing the appropriate commands.

locomotive: A specialized type of railroad car, also known as an *engine,* that propels other railroad cars along the track.

log file: A file that records activity. A Web server log file, for example, records the origin of anyone who looks at a Web page, the type of browser the person is using, and so on. Log-file analyzer programs, such as Statbot, are useful to Webmasters in figuring out peak times of usage, number of hits per day, which other sites are referring visitors to this site, and so on.

mailing list: A discussion group in which the members post messages that a list server relays to them via e-mail. *Open mailing lists* can be joined by anyone; *closed mailing lists* require approval to join.

markup language: A computer programming language that is dedicated to the layout and function of elements on-screen. HTML is the best-known markup language, although there are many others for specialized purposes, such as the Astronomical Markup Language (ASML), the Bioinformatic Sequence Markup Language (BSML), and the Math Markup Language (MATHML), as well as some that hope to compete with HTML to become the new lingua franca of Web development authors. See also ***eXtensible Markup Language, eXtensible HyperText Markup Language,*** and ***HyperText Markup Language.***

marquee: A scrolling message such as the ones that were once common on the signs (marquees) outside theaters.

merchant account: An arrangement with a bank or a bank's sales organization for you to accept credit cards in payment for goods or services.

message board: Similar to a newsgroup but operates on an individual Web site. Message boards, sometimes known as *graffiti walls,* enable site visitors to leave messages for other visitors to read.

metadata: Information beyond what is necessary for the display of a Web page. Common uses of metadata, for example, are the inclusion of the author's name and a content description in the HEAD section of a Web page.

modem (*m*odulator/*dem*odulator): Device that enables a computer to send signals over a telephone line.

moderator: Person who controls the content of a mailing list or newsgroup. In extreme cases, this control can amount to censorship, but reasonable moderation simply results in the removal of extraneous material, such as sales pitches for products and services that don't relate to the topic. A moderator may also play peacemaker, attempting to keep tempers in check among the members of the mailing list or newsgroup, thus avoiding flame wars.

Modesty Blaise: Popular adventure character first appearing in a 1962 comic strip and later the subject of about a dozen novels and at least one movie.

netiquette (Inter*net* et*iquette*): A series of customs that enable people to get along while living in cyberspace. Basically, you want to be nice and consider how your actions may affect other people.

newline: A programming instruction in the form of \n to move the next bit of text down one line.

Northwest Passage: Channel leading from the Atlantic to the Pacific Ocean north of North America. Much sought after since the fifteenth century, but not successfully negotiated until 1906.

online service: Sort of a mini-Internet; services such as CompuServe, America Online, and so on provide many of the functions that the Internet does but on a smaller scale. In recent years, the online services have lost much business to the Internet and now provide Internet access as part of their services.

opt-in mailing list: A mailing list that you subscribe to by entering your e-mail address in a form. You then receive a message in your mailbox asking you to confirm the subscription. If you don't reply to that message, your address doesn't go into the system. This sign-up method makes it difficult for anyone else to sign you up for the list.

page generation program: Software that uses a WYSIWYG (what you see is what you get), point-and-click interface for creating Web pages.

parameter: Information that you add to the HTML code that calls a Java applet. This information sets variable values for the applet's use, and you add it through the PARAM element.

password: Secret word that you use to gain computer access. Sometimes you choose a password; sometimes someone else assigns you one. Two schools of thought on passwords offer contradictory advice. One says to make them so difficult to imagine that no one else can possibly guess yours in a million years. The other school of thought says to make them easy enough that you can remember them.

Pausanias: General of the Greek army in the Battle of Plataea in 479 B.C.

PDF: See *Portable Document Format.*

plug-in: A small program which provides additional functionality to a larger program, such as letting a Web browser use Flash or adding a filter to a graphics program.

podcast: An audio broadcast included as a part of an RSS feed.

pop-up: A separate window in which a Web browser displays additional information not found on the Web page that the visitor originally accessed. Pop-up windows are used for a variety of purposes — some are considered legitimate, while others often are not. Pop-up windows, in their best and highest usage, are useful adjuncts to a normal Web page, adding helpful information or additional capabilities. Their common usage as advertising billboards, however, has given them a bad reputation, and programs called *pop-up blockers,* which prevent all pop-up windows from materializing, are becoming increasingly popular. Savvy Web designers should look for ways to avoid using pop-ups.

Portable Document Format (PDF): A proprietary document display format developed by Adobe Systems, Inc. Although it allows people to easily transfer existing documents into a form that's viewable on the Web, visitors need a separate plug-in in order to view those documents.

public domain: The group of all created works that copyright law no longer protects (or never did).

Quimper: French city on the Odet River.

Really Simple Syndication (RSS): A method for providing a continuously-updated source of text, images, or audio. Commonly used for news stories and blogs.

reciprocal link: A link to a Web page that also displays a link back to your Web page. Hyperlinking is a common practice for building traffic among Web sites. If you want to establish a reciprocal link with someone else's site, add a link to that site on your own and then send an e-mail message asking the site's owner to reciprocate.

registrar: A company approved by the Internet Corporation for Assigned Names and Numbers (ICANN) to keep track of domain names on the Internet. A domain name that you register must point to an active Web site. You may also *reserve* or *park* domain names if you have no current site active for that name but still want to prevent anybody else from registering the name. See also ***Domain Name System, Internet Corporation for Assigned Names and Numbers.***

RGB triplet: A method of denoting colors by specifying the amount of red, green, and blue in the color. Java applets often utilize this method. The possible values range from 0 to 255. Thus, if you want red lettering, you use a value of 255,0,0. This setting tells the applet to use as much red as possible but no green and no blue.

ring: A series of Web sites that connect together through links that lead from one to the other until visitors who follow all the links go full circle and return to their starting place.

robot: A program, also known as a *spider,* that automatically surfs the Web, indexing Web pages and adding information from those pages to a search site's database.

RSS: See ***Really Simple Syndication.***

Runic alphabet: Characters that the Teutonic peoples of early Europe used; also known as *futhark.*

safety paper: The kind of paper on which you print a draft or check.

script: A short program.

search engine optimization (SEO): The process of designing a Web page so that it gets the highest possible ranking in a search.

Secure Sockets Layer (SSL): An encryption system originally developed by Netscape that allows visitors to enter information into online forms and submit that information without allowing anyone else to read it. It's commonly used in processing order forms and other online forms that contain private information.

SEO: See ***search engine optimization.***

server: See ***client/server.***

Server Side Includes (SSI): The capability of a server that processes a CGI script to include data of its own that it sends back to the Web browser.

SGML: See *Standard Generalized Markup Language.*

shopping cart: A program that visitors to your site use to keep track of which items they want to purchase. The shopping cart metaphor extends to the visitor's capability to put items into the cart and remove them before making a final purchasing decision.

sleep: A common practice utterly unknown to authors trying to meet a deadline.

spam: Unsolicited e-mail messages that someone sends in bulk quantities to several addresses; also the same message posted to multiple newsgroups simultaneously.

spider: See *robot.*

SSI: See *Server Side Includes (SSI).*

SSL: See *Secure Socket Layers.*

standard: Also known as *specifications.* Generic term for anything that lots of people agree on. It may apply to a way to transfer files from one system to another, the exact structure and function of a computer language, or a method of compressing video images. If a recognized, organized group develops it, it's known as an *official standard.* If it's just something that the market leader develops, and most of the people in a particular field use it, it's known as a *de facto standard.*

Standard Generalized Markup Language (SGML): The original markup language from which HTML was developed. See also *markup language.*

start tag: See *tag.*

style sheets: See *Cascading Style Sheet.*

subscriber: A member of a mailing list. Also known, amazingly enough, as a list member.

syndicate: A content provider that represents several different sources of content, such as comics, opinion columns, horoscopes, and articles.

tag: You indicate the beginning of each element in HTML by placing the name of that element within angle brackets. This part of the element is known as a *start tag.* You indicate the end of the element by using an *end tag,* which looks just like the start tag except that you add a slash before the element's name. The start and end tags for the TABLE element, for example, are <TABLE> and </TABLE>.

telepathy: Ability to transfer thoughts from one mind to another.

text editor: A simple form of word processor that saves text files without formatting.

text file: A file of text. (No kidding.) In transferring text files via FTP, you want to be careful to send them as such rather than as binary files because text files often require conversion in transferring between Windows and UNIX systems, which use slightly different text formats. See also *ASCII.*

thread: Hierarchy that shows the relationship of a series of messages on a message board. See also *message board.*

tiling: The repetition of a background image across a Web page until it reaches the edge of the screen. It then begins tiling again in the next available space below the first line of images — and so on until it fills the entire page with multiple copies of the image.

top-level domain (TLD): The final letters at the end of an Internet address. You consider them *top level* because you read Internet addresses in steps from right to left, with the part after the last dot on the right being the highest step in a hierarchy that eventually leads down, step by dotted step, to a particular computer. The four most common TLDs are `.com`, `.net`, `.edu`, and `.org`. These TLDs are known as the *generic TLDs* or *gTLDs;* those that specify a country in which a site originates are known as *country-level TLDs* or *CLTLDs.*

traffic: The number of visits to an Internet site, as in "Our traffic increased by 100,000 visitors last week."

Uncertainty Principle: Fundamental theorem of quantum physics that states that knowing both the direction of travel and the location in space-time of an atomic particle is impossible.

uniform resource locator (URL): The address of a file (or other resource) on the Internet. The URL for a file on a Web server is formed by putting together a series of directions to the file, as in the following example:

```
http://www.someschool.edu/graphics/logo.png
```

Here's a breakdown of the preceding URL:

- ✔ The `http://` specifies the HyperText Transfer Protocol (the Web's native method of information exchange).

- ✔ The `www` tells you that the computer that holds the file is a Web server. Actually, you already know that from the first part — that's why a lot of Web sites don't use the `www` prefix anymore.

✔ The `someschool` segment gives the *subdomain,* which is what people usually think of as the name of the Web site. The Wiley Web site, for example, is located at `www.wiley.com`, and its subdomain is `wiley`.

✔ The three-letter extension represents the *top-level domain.* In this case, the subdomain is followed by `.edu`, meaning that this Web site is in the education domain.

✔ The `graphics` part leads to a particular directory on the specified Web server.

✔ The final portion, `logo.png`, is a file within that directory.

Files located within the same server as a Web page can be referenced in a simpler way by using *relative URLs.* Instead of fully specifying how to find the file from anywhere on the Internet, relative URLs only specify how to find it from the Web page that refers to it. The file in the preceding example could be linked to from the school's home page by using the following relative URL:

```
<IMG src="graphics/logo.png">
```

Because the Web browser that you use to view the home page already knows where it is, it can perform a bit of cutting and pasting to come up with the right URL. The browser "reasons" that it is currently viewing a Web page located at `http://www.someschool.edu/index.html`. It strips off everything after the final slash to arrive at `http://www.someschool.edu/` and then adds `graphics/logo.png` to that to arrive at `http://www.someschool.edu/graphics/logo.png`. See also ***top-level domain.***

upload: To transfer a file from your computer to another computer. Also the file that you upload. See also ***download.***

URL: See ***Uniform Resource Locator.***

Van de Graaff generator: A primitive device that generates millions of volts of static electricity.

VBScript: The Visual Basic scripting language from Microsoft. As the name suggests, it is a version of the simple BASIC programming language, but geared toward Web site development rather than general software development.

virtual server: A directory on a computer that simulates the existence of a separate computer. See also ***dedicated server.***

visited link: See ***link.***

Webmaster: The person in control of a Web site. A Webmaster may be an individual with only a single Web page or the manager of a large team of developers who create and maintain Web sites.

Web browser: A program such as Internet Explorer or Firefox that displays Web pages.

Web ring: See *ring*.

Web site: Any presence on the World Wide Web. Usually applies to a collection of Web pages.

William Kidd: Eighteenth-century English privateer who went down in history as the pirate Captain Kidd. He provided documents to political authorities that showed that he'd attacked only ships carrying papers that showed they were at war with England, but the papers were lost until the 1970s.

x-axis: See *axis*.

XHTML: See *eXtensible HyperText Markup Language*.

XML: See *eXtensible Markup Language*.

XSL: See *eXtensible Style Language*.

y-axis: See *axis*.

ytterbium: A rare earth element that you often find in combination with gadolinite.

z-axis: See *axis*.

zymurgy: The study of the fermentation process.

Appendix B

About the CD

*H*ere is some of the cool stuff that you'll find on the *Building a Web Site For Dummies* CD-ROM:

- ✔ Links to all the sites mentioned in the book

- ✔ An incredible array of evaluation, trial, and freeware versions of Web-site creation tools

- ✔ Trial versions of fabulous graphics tools

System Requirements

Make sure that your computer meets the minimum system requirements shown in the following list. If your computer doesn't match up to most of these requirements, you may have problems using the software and files on the CD. For the latest and greatest information, please refer to the ReadMe file located at the root of the CD-ROM.

- ✔ A PC with a Pentium III or faster processor; or a Mac OS computer with a G3 or faster processor

- ✔ Microsoft Windows 2000, XP or Vista; or Mac OS X 10.4.0 or later

- ✔ At least 128MB of total RAM installed on your computer; for best performance, we recommend at least 256MB

> ✔ A CD-ROM drive
>
> ✔ A sound card for PCs; Mac OS computers have built-in sound support
>
> ✔ A monitor capable of displaying at least 16 million colors
>
> ✔ An Internet connection via cable modem, DSL, or higher speed.

If you need more information on the basics, check out these books published by Wiley Publishing: *PCs For Dummies,* by Dan Gookin; *Macs For Dummies,* by Edward C. Baig; *iMacs For Dummies,* by Mark L. Chambers; *Windows 2000 Professional For Dummies, Windows XP For Dummies, Windows Vista For Dummies* all by Andy Rathbone.

Using the CD with Microsoft Windows

To install from the CD to your hard drive, follow these steps:

1. **Insert the CD into your computer's CD-ROM drive.**

   A window appears with the following options: HTML Interface, Browse CD, and Exit.

2. **Click the Start button and choose Run from the menu.**

3. **In the dialog box that appears, type** *d*:\Start.exe.

   Replace *d* with the proper drive letter for your CD-ROM if it uses a different letter. (If you don't know the letter, double-click My Computer on your desktop and see what letter is listed for your CD-ROM drive.)

   Your browser opens, and the license agreement is displayed.

4. **Read through the license agreement, nod your head, and click the Agree button if you want to use the CD.**

   After you click Agree, you're taken to the Main menu, where you can browse through the contents of the CD.

5. **To navigate within the interface, click a topic of interest to take you to an explanation of the files on the CD and how to use or install them.**

6. **To install software from the CD, simply click the software name.**

Using the CD with Mac OS

To install items from the CD to your hard drive, follow these steps:

1. **Insert the CD into your computer's CD-ROM drive.**

   In a moment, an icon representing the CD you just inserted appears on your Mac desktop. Chances are, the icon looks like a CD-ROM.

2. **Double-click the CD icon to show the CD's contents.**

3. **Double-click Start to launch the interface and display the license agreement.**

4. **Read through the license agreement, nod your head, and click the Accept button if you want to use the CD.**

   After you click Accept, you're taken to the Main menu. This is where you can browse through the contents of the CD.

5. **To navigate within the interface, click any topic of interest, and you're taken to an explanation of the files on the CD and how to use or install them.**

6. **To install software from the CD, simply click the software name.**

What You'll Find on the CD

The following sections are arranged by category and provide a summary of the software and other goodies you'll find on the CD. If you need help with installing the items provided on the CD, refer back to the installation instructions in the preceding section.

Shareware programs are fully functional, free, trial versions of copyrighted programs. If you like particular programs, register with their authors for a nominal fee and receive licenses, enhanced versions, and technical support. *Freeware programs* are free, copyrighted games, applications, and utilities. You can copy them to as many PCs as you like — for free — but they offer no technical support. *GNU software* is governed by its own license, which is included inside the folder of the GNU software. There are no restrictions on distribution of GNU software. See the GNU license at the root of the CD for more details. *Trial, demo,* or *evaluation* versions of software are usually limited either by time or functionality (such as not letting you save a project after you create it).

Coffee Cup HTML Editor 2007

Shareware

For Windows. The venerable Coffee Cup HTML Editor just keeps getting better and better. Whether you prefer visual editing or getting under the hood to monkey with the code, this is the way to go.

For more information and updates, visit the Coffee Cup site: `www.coffeecup.com/html-editor`.

For more information and updates, visit the DAZ Bryce site: `www.daz3d.com/i.x/software/bryce`.

IrfanView

Freeware

For Windows. The handiest little image manipulation program from Irfan Skiljan for quick and easy adjustments.

For more information and updates, visit the IrfanView Web site: `www.irfanview.net`

Site Studio 6

30-Day Trial

For Windows. With two versions (Home and Pro), this slick Web site editor has what it takes to satisfy everyone.

For more information and updates, visit the Site Studio site: `www.effectivestudios.com`.

SiteSpinner

15-Day Trial

For Windows. You don't have to know a thing about HTML coding to make your own Web site with this program. Just sit down and spin your own web today!

For more information and updates, visit the SiteSpinner site: `www.virtualmechanics.com`.

WYSIWYG Web Builder

30-Day Trial

For Windows. I wish I'd had this program when I first started building Web sites. It has a nice clean user interface: Everything you need to do is on the left, your Web page in progress is in the center, and every file you need to add is on the right. Creating sites just doesn't get any easier!

For more information and updates, visit the WYSIWYG Web Builder site: `www.pablosoftwaresolutions.com/html/wysiwyg_web_builder.html`.

Author-created links pages

For Windows and Mac. These files contain links to the sites mentioned in each chapter. The structure of the links directory is

```
Author/Chapter1
Author/ChapterX
```

Troubleshooting

I tried my best to compile programs that work on most computers with the minimum system requirements. Alas, your computer may differ, and some programs may not work properly for some reason.

The two likeliest problems are that you don't have enough memory (RAM) for the programs you want to use, or you have other programs running that are affecting installation or running of a program. If you get an error message such as `Not Enough Memory` or `Setup Cannot Continue`, try one or more of the following suggestions and then try using the software again:

- ✔ **Turn off any antivirus software running on your computer.** Installation programs sometimes mimic virus activity and may make your computer incorrectly believe that it's being infected by a virus.

- ✔ **Close all running programs.** The more programs you have running, the less memory is available to other programs. Installation programs typically update files and programs; so if you keep other programs running, installation may not work properly.

✔ **Have your local computer store add more RAM to your computer.** This is, admittedly, a drastic and somewhat expensive step. However, if you have a computer that's a few years old, adding more memory can really help the speed of your computer and allow more programs to run at the same time. This may include closing the CD interface and running a product's installation program from Windows Explorer.

Customer Care

If you have trouble with the CD-ROM, please call the Wiley Product Technical Support phone number at (800) 762-2974. Outside the United States, call 1(317) 572-3994. You can also contact Wiley Product Technical Support at `http://support.wiley.com`. John Wiley & Sons will provide technical support only for installation and other general quality control items. For technical support on the applications themselves, consult the program's vendor or author.

To place additional orders or to request information about other Wiley products, please call (877) 762-2974.

Index

Notes

Notes

BUSINESS, CAREERS & PERSONAL FINANCE

0-7645-9847-3

0-7645-2431-3

Also available:
- Business Plans Kit For Dummies
  0-7645-9794-9
- Economics For Dummies
  0-7645-5726-2
- Grant Writing For Dummies
  0-7645-8416-2
- Home Buying For Dummies
  0-7645-5331-3
- Managing For Dummies
  0-7645-1771-6
- Marketing For Dummies
  0-7645-5600-2

- Personal Finance For Dummies
  0-7645-2590-5*
- Resumes For Dummies
  0-7645-5471-9
- Selling For Dummies
  0-7645-5363-1
- Six Sigma For Dummies
  0-7645-6798-5
- Small Business Kit For Dummies
  0-7645-5984-2
- Starting an eBay Business For Dummies
  0-7645-6924-4
- Your Dream Career For Dummies
  0-7645-9795-7

HOME & BUSINESS COMPUTER BASICS

0-470-05432-8

0-471-75421-8

Also available:
- Cleaning Windows Vista For Dummies
  0-471-78293-9
- Excel 2007 For Dummies
  0-470-03737-7
- Mac OS X Tiger For Dummies
  0-7645-7675-5
- MacBook For Dummies
  0-470-04859-X
- Macs For Dummies
  0-470-04849-2
- Office 2007 For Dummies
  0-470-00923-3

- Outlook 2007 For Dummies
  0-470-03830-6
- PCs For Dummies
  0-7645-8958-X
- Salesforce.com For Dummies
  0-470-04893-X
- Upgrading & Fixing Laptops For Dummies
  0-7645-8959-8
- Word 2007 For Dummies
  0-470-03658-3
- Quicken 2007 For Dummies
  0-470-04600-7

FOOD, HOME, GARDEN, HOBBIES, MUSIC & PETS

0-7645-8404-9

0-7645-9904-6

Also available:
- Candy Making For Dummies
  0-7645-9734-5
- Card Games For Dummies
  0-7645-9910-0
- Crocheting For Dummies
  0-7645-4151-X
- Dog Training For Dummies
  0-7645-8418-9
- Healthy Carb Cookbook For Dummies
  0-7645-8476-6
- Home Maintenance For Dummies
  0-7645-5215-5

- Horses For Dummies
  0-7645-9797-3
- Jewelry Making & Beading For Dummies
  0-7645-2571-9
- Orchids For Dummies
  0-7645-6759-4
- Puppies For Dummies
  0-7645-5255-4
- Rock Guitar For Dummies
  0-7645-5356-9
- Sewing For Dummies
  0-7645-6847-7
- Singing For Dummies
  0-7645-2475-5

INTERNET & DIGITAL MEDIA

0-470-04529-9

0-470-04894-8

Also available:
- Blogging For Dummies
  0-471-77084-1
- Digital Photography For Dummies
  0-7645-9802-3
- Digital Photography All-in-One Desk Reference For Dummies
  0-470-03743-1
- Digital SLR Cameras and Photography For Dummies
  0-7645-9803-1
- eBay Business All-in-One Desk Reference For Dummies
  0-7645-8438-3
- HDTV For Dummies
  0-470-09673-X

- Home Entertainment PCs For Dummies
  0-470-05523-5
- MySpace For Dummies
  0-470-09529-6
- Search Engine Optimization For Dummies
  0-471-97998-8
- Skype For Dummies
  0-470-04891-3
- The Internet For Dummies
  0-7645-8996-2
- Wiring Your Digital Home For Dummies
  0-471-91830-X

* Separate Canadian edition also available
† Separate U.K. edition also available

Available wherever books are sold. For more information or to order direct: U.S. customers visit www.dummies.com or call 1-877-762-2974.
U.K. customers visit www.wileyeurope.com or call 0800 243407. Canadian customers visit www.wiley.ca or call 1-800-567-4797.

SPORTS, FITNESS, PARENTING, RELIGION & SPIRITUALITY

0-471-76871-5

0-7645-7841-3

Also available:
- Catholicism For Dummies
  0-7645-5391-7
- Exercise Balls For Dummies
  0-7645-5623-1
- Fitness For Dummies
  0-7645-7851-0
- Football For Dummies
  0-7645-3936-1
- Judaism For Dummies
  0-7645-5299-6
- Potty Training For Dummies
  0-7645-5417-4
- Buddhism For Dummies
  0-7645-5359-3

- Pregnancy For Dummies
  0-7645-4483-7 †
- Ten Minute Tone-Ups For Dummies
  0-7645-7207-5
- NASCAR For Dummies
  0-7645-7681-X
- Religion For Dummies
  0-7645-5264-3
- Soccer For Dummies
  0-7645-5229-5
- Women in the Bible For Dummies
  0-7645-8475-8

TRAVEL

0-7645-7749-2

0-7645-6945-7

Also available:
- Alaska For Dummies
  0-7645-7746-8
- Cruise Vacations For Dummies
  0-7645-6941-4
- England For Dummies
  0-7645-4276-1
- Europe For Dummies
  0-7645-7529-5
- Germany For Dummies
  0-7645-7823-5
- Hawaii For Dummies
  0-7645-7402-7

- Italy For Dummies
  0-7645-7386-1
- Las Vegas For Dummies
  0-7645-7382-9
- London For Dummies
  0-7645-4277-X
- Paris For Dummies
  0-7645-7630-5
- RV Vacations For Dummies
  0-7645-4442-X
- Walt Disney World & Orlando
  For Dummies
  0-7645-9660-8

GRAPHICS, DESIGN & WEB DEVELOPMENT

0-7645-8815-X

0-7645-9571-7

Also available:
- 3D Game Animation For Dummies
  0-7645-8789-7
- AutoCAD 2006 For Dummies
  0-7645-8925-3
- Building a Web Site For Dummies
  0-7645-7144-3
- Creating Web Pages For Dummies
  0-470-08030-2
- Creating Web Pages All-in-One Desk
  Reference For Dummies
  0-7645-4345-8
- Dreamweaver 8 For Dummies
  0-7645-9649-7

- InDesign CS2 For Dummies
  0-7645-9572-5
- Macromedia Flash 8 For Dummies
  0-7645-9691-8
- Photoshop CS2 and Digital
  Photography For Dummies
  0-7645-9580-6
- Photoshop Elements 4 For Dummies
  0-471-77483-9
- Syndicating Web Sites with RSS Feeds
  For Dummies
  0-7645-8848-6
- Yahoo! SiteBuilder For Dummies
  0-7645-9800-7

NETWORKING, SECURITY, PROGRAMMING & DATABASES

0-7645-7728-X

0-471-74940-0

Also available:
- Access 2007 For Dummies
  0-470-04612-0
- ASP.NET 2 For Dummies
  0-7645-7907-X
- C# 2005 For Dummies
  0-7645-9704-3
- Hacking For Dummies
  0-470-05235-X
- Hacking Wireless Networks
  For Dummies
  0-7645-9730-2
- Java For Dummies
  0-470-08716-1

- Microsoft SQL Server 2005 For Dummies
  0-7645-7755-7
- Networking All-in-One Desk Reference
  For Dummies
  0-7645-9939-9
- Preventing Identity Theft For Dummies
  0-7645-7336-5
- Telecom For Dummies
  0-471-77085-X
- Visual Studio 2005 All-in-One Desk
  Reference For Dummies
  0-7645-9775-2
- XML For Dummies
  0-7645-8845-1

HEALTH & SELF-HELP

0-7645-8450-2   0-7645-4149-8

Also available:

- Bipolar Disorder For Dummies
  0-7645-8451-0
- Chemotherapy and Radiation
  For Dummies
  0-7645-7832-4
- Controlling Cholesterol For Dummies
  0-7645-5440-9
- Diabetes For Dummies
  0-7645-6820-5* †
- Divorce For Dummies
  0-7645-8417-0 †

- Fibromyalgia For Dummies
  0-7645-5441-7
- Low-Calorie Dieting For Dummies
  0-7645-9905-4
- Meditation For Dummies
  0-471-77774-9
- Osteoporosis For Dummies
  0-7645-7621-6
- Overcoming Anxiety For Dummies
  0-7645-5447-6
- Reiki For Dummies
  0-7645-9907-0
- Stress Management For Dummies
  0-7645-5144-2

EDUCATION, HISTORY, REFERENCE & TEST PREPARATION

0-7645-8381-6   0-7645-9554-7

Also available:

- The ACT For Dummies
  0-7645-9652-7
- Algebra For Dummies
  0-7645-5325-9
- Algebra Workbook For Dummies
  0-7645-8467-7
- Astronomy For Dummies
  0-7645-8465-0
- Calculus For Dummies
  0-7645-2498-4
- Chemistry For Dummies
  0-7645-5430-1
- Forensics For Dummies
  0-7645-5580-4

- Freemasons For Dummies
  0-7645-9796-5
- French For Dummies
  0-7645-5193-0
- Geometry For Dummies
  0-7645-5324-0
- Organic Chemistry I For Dummies
  0-7645-6902-3
- The SAT I For Dummies
  0-7645-7193-1
- Spanish For Dummies
  0-7645-5194-9
- Statistics For Dummies
  0-7645-5423-9

Get smart @ dummies.com®

- **Find a full list of Dummies titles**
- **Look into loads of FREE on-site articles**
- **Sign up for FREE eTips e-mailed to you weekly**
- **See what other products carry the Dummies name**
- **Shop directly from the Dummies bookstore**
- **Enter to win new prizes every month!**

Wiley Publishing, Inc.
End-User License Agreement

READ THIS. You should carefully read these terms and conditions before opening the software packet(s) included with this book "Book". This is a license agreement "Agreement" between you and Wiley Publishing, Inc. "WPI". By opening the accompanying software packet(s), you acknowledge that you have read and accept the following terms and conditions. If you do not agree and do not want to be bound by such terms and conditions, promptly return the Book and the unopened software packet(s) to the place you obtained them for a full refund.

1. **License Grant.** WPI grants to you (either an individual or entity) a nonexclusive license to use one copy of the enclosed software program(s) (collectively, the "Software") solely for your own personal or business purposes on a single computer (whether a standard computer or a workstation component of a multi-user network). The Software is in use on a computer when it is loaded into temporary memory (RAM) or installed into permanent memory (hard disk, CD-ROM, or other storage device). WPI reserves all rights not expressly granted herein.

2. **Ownership.** WPI is the owner of all right, title, and interest, including copyright, in and to the compilation of the Software recorded on the physical packet included with this Book "Software Media". Copyright to the individual programs recorded on the Software Media is owned by the author or other authorized copyright owner of each program. Ownership of the Software and all proprietary rights relating thereto remain with WPI and its licensers.

3. **Restrictions on Use and Transfer.**

   (a) You may only (i) make one copy of the Software for backup or archival purposes, or (ii) transfer the Software to a single hard disk, provided that you keep the original for backup or archival purposes. You may not (i) rent or lease the Software, (ii) copy or reproduce the Software through a LAN or other network system or through any computer subscriber system or bulletin-board system, or (iii) modify, adapt, or create derivative works based on the Software.

   (b) You may not reverse engineer, decompile, or disassemble the Software. You may transfer the Software and user documentation on a permanent basis, provided that the transferee agrees to accept the terms and conditions of this Agreement and you retain no copies. If the Software is an update or has been updated, any transfer must include the most recent update and all prior versions.

4. **Restrictions on Use of Individual Programs.** You must follow the individual requirements and restrictions detailed for each individual program in the "About the CD" appendix of this Book or on the Software Media. These limitations are also contained in the individual license agreements recorded on the Software Media. These limitations may include a requirement that after using the program for a specified period of time, the user must pay a registration fee or discontinue use. By opening the Software packet(s), you agree to abide by the licenses and restrictions for these individual programs that are detailed in the "About the CD" appendix and/or on the Software Media. None of the material on this Software Media or listed in this Book may ever be redistributed, in original or modified form, for commercial purposes.

5. **Limited Warranty.**

   (a) WPI warrants that the Software and Software Media are free from defects in materials and workmanship under normal use for a period of sixty (60) days from the date of purchase of this Book. If WPI receives notification within the warranty period of defects in materials or workmanship, WPI will replace the defective Software Media.

   (b) WPI AND THE AUTHOR(S) OF THE BOOK DISCLAIM ALL OTHER WARRANTIES, EXPRESS OR IMPLIED, INCLUDING WITHOUT LIMITATION IMPLIED WARRANTIES OF MERCHANTABILITY AND FITNESS FOR A PARTICULAR PURPOSE, WITH RESPECT TO THE SOFTWARE, THE PROGRAMS, THE SOURCE CODE CONTAINED THEREIN, AND/OR THE TECHNIQUES DESCRIBED IN THIS BOOK. WPI DOES NOT WARRANT THAT THE FUNCTIONS CONTAINED IN THE SOFTWARE WILL MEET YOUR REQUIREMENTS OR THAT THE OPERATION OF THE SOFTWARE WILL BE ERROR FREE.

   (c) This limited warranty gives you specific legal rights, and you may have other rights that vary from jurisdiction to jurisdiction.

6. **Remedies.**

   (a) WPI's entire liability and your exclusive remedy for defects in materials and workmanship shall be limited to replacement of the Software Media, which may be returned to WPI with a copy of your receipt at the following address: Software Media Fulfillment Department, Attn.: *Building a Web Site For Dummies,* 3rd Edition, Wiley Publishing, Inc., 10475 Crosspoint Blvd., Indianapolis, IN 46256, or call 1-800-762-2974. Please allow four to six weeks for delivery. This Limited Warranty is void if failure of the Software Media has resulted from accident, abuse, or misapplication. Any replacement Software Media will be warranted for the remainder of the original warranty period or thirty (30) days, whichever is longer.

   (b) In no event shall WPI or the author be liable for any damages whatsoever (including without limitation damages for loss of business profits, business interruption, loss of business information, or any other pecuniary loss) arising from the use of or inability to use the Book or the Software, even if WPI has been advised of the possibility of such damages.

   (c) Because some jurisdictions do not allow the exclusion or limitation of liability for consequential or incidental damages, the above limitation or exclusion may not apply to you.

7. **U.S. Government Restricted Rights.** Use, duplication, or disclosure of the Software for or on behalf of the United States of America, its agencies and/or instrumentalities "U.S. Government" is subject to restrictions as stated in paragraph (c)(1)(ii) of the Rights in Technical Data and Computer Software clause of DFARS 252.227-7013, or subparagraphs (c) (1) and (2) of the Commercial Computer Software - Restricted Rights clause at FAR 52.227-19, and in similar clauses in the NASA FAR supplement, as applicable.

8. **General.** This Agreement constitutes the entire understanding of the parties and revokes and supersedes all prior agreements, oral or written, between them and may not be modified or amended except in a writing signed by both parties hereto that specifically refers to this Agreement. This Agreement shall take precedence over any other documents that may be in conflict herewith. If any one or more provisions contained in this Agreement are held by any court or tribunal to be invalid, illegal, or otherwise unenforceable, each and every other provision shall remain in full force and effect.